D1347911

Clint Eastwood

Film-Maker

NORTHERN COLLEGE

LIBRARY AND LEARNING RESOURCES CENTRE
Northern College, Barnsley. S75 3ET

Please return this book by the last date stamped below.

22.5.98	27/2/04	20/12/11
19.4.99	26/04/04	14.2.13
19 APR 1999	15/12/04	7.5.15
30.3.00	10.1.05	17.5.17.
7.4.00	11/2/05.	
26 5 00	20/4/05.	
27/3/01	30/11/05	
23/4/01	16/12/05	
23.5.01	15/3/07	
29/5	26 3.07	
5 3 03	25/5/07	
3.4.03	31/3/08.	
14/5/03	3/4/09.	
6/02/04.	12.5.10	
	3.5.11	

Clint Eastwood

Film-Maker

Daniel O'Brien

B.T. Batsford Ltd, London

First published 1996
© Daniel O'Brien 1996

Printed in the UK by Butler & Tanner

for the Publishers

B.T. Batsford Ltd
4 Fitzhardinge Street
London W1H 0AH

A CIP catalogue record for this book is available
from the British Library

ISBN 0 7134 7839 X

Contents

Acknowledgements

My thanks to the following for offering their thoughts on both Clint Eastwood and this book: Elisabeth le Gonidec de Kerhalic, Gary Kramer, Mark Lonsdale (who also lent me his copy of *Bird*) and my agent David O'Leary. Thanks also to Richard Reynolds at Batsford and Dominic Hickie.

Illustrations: Stills supplied by the British Film Institute Stills, Posters and Designs department. All the photographs were originally issued as publicity material by copyright holders Universal-International (*Revenge of the Creature*, *Tarantula*, *Francis in the Navy*), RKO (*The First Traveling Saleslady*), Regal Pictures/Twentieth Century Fox (*Ambush at Cimarron Pass*), CBS (*Rawhide*), United Artists (*A Fistful of Dollars*, *For a Few Dollars More*, *The Good The Bad and The Ugly*, *Hang 'Em High*, *Thunderbolt and Lightfoot*), Toho (*Yojimbo*), Malpaso/Universal (*Coogan's Bluff*, *The Beguiled*, *Play Misty for Me*), Metro Goldwyn Mayer (*Where Eagles Dare*), Malpaso/Warner (*Dirty Harry*, *Magnum Force*, *The Outlaw Josey Wales*, *The Enforcer*, *The Gauntlet*, *Every Which Way But Loose*, *Honkytonk Man*, *Tightrope*, *Pale Rider*, *Bird*, *White Hunter Black Heart*, *Unforgiven*), Malpaso/Paramount (*Escape from Alcatraz*), Second Street/Warner (*Bronco Billy*) and Columbia Tri-Star (*In the Line of Fire*).

Introduction

My involvement goes deeper than acting or directing. I love every aspect of the creation of motion pictures and I guess I'm committed to it for life.
Clint Eastwood

I intend to live it out on my own terms or I ain't gonna live it at all.
Red Stovall, *Honkytonk Man*

A man's got to know his limitations.
Inspector Harry Callahan, *Magnum Force*

Clint Eastwood is an impressive, if curious, phenomenon: producer, director, top box-office star, cultural icon and the cinema's ultimate tight-lipped (yet sensitive) macho man. Over four decades, Eastwood has progressed from unnoticed 'B' movie bit player to internationally acclaimed film-maker, one of Hollywood's most powerful and respected elder statesmen. His career has been an astute, largely successful balancing of ambitious, thoughtful genre works (such as *High Plains Drifter*, 1973), with blatantly commercial vehicles of dubious quality (such as *The Enforcer*, 1976). Though his films are distributed by the major studios (latterly Warner Bros), Eastwood has usually worked through his own, independent production company, confining himself to medium budgets and tight schedules (not always to the films' advantage). After more than two decades as a Hollywood star, he finally achieved official industry recognition, earning two Academy Awards for the dark, revisionist western *Unforgiven* (1992), fifteen years after he should have won for *The Outlaw Josey Wales* (1976), still Eastwood's finest hour as a director-star. Once described as the macho equivalent of Woody Allen, Eastwood occupies a unique place within the American film industry, an independent film-maker with mainstream appeal, a populist responsible for some of the most unusual films to emerge from post-sixties Hollywood. The aim of this book is to trace the development of Eastwood's relationship with the cinema, both as creative talent and businessman (a precarious combination), documenting his gradual, often low-key mastery of the medium. Set against this is Eastwood's much commented-on private life, which takes in a thirty year 'open' marriage, numerous affairs (some fleeting, some years in duration), four children (from three relationships) and a bitter palimony lawsuit. Always at pains to keep his off-camera activities hidden from public scrutiny, Eastwood remained relatively untroubled until 1989, when his bust-up with former co-star and lover Sondra Locke brought his professional and personal worlds together in a way he could never have intended. An unpleasant episode for the star, no doubt, yet perhaps not unexpected in a life where the desire to be leader of the gang has left little room for compromise. Many have traced this attitude back to Eastwood's disrupted, often solitary childhood during the Depression-hit 1930s. Just as likely a factor is the decade of frustrations

● **Clint Eastwood directing *Play Misty for Me*, his official behind-the-camera debut.**

and false starts he had to endure before film success beckoned. There is a certain irony in the fact that this archetypal American boy made good should have to travel halfway across the world before America would take any real notice of him.

Arriving in Hollywood in 1954, Eastwood found work as a supporting actor in Universal-International second features such as *Revenge of the Creature* (1955), *Tarantula* (1955) and *Francis in the Navy* (1955). Apart from a friendship with veteran producer-director Arthur Lubin, who cast Eastwood as the junior romantic lead in the RKO comedy western *The First Traveling Saleslady* (1956), this early film career proved largely unrewarding. When the already minimal film work dried up, Eastwood departed for television and a co-starring role (as Rowdy Yates) in the CBS western series *Rawhide* (1959-66), which after a very hesitant start went on to enjoy worldwide success. During this period in the largely unexciting world of conveyor-belt television production, Eastwood took the opportunity to pursue his growing interest in the technical side of filming. He suggested more adventurous techniques (such as strapping a camera to the saddle of a galloping horse) and would have directed some episodes himself, had CBS not decided that actors couldn't be trusted behind the camera.

After five increasingly dreary years on *Rawhide*, Eastwood's moribund film career was resurrected in the unlikely setting of Italy, collaborating with director Sergio Leone on the groundbreaking spaghetti westerns *A Fistful of Dollars* (1964), *For a Few Dollars More* (1965) and *The Good The Bad and The Ugly* (1966). Having first offered the leading role in *A Fistful of Dollars* to James Coburn and Charles Bronson (who described the script as the worst he'd ever read), Leone had been reduced to looking for a star among the expatriate American actors working in Italian 'sword and sandal' epics. One of these, Richard Harrison, turned the film down but suggested Eastwood as an alternative. Leone looked at a dubbed episode of *Rawhide* and was impressed by the actor's charisma and unselfconscious grace of movement (which he likened to a cat), even when confined in a stereotyped, juvenile cowboy role. Against the advice of his business manager, who regarded the film as a bad career move, Eastwood accepted Leone's offer of a starring role in an Italian-German-Spanish western, reasoning that if it turned out to be a disaster, no-one in the United States would ever hear of it. Cast as the taciturn, enigmatic, amoral 'Man With No Name' (a marketing gimmick devised by United Artists for the film's belated English-language release), Eastwood found an ideal screen image, one which he would continue to employ, in refined and mutated forms, throughout his career. Both Leone and Eastwood later claimed the bulk of the credit for the development of the character (Eastwood allegedly 'borrowed' several key props, such as his pistol and gunbelt, from the *Rawhide* set), though much of it was taken from the film's Japanese inspiration, Akira Kurosawa's lone-samurai classic *Yojimbo* (1960). What is not disputed is Eastwood's vital contribution to the script, paring down his character's dialogue to the bare minimum (he later employed a similar trick in *Where Eagles Dare* 1968, giving many of his lines to co-star Richard Burton). Never entirely at ease with overly articulate characters (such as John Wilson in *White Hunter Black Heart* 1990), Eastwood is at his most intriguing when least verbose. Equally important was Leone's tremendous sense of style and energy, qualities sometimes lacking in Eastwood's later homegrown films.

The success of *A Fistful of Dollars* and its sequels in the United States enabled Eastwood to return home for his first American starring vehicle, *Hang 'Em High* (1968). A solid, if unremarkable western, the film was also the first produced through Eastwood's own company, Malpaso (named after a creek in Eastwood's adopted home

● *For a Few Dollars More*

town of Carmel; also Spanish for 'bad move'). Determined to keep as tight a control on the film as possible, Eastwood hired television director and fellow *Rawhide* veteran Ted Post, ensuring that his own creative input would be given a fair hearing. While this proved to be the right decision at the time, Eastwood can be criticized for continuing to employ pedestrian, second rate directors, such as James Fargo and Wayne Van Horn, on later vehicles. Both Fargo and Van Horn were promoted to the job from within the ranks of Malpaso, revealing an extreme reluctance on Eastwood's part to hand over nominal control of his films to anyone who might dare to disagree with him. Even when he decided to employ more distinguished film-makers, terminal 'creative differences' could set in very quickly. Respected directors Philip Kaufman and Blake Edwards found their attempts at collaboration with the star brought to a rapid and undignified halt.

Eastwood followed the commercial success of *Hang 'Em High* with the police drama *Coogan's Bluff* (1968), the first of his collaborations with maverick action director Don Siegel (later to include the legendary *Dirty Harry* 1971). Despite an initial personality clash (and major problems with the script), Siegel's expertise with violent, 'lone wolf' characters enabled Eastwood to add a measure of depth to his screen persona largely absent from his other late-sixties vehicles. Eastwood further consolidated his star status with two comic-book style war films, *Where Eagles Dare* and *Kelly's Heroes* (1970), though studio interference on the latter left him embittered. His only miscalculation during this crucial period was agreeing to co-star with Lee Marvin in *Paint Your Wagon* (1969), an overblown megabudget musical which died at the box-office. To Eastwood, the film represented an object lesson in the perils of ill-planned, undisciplined film-making: 'It was a disaster, but it didn't have to be such an expensive disaster.'

By the early seventies, Eastwood felt ready to exercise a further degree of control over his career, making his directorial debut with *Play Misty for Me* (1971). A tense, if far from flawless psychological thriller, the film marked a move away from the action man vehicles (westerns, police dramas, war films) which had made him a star. Later self-directed efforts include a romantic drama (*Breezy* 1973), a screwball satirical comedy (*Bronco Billy* 1980), a Depression era comedy-drama (*Honkytonk Man* 1982), a biopic of jazz legend Charlie Parker (*Bird* 1988) and a character study of an obsessed film director based on John Huston (*White Hunter Black Heart*). That said, it took another action movie, also released in 1971, to propel Eastwood into the top flight of Hollywood names. With *Dirty Harry*, he progressed from star to superstar, unperturbed by protests that the film was a sadistic right-wing fantasy of law enforcement through thuggery (slightly toned down in its native country to avoid a commercially detrimental X-rating, a category usually reserved for pornography). Aside from No Name and Philo Beddoe, the bare-knuckle fighter/knucklehead in the comedies *Every Which Way But Loose* (1978) and *Any Which Way You Can* (1980), Harry Callahan is the only Eastwood character to merit a sequel or four. The action-oriented films kept on coming, some (*Joe Kidd* 1972, *Magnum Force* 1973, *The Eiger Sanction* 1975) fairly conventional, others decidedly offbeat. Both *High Plains Drifter* (1973) and *Pale Rider* (1985) are supernatural revenge westerns, where the central character turns out to be either a ghost or an avenging angel.

Eastwood's success as a director is due in no small part to the influence of his two mentors, Leone and Siegel (*Unforgiven* is dedicated to them). If Leone showed him the possibilities of natural landscape (beautifully used in *High Plains Drifter* and *The Outlaw Josey Wales*) and the ultra-widescreen 'Scope format (Techniscope /Panavision), Siegel's hand can be detected in Eastwood's taut staging of action sequences (very different to Leone's highly stylized and ritualized use of violence) and his aptitude for economically sketched characterization. Another notable Eastwood trait is his refusal (in his best work) to glamorize or wallow in violence, avoiding the slow motion bloodspurting beloved of the Sam Peckinpah school of action film-making. The low key shootout at the climax of *Pale Rider* is a case in point. Undeniably gifted, Eastwood has never quite attained the same league as Leone and an on-form Siegel and his understated style can produce problems. Favouring subdued lighting and unhurried pacing, Eastwood's direction can seem ponderous and lacking in vitality. He does not possess Leone's unerring sense of rhythm and tempo; subsequently a number of his films are sadly short of humour and excitement. The downbeat subject matter of *Bird* or *Unforgiven* is a suitable vehicle for Eastwood's talents. Applying a similar style to a thriller (*Firefox* 1982) or a comedy (*Bronco Billy*) produces unhappy results.

During the seventies and early eighties, Eastwood built up a virtual repertory company of actors (including John Mitchum (brother of Robert), Sondra Locke, Geoffrey Lewis and Bill McKinney) and technicians (cameramen Bruce Surtees and Jack N. Green, composers Lalo Schifrin, Jerry Fielding and Lennie Niehaus, editors Ferris Webster and Joel Cox, production designer Edward Carfagno and special effects man Chuck Gaspar) with whom he collaborated on a number of films. Between 1971 and 1982, when he became his own producer, nearly all of Eastwood's vehicles were produced by Robert Daley. This 'team' approach, with its accompanying loyalty and dedication to duty, seems to have inspired him to take a few risks with his star image (as in

● **Eastwood finds his star status challenged during the filming of *Magnum Force*.**

Honkytonk Man and *Tightrope* 1984, an effective police procedural treading the dark waters of perverse sexuality) and, occasionally, to share centre stage with his co-stars, notably Jessica Walter (*Play Misty for Me*), Chief Dan George (*The Outlaw Josey Wales)* and Sondra Locke (*The Gauntlet, Sudden Impact*). Curiously, Eastwood's desire for regular collaborators has never extended to writers. Only a handful, such as Dean Riesner (*Coogan's Bluff*, *Play Misty for Me*, *Dirty Harry*, *The Enforcer*), Michael Cimino (*Magnum Force*, *Thunderbolt and Lightfoot*) and Richard Tuggle (*Escape from Alcatraz*, *Tightrope*), have worked on more than one of his films, with both Cimino and Tuggle graduating to writer-director for their second Eastwood project. More cynical observers have claimed that this is simply a result of a budget-conscious star refusing to pay more than the bare minimum for his scripts, yet this economy does not appear to have deterred talent from other departments.

Following the mid-seventies peak of *Josey Wales*, Eastwood's output suffered a decline in overall quality, not helped by the miscasting of girlfriend Sondra Locke in several films. A competent actress, Locke's limited range and rather remote on-screen persona did little to grab audience sympathy. Cinemagoers appeared not to mind and *Every Which Way But Loose*, Eastwood's first 'family' offering, became his biggest hit of the decade. Alternating his more personal films with slick, undemanding action-adventures (the more routine outings, such as *Any Which Way You Can* and *City Heat* 1984, were usually assigned to other directors), Eastwood sustained his career throughout the eighties, coming unstuck only when *Pink Cadillac* (1989), a vacuous chase movie, failed to draw the expected crowds (a fate shared by the more interesting *White Hunter Black Heart*). *The Rookie* (1990), while a solid commercial success, betrayed a certain weariness with the cop-movie format (already evident in the Dirty Harry outings *Sudden Impact* and *The Dead Pool* 1988). Both as director and star, Eastwood seemed to be reworking old material with little enthusiasm. While the star's offscreen battles with Locke produced more heated drama than many of his films, several observers questioned Eastwood's ability to hold on to his already waning box office appeal.

His belated follow-up to *The Rookie*, *Unforgiven*, appeared a serious risk at a time when Eastwood could least afford one. Despite the success of *Pale Rider* seven years previously, the western had remained a moribund genre. Moreover, *Unforgiven* was an unusually downbeat script (by David Webb Peoples), depicting gunplay as no more than wholesale slaughter. Two decades earlier, Eastwood had paid the price of opting for quality over commercial viability when *The Beguiled* (1971), a bizarre Civil War melodrama directed by Don Siegel, failed at the box office. This time round, his decision to tackle a difficult project paid off, with critical praise, a substantial commercial hit and top awards. Following on from the surprise success of Kevin Costner's eco-friendly western *Dances with Wolves* (1990), *Unforgiven*'s box-office impact was sufficient to revitalize the western genre, inspiring productions such as *Posse* (1993) and *Tombstone* (1993). Eastwood's post-*Unforgiven* output has been uneven. *In the Line of Fire* (1993) is a well crafted thriller where the star's advancing years are a key plot point. *A Perfect World* (1993), a protracted melodrama involving an escaped convict and his child hostage, deserves marks for effort rather than achievement. Casting himself in a secondary role, Eastwood constructed an ambitious vehicle for the then current industry golden boy Costner, who couldn't meet the demands of his part. Mediocre reviews and box-office underlined the film's inadequacies and Eastwood's latest venture, an adaptation of the bestselling romantic novel *The Bridges of Madison County* (1995), is a blatant return to commercial fodder. Playing opposite Meryl Streep, queen of the serious-accent school of acting, the role of dashing lover is a first for Clint Eastwood (onscreen at any rate). Better late than never?

There is always a slight feeling of disappointment looking back over Eastwood's career, not so much a case of early promise unfulfilled as talent deliberately slumming it at regular intervals. When an offbeat, adventurous 'road movie' like *Thunderbolt and Lightfoot* is followed by the utterly fatuous *Eiger Sanction*, the accountant is winning out over the film-maker. From a commercial point of view, this is fair enough, if we accept that the dross pays for the interesting stuff (though Eastwood's personal efforts have occasionally exhibited more enthusiasm than sound judgement). Whatever one's reservations about the end results, there is little doubt that projects such as *Bird* and *White Hunter Black Heart* would not have seen the light of day without the financial muscle provided by the megahits *Sudden Impact* and *Heartbreak Ridge* (1986). Yet there is no good reason why so many of the shoot-em-ups/punch-em-ups/kick-em-ins should be so dull. Routine film-making does not have to be lazy film-making. It is difficult to believe that Eastwood is genuinely proud of movies like *Firefox* and *The Dead Pool*. Making a buck is one thing; making a buck with shoddy goods shows both complacence and contempt for the paying public.

This aside, there is much to be grateful for. In a 40-year career totalling 52 films, Eastwood has had his share of great moments. The *Dollars* trilogy has stood the test of time, with *The Good The Bad and The Ugly* now regarded as a modern classic. *Coogan's Bluff* and *Where Eagles Dare* stand out as the best of Eastwood's late sixties vehicles. The seventies brought *The Beguiled*, *Dirty Harry*, *High Plains Drifter*, *Thunderbolt and Lightfoot*, *The Outlaw Josey Wales* and *Escape from Alcatraz*. If the ground has been thinner since, we can still appreciate *Tightrope*, *Bird* and *White Hunter Black Heart*, with *Unforgiven* serving as an impressive reminder of its creator's talent. Clint Eastwood keeps blazing away.

● Lining up a shot for *Unforgiven*.

1

Universal Years

Pleased to meet you, all of you.
Rose Gillray, *The First Traveling Saleslady*

In the mid-1940s, an English teacher at Oakland Technical High School, Oakland California, talked a very reluctant fifteen-year-old Clint Eastwood into taking the lead role in a class play. Having considered running away before the performance, young Eastwood decided to go through with it, reasoning that he would be jeered at more for quitting than for making a fool of himself on stage. Cast as an aggressive, self-assured teen rebel, he was surprised to find that his dramatic debut went rather well. The laughs came in the right places and his audience appeared to sympathize with him. If nothing else, the experience was a valuable lesson in the importance of self-confidence (or the appearance of it). Nevertheless, Eastwood did not really enjoy himself and vowed that his first stab at acting would also be his last.

Twelve years on, a discontented and impoverished Eastwood would probably have agreed that his initial decision was the right one. Based in Los Angeles since the early 1950s, this aspiring leading man had seen his early film career go nowhere and most of his income now came from digging swimming pools for the wealthy residents of the Beverly Hills suburbs. He'd pursued an acting career against the wishes of his wife and her family, whose reservations now appeared amply justified. To make matters a great deal worse, it seemed that his one chance of a decent break was now lost forever. The CBS television network had informed his agent that their proposed Western series, in which he had a leading role, was to be cancelled. Hour-long cowboy shows were going out of fashion and sponsors didn't want to know. CBS weren't even going to screen the ten trial episodes already filmed. Faced with indifference from both the film and television industries, Clint Eastwood was running out of options. Perhaps it was time to admit defeat and go back to his unfinished course in business studies at Los Angeles City College. Yet this, he felt, was really for people who didn't know what they wanted to do with their lives. He knew.

By the time Clinton junior was born on 31 May 1930, the middle-class Eastwood family had been living with the effects of the disastrous 1929 Wall Street Crash for just over seven months. Clinton senior, formerly a stockbroker, was taking whatever jobs he could find (often menial work such as pumping gas/petrol), travelling hundreds of miles with his wife, Ruth, and daughter, Jean, to wherever work was available. The family was currently based in the town of Oakland, near San Francisco, though it quickly became just another pitstop in the unceasing search for a regular income. Eastwood has always played down the hardship element of his early childhood, perhaps concerned that people might associate his family's plight with the dust-bowl hell on earth existence immortalized in John Steinbeck's 1939 novel *The Grapes of Wrath*. While the Eastwoods did have to move up and down the West Coast, disrupting friendships and the children's education, he insists there was never any danger of starvation. Any tensions and stress that Clinton Sr and Ruth suffered (and there must have been plenty) were kept hidden from

Jean and Clinton Jr. A measure of stability was provided by regular visits to their grand-mother's chicken farm, near Livermore. It has been commented on that Eastwood's childhood memories tend to focus round his father (who taught him the basics of swimming, hunting and fishing, as well as instilling the value of independence) and grand-mother, rather than his mother, but there seems no reason to doubt his assertion that all the family members were close. At the 1993 Academy Award ceremony, Ruth Wood (she remarried after Clinton Sr's death in 1970) was Eastwood's guest of honour. Circumstances obliged Eastwood to become something of a loner right through to early adulthood (he has described his teenage years as living 'within my imagination'). While one might question his attitude to long-term relationships, especially with women (he now admits that his one marriage was possibly a mistake), anyone looking for mental scars resulting from Eastwood's formative years would have a hard time making a convincing case (though he wasn't too keen on being a Jr). The most visible long term effects (in his professional life at any rate) are a respectful attitude towards money, a strong desire to keep working, an insistence on absolute loyalty from his employees and an unshakeable belief in his own instinct.

By the time Eastwood reached college age, his family life was a little more settled. The Eastwoods were back in Oakland, where Clinton Sr had secured a job as an industrial efficiency expert, while Ruth found a post at IBM (International Business Machines). Clinton Jr began to form more lasting friendships, including one with fellow high school student Fritz Manes, who later became a film stuntman before joining the Malpaso company in the mid-1970s as an associate producer (which usually means location manager). No-one could ever accuse Eastwood of lacking a sense of professional loyalty. During the summer vacations, he took on a series of outdoor jobs, usually involving heavy manual labour, including working as a farmhand, a lumberjack (narrowly avoiding being crushed by falling logs) and a forest-firefighter (narrowly avoiding being scorched). His college grades proved acceptable, if hardly spectacular, and his undeniable athletic prowess was felt to be undermined by his reluctance to participate as a team player (leader or nothing at all: 'I'm not the gang type'). One of Eastwood's developing interests at this time was music, especially jazz, partly inspired by attending a live performance given by Charlie Parker, Coleman Hawkins and Lester Young in 1946. He learned to play the trumpet and piano, putting the latter skill to lucrative use at the Omar Club, Oakland, where at weekends he played jazz in return for food, beer and tips (Eastwood's age made this sideline slightly illegal). On graduating from Oakland Technical High in 1948, Eastwood took on a few more dead-end jobs (such as steel-furnace stoker) before making a decision to pursue his musical studies at Seattle University. This ambition was thwarted by his call up for military service in 1950. America had decided to get serious in Korea (the war would last until 1953) and Eastwood found himself posted to Fort Ord training camp, on the Monterey Peninsula.

Stuck in the army for two years, Eastwood had little option but to adjust to the tedious routine of military life. He escaped being posted to the war zone ('my number never came up'), serving his country largely as an army swimming instructor. The only real brush with danger came when, having taken a little home leave, he rashly hitched a lift back to the camp in an aeroplane radar compartment with a defective door catch. Having spent an agonising period of time either passing out (through lack of oxygen) or nearly falling out, Eastwood was then obliged to swim several miles in rough sea after the aeroplane ran out of fuel and ditched in the ocean. Whether or not he felt able to laugh about it later is uncertain.

Off duty, Eastwood found time to continue with his musical enthusiasms, teaming up with fellow conscript Lennie Niehaus, a gifted saxophone player, in the army jazz band. Like Fritz Manes, Niehaus would later receive the call to join Malpaso, initially as musical arranger on *The Outlaw Josey Wales*. Eastwood's army stint also introduced him to the coastal town of Carmel, 120 miles south of San Francisco, which he first encountered in 1951 on a Saturday night out. He claims to have decided that, should he ever make any real money, he would settle there. All he needed was the right career.

Aside from Niehaus, Eastwood's army acquaintances included two ambitious young actors, David Janssen and Martin Milner, who suggested he might look for a break into films when his military service came to an end. Both former child actors, Janssen and Milner already had a number of Hollywood credits to their names (Milner had enough clout to land a job directing training films for the US Army). Janssen had appeared in the melodrama *Swamp Fire* (1946), billed some way below stars Johnny Weismuller and Buster Crabbe, while Milner could be seen in *Life With Father* (1947), with William Powell and a young Elizabeth Taylor, and *Sands of Iwo Jima* (1949), one of John Wayne's finest hours. While neither of them were ever to achieve much success in films, television later offered a more fleeting taste of fame and fortune, Milner co-starring in *Route 66* (1960-63), Janssen starring in *The Fugitive* (1963-66). Though not entirely uninterested (being a keen filmgoer), Eastwood still regarded acting with some wariness. When he did head out to Los Angeles following his Army discharge, it was for reasons unconnected with Hollywood. Out on a double date with a friend, Eastwood found himself paired off with Maggie Johnson, a final year student at the University of California. A serious relationship followed and when Maggie announced her intention to return home to LA following graduation, Eastwood decided to use the money allotted him by the GI Bill to take a business course at the Los Angeles City College. They married in December 1953, choosing Carmel as their honeymoon location.

Setting up home in a modest rented apartment, Eastwood demonstrated that he already had a fair amount of business acumen by negotiating a deal with the landlord whereby he would act as manager for the entire building in return for 50 percent off his and Maggie's rent. If the business course failed to inspire, the Eastwoods could at least enjoy a lively social life, often mixing with people connected to the all-pervasive film industry. One of Maggie's close friends was Sonia Chernus, a story consultant working for the CBS (Columbia Broadcasting System) television network. On the domestic front, life could get a little strained. Eastwood later confessed that he found marriage very hard to adjust to, resenting the way it restricted his freedom. Early on it became obvious that Maggie would have to make all the necessary compromises if the union was to last. Eastwood felt no inclination to give way to her wishes, reasoning that Maggie knew what she was getting when she married him. This stubborn 'master of the house' attitude cannot have been helped by Eastwood's awareness that Maggie supplied the bulk of their income, working for a car parts firm called Industria Americana. For a man brought up to value independence and self-sufficiency above all else, this might well have appeared as a humiliation (though one would hope that Eastwood was never that insecure). His own financial contributions derived mostly from regular stints as a pool digger/maintenance man and gas/petrol pump operator (much like his father twenty years earlier). While pumping fuel one tedious day, Eastwood met Arthur Lubin, the man who would put him on the road to stardom. A long and meandering road, admittedly, but it is not unreasonable to say that without Lubin, Clint Eastwood Superstar could never have existed.

Though unlikely to figure on any list of great American film-makers, Arthur Lubin deserves some kind of niche in cinema history. In Hollywood from the mid-1920s, Lubin began his film career as an actor, turning to directing in 1934. Based largely at Universal Studies, smallest of the major companies, he specialised in low budget comedies and exotic 'B' pictures. Two of his more notable early efforts are *California Straight Ahead* (1937), an above average star vehicle for a pre-*Stagecoach* John Wayne, and *Black Friday* (1940), a bizarre brain transplant horror-thriller starring Boris Karloff and Bela Lugosi. In 1941, Lubin hit the big(gish) time, directing *Buck Privates* (1941), the first film showcase for comedians Bud Abbott and Lou Costello (their initial stab at cinema greatness, as supports in *One Night in the Tropics* 1940, had sunk without trace). *Buck Privates* (retitled *Rookies* for British audiences) made $10 million at the box-office and Lubin was rewarded with four more Abbott and Costello vehicles: *In the Navy* (1941), *Hold That Ghost* (1941), *Keep 'Em Flying* (1941) and *Ride 'Em Cowboy* (1942). Universal then moved him upmarket, assigning him to two Technicolor spectaculars: a $1.5 million remake of *The Phantom of the Opera* (1943), with Claude Rains, and *Ali Baba and the 40 Thieves* (1944). In 1946, Universal merged with International Films (becoming Universal-International), and began to concentrate almost entirely on 'B' films, a long way from such 1930s triumphs as *All Quiet on the Western Front* (1930), *Waterloo Bridge* (1931) and *Frankenstein* (1931). Lubin stayed on as a contract director, enjoying his biggest success with a series of family comedies featuring Francis the Talking Mule. Produced by Robert Arthur, the series kicked off (so to speak) with *Francis* (1950), starring Donald O'Connor (still two years away from *Singin' in the Rain* 1952), Chill Wills (as the mule's voice) and a young Tony Curtis (who claims that the film grossed $3 million). Sequels followed at a rate of one a year: *Francis Goes to the Races* (1951), *Francis Goes to West Point* (1952), *Francis Covers the Big Town* (1953) and *Francis Joins the Wacs* (1954). Lest anyone should think he had a mule fixation, Lubin also directed *Rhubarb* (1951), a Paramount comedy starring Ray Milland and a cat. During the production of *Francis Joins the Wacs* Lubin encountered Eastwood and suggested he take a screen test.

There are, of course, alternative versions of the events leading up to Eastwood's first on-camera performance. Some sources claim that he met Lubin while still stationed at Fort Ord, chancing upon the director during a location shoot (if so, Eastwood was a little slow to take up the offer of a break into films). There is also the figure of Irving Lasper, an army friend of Eastwood's, who'd found work at Universal-International as a stills photographer. According to Lasper, he encouraged a still-reluctant Eastwood to take the proffered screen test. Taking into consideration Maggie's lack of enthusiasm for the profession, this may well be true, though it would have been one of the few times that Mrs Eastwood's wishes deterred her husband from his desired course of action. Whatever the case, Eastwood took the test, which amounted to little more than posing for the camera while responding to questions about himself. Lubin had something of a reputation for discovering new talent (he is supposed to have picked Rock Hudson for his screen test), and after a week or so of figurative nail-biting, Eastwood heard back from the studio. Universal-International was prepared to offer him a six month contract at $75 a week, rising to $100 per week if the contract was extended beyond the initial trial period. All this and a place on the studio's training/talent programme for 1954-55. A modest start, certainly, but Eastwood quickly found himself drawn to the business of film production, spending as much time as possible watching the various studio personnel at work. It is significant that, even at this early stage, he felt as much interest in the behind-the-camera technicalities as the acting he was being paid for. Aware of the limitations of the studio training (how to look good in period costume), Eastwood decided to take extra-curricular drama lessons at night school (at his own expense). Having committed himself to the movies (at least for six months), he did not intend to lose out through lack of effort. When the time came for his motion picture debut, Eastwood discovered how little his efforts could count for when control of a film lay in other hands.

Anxious to make their new investment work for them, Universal-International cast Eastwood as a laboratory technician in *Revenge of the Creature* (1955), the first sequel to *The Creature from the Black Lagoon* (1954), a *King Kong*-inspired horror-fantasy (in glorious 3-D) which had gone down well with drive-in audiences. Both films were directed by science-fiction specialist Jack Arnold, who at one time enjoyed a high reputation among fantasy cultists. Justly praised for efforts such as *It Came from Outer Space* (1953) and *The Incredible Shrinking Man* (1957), Arnold had struggled to do anything of great interest with *Black Lagoon*. Apart from moody underwater photography and a striking, if blatantly man-in-a-suit creature (designed by top make-up artist Bud Westmore), the film is competent rather than inspired. *Revenge of the Creature* is nothing more than a second-rate carbon copy, further doomed by the casting of ultimate non-star John Agar in the lead role. Having cannily launched himself into a film career by marrying child-star-turned-teenage-starlet Shirley Temple, Agar won co-starring roles in the John Ford-John Wayne classics *Fort Apache* (1948) and *She Wore a Yellow Ribbon* (1949), also standing tall with Wayne in *Sands of Iwo Jima*. Following his divorce from Temple in 1949, Hollywood suddenly noticed that Agar had no talent and his career took a big slide downwards. Hence *Revenge of the Creature*.

Whatever initial reservations Eastwood may have had about the film (not that he had any choice), he soon realized that even a straightforward 'B' movie sequel could provoke creative differences. His brief role (a character named Jennings, though he received no screen credit) required him to waffle on about losing one of his laboratory rats, only to have it turn up in a pocket of his white coat (standard issue to all 'B' film scientists). Less than impressed by this feeble piece of comedy relief (essential to all scary films, for some elusive reason), Jack Arnold demanded that the scene should be cut from the script. His regular producer, William Alland, insisted that it remained, presumably to pad the film out to its required running time. While Eastwood may well have agreed with Arnold, the loss of his only scene in his film debut would have been just about the worst start possible. Fortunately, Alland got his way.

Eastwood's second film appearance, *Tarantula*, went more smoothly, though his role was an even briefer walk on (or sit-down in this case). Another outing from the Arnold-Alland team, *Tarantula* offered assorted giant sized animals (with the title spider dominating) and several humans afflicted by acromegaly, a disease which causes the facial bones of fully grown adults to enlarge in a grotesque and painful manner ('B' horror star Rondo Hatton suffered from the condition). As usual, the cause is a mysterious chemical formula with potent mutating effects. An improvement on *Revenge of the Creature*, *Tarantula* ultimately fails for the simple reason that the monster spider (achieved with a genuine specimen magnified and a slightly less convincing model) seems a little tame compared with the more intimate horror of human metamorphosis. John Agar again took the dashing lead, with Mara Corday (born Marilyn Watts) as his romantic interest and Leo G. Carroll as the misguided scientist who only wanted to boost the world's dwindling food supply. A gifted actor (well used by Alfred Hitchcock in the films *Spellbound* 1945, *Strangers on a Train* 1951 and *North by Northwest* 1959),

● *Revenge of the Creature:* a short lived romantic interlude for Clete Ferguson (John Agar) and Helen Dobson (Lori Nelson).

Carroll brings a measure of pathos to his role largely absent in the script, especially when infected by the drug (make-up courtesy of Bud Westmore). Eastwood didn't get to join in until the end, playing the army jet pilot who drops napalm on the rampaging tarantula. Largely obscured by a flying helmet and oxygen mask, he had only two lines to speak, though on balance this seems an improvement on a junior scientist a test-tube short of a chemistry set. Eastwood appears to have a certain affection for *Tarantula*, paying homage to the film in *Coogan's Bluff* and *The Rookie* (via clips on a disco wall and television set). His brief role did not allow him much opportunity to mix with the rest of the cast (it is likely that his segments in a mock-up cockpit were filmed in half a day), yet he seems to have struck up more than a passing friendship with leading lady Mara Corday. An attractive, if not exceptional actress confined mainly to low budget science fiction (*The Black Scorpion* 1957, *The Giant Claw* 1957), with occasional supporting roles in more upmarket films such as *Man Without a Star* (1955), with Kirk Douglas, and *Foxfire* (1955), with Jane Russell, Corday's film career went a little quiet after the late fifties. Twenty years on, Eastwood engineered a modest bigscreen comeback for her, with a small role in *The Gauntlet*, the first of four appearances in Malpaso productions.

Following his taste of science-fiction (a genre he never returned to, except, very marginally, in the dismal *Firefox*), Eastwood found himself reunited with Arthur Lubin, who cast him in *Lady Godiva* (1955, released in Britain as *Lady Godiva of Coventry*). A modest (and disappointingly demure) historical drama, the film at least boasted a couple of name actors, John Ford regulars Maureen O'Hara (as Lady G) and Victor McLaglen (as an old rogue named Grimald). Alas, the budget didn't run to an 'A' picture leading man, and Lubin had to make do with George Nader, who apart from an impressive performance in the British crime melodrama *Nowhere to Go* (1958, with a young Maggie

Smith), spent most of his career in the likes of *Rustlers on Horseback* (1950), *Sins of Jezebel* (1953) and *Robot Monster* (1953). Still, *Lady Godiva* gave Eastwood three career firsts: his first film in colour, his first role in period costume and his first screen billing (as First Saxon, appropriately enough).

It was back to black and white for *Francis in the Navy*, penultimate in the series and the last on which Lubin (and Donald O'Connor) worked. Cast as a sailor named Jonesy, Eastwood met up with old friends David Janssen (another Lubin discovery, by all accounts), playing a naval lieutenant, and Martin Milner. None of them had much to do except stand around looking bemused as O'Connor (in a dual role) and the mule went through their usual repertoire of antics, pausing only for O'Connor to romance leading lady Martha Hyer (later one of the many 'guest stars' on *Rawhide*).

At this point, Eastwood's film career was moving along in satisfactory fashion. After the initial six months, Universal-International renewed his contract, increasing his salary by the agreed $25 a week, with a further raise promised once he had completed a full year at the studio. What stifled this early progress had little to do with his talent or even Universal's admittedly uncertain opinion of him. Eastwood's continued success entirely depended on the company's 'B' movie output and the accompanying training/talent programme. In the mid-fifties, the film industry had still not recovered from the post-World War II drop in audiences, which allied with the rising popularity of television and the 1949 antitrust laws (forbidding studios to act as their own film exhibitors) left all the companies on uncertain financial ground. One consequence of this was that the second feature, or 'B' film, rapidly ceased to hold much commercial attraction. Cheap as they were, these films could never generate sufficient revenue to keep a studio profitable. In the early fifties, Decca Records acquired a controlling interest in Universal-International, immediately implementing a major change in production

● *Tarantula.*

policy. 'B' films were to be phased out altogether (along with the training for prospective new stars), replaced by glossy melodramas (such as the Rock Hudson-Jane Wyman vehicles *Magnificent Obsession* 1954 and *All That Heaven Allows* 1955) and innocuous bedroom farces (such as the Rock Hudson-Doris Day vehicles *Pillow Talk* 1959 and *Lover Come Back* 1961). Despite these measures, only the international success of the Hammer horror film *Dracula* (1958), distributed by Universal, saved the studio from bankruptcy.

While Eastwood almost certainly knew about his studio's difficulties through industry gossip, he didn't get his first direct indication that things were turning bad until, after the agreed twelve months, Universal refused to increase his salary to $125 per week. Citing the awkward financial climate, the studio announced that a further six month contract could only be viable at his current wage. Explanations were little more than a formality, as an understandably annoyed Eastwood had no options other than to accept the new conditions or quit altogether. There had already been mumblings about his unsuitability as leading man material. He was too lean, too gaunt, too narrow-eyed. Worst of all, he bore no resemblance to either Tony Curtis or Rock Hudson, the studio's topline male stars. To add insult to insult, Hudson starred in Eastwood's last film as a Universal-International contract player, *Never Say Goodbye* (1956), a remake of the studio's minor hit *This Love of Ours* (1945). Finishing as he'd started, Eastwood played another laboratory assistant, this time to Hudson's dedicated doctor, who in a standard 'weepie' storyline encounters his lost wartime love nine years on. Eastwood had more reason to lament his lost glasses. Noticing the prop spectacles worn by Eastwood in his one scene, Hudson demanded a pair for himself, presumably wishing to look more intellectual. Ignoring director Jerry Hopper's entreaty that a bespectacled Rock Hudson was not what his female fans wanted (Hudson, after all, did not have a great deal of time for women), he got his way, choosing the pair balanced on Eastwood's nose. Co-star David Janssen no doubt offered Eastwood his sympathies. The final six months ran its dismal course, and, after a year and a half at Universal-International, Eastwood received notice that his services were no longer required. Another casualty of the studio's upmarket revamping was Arthur Lubin, whose long standing reputation as an expert 'B' craftsman had finally worked against him. Fired by Universal-International within a few days of Eastwood, Lubin reaffirmed his faith in the young actor's ability by offering him a role in a film he'd agreed to make for the RKO studio, *The First Traveling Saleslady*.

RKO (Radio Keith Orpheum) was in an even worse state than Universal-International. Controlled since 1948 by eccentric millionaire and amateur movie mogul Howard Hughes, the company had never enjoyed real financial stability. Sued by his fellow stockholders for mismanagement in the early fifties, Hughes responded by buying up all their shares at a ridiculously inflated price. He then sold the original studio buildings to the Lucille Ball/Desi Arnaz television company Desilu in 1953. Lubin's decision to work with this moribund outfit as a director-producer (he now had his own company, Arthur Lubin Productions Incorporated) can't have been anything more than a stop-gap measure. If Eastwood didn't care for Lubin's new business partner any more than Lubin did, he could at least admire his mentor's survival instinct and ability to adjust to less than favourable circumstances. Besides, he needed work and the part on offer was his biggest to date.

The First Traveling Saleslady began life as a straight Wild West historical drama concerning the efforts of female sales representatives to interest Texas cattle barons in the modern miracle of barbed wire. The manufacturers have discovered that the landowners treat their regular salesmen with hostility at best and violence (even murder) at

● *Francis in the Navy*: **four men and a mule.**

worst. Salesladies might at least make it back home alive. RKO bought this rather sombre script, by Stephen Longstreet (best remembered for *The Jolson Story* 1946), only to
decide that it needed a lot more humour, plus a song or two. Longstreet being either
unable or unwilling to make the required changes, Lubin hired another writer, Devery
Freeman (who'd worked with the director on *Francis in the Navy*), to transform the script
into an easy-going comedy (i.e. not many laughs). Veteran star Ginger Rogers was cast
as the title character, a bankrupt New York corset entrepreneur turned saleslady, with
Broadway actress Carol Channing co-starring as her gawky, comedy-relief sidekick
(Lubin originally wanted Mae West for the lead role, but the 64-year-old sex goddess
proved unavailable, as did *Lady Godiva* star Maureen O'Hara.) The slightly less prominent male leads were James Arness, steadily gaining in popularity as the star of the television western series *Gunsmoke* (1955-75), and Barry Nelson, who a few years earlier
had made a piece of virtually unnoticed screen history as the first actor to play James
Bond (in an hour long television adaptation of *Casino Royale* 1954). Sixth down the cast
list (though first in the 'featuring' section of the credits), Eastwood played Lieutenant
Jack Rice of Roosevelt's Rough Riders, a cavalry division made up of volunteers. When
it came to persuading RKO to let him cast Eastwood, Lubin had luck on his side. The
character of Rice served mainly as Channing's romantic interest. Channing was/is taller
than the average starlet and at 6 feet 4 inches Eastwood measured up nicely.

Saddled with a flat script, awful songs (including 'A Corset Can Do a Lot for a
Girl'), overemphatic acting and a snail's pace, *The First Traveling Saleslady* is by no means
a high point in Eastwood's early career. There is an element of half-baked feminism in
the story, as the independent, progressive Rose Gillray (Rogers) clashes with rugged,
sexist cattle baron Joel Kingdom (Arness), who (surprise) falls in love with her. Nelson
plays a motor car pioneer, which allows for plenty of feeble jokes about women drivers.
The native Indians on display are depicted as simple-minded children (Eastwood would

always try to avoid this in his own westerns) and overall the film has a smug, patronising tone (all women really need is a strong man) that now seems a little offensive. Lubin employs his usual straightforward, unshowy style of direction (mostly medium shots), which without a half-decent screenplay is insufficient to hold back the tedium.

Stuck in a dud production, Eastwood obviously did what he could with his scenes. Rice first appears half an hour into the film, recruiting for the Rough Riders in the unlikely setting of a hotel lobby. Bashful, soft spoken and most definitely good looking, Rice is encountered by Molly Wade (Channing), who immediately takes a shine to him. Following this grand entrance (lasting less than a minute of screen time), Eastwood has little to do other than sweet-talk Channing, ride a horse, sit in a courthouse (for the drawn-out grand finale) and generally look good in his uniform. Needless to say, Rice and Molly end up together, while Rose chooses her automobile inventor rather than the now chastened Joel Kingdom (just about the only positive aspect of the film). Interestingly, both leading ladies are paired off with men nearly ten years their junior (Channing was born in 1921), unusual at the time and still a rarity in American films forty years later.

Confined to eleven lines of dialogue and less than five minutes of screen-time, Eastwood's efforts were sufficient to merit a favourable (if brief) mention in *The Hollywood Reporter* (one of the movie industry's trade journals) when it reviewed the film. Other than Eastwood, the only actor to emerge with much credit was Barry Nelson, who later made a more memorable appearance as the smug hotel manager in Stanley Kubrick's *The Shining* (1980). For Ginger Rogers, *The First Traveling Saleslady* marked a sad return to the studio where she'd enjoyed the cinema's greatest dancing partnership with Fred Astaire (in *The Gay Divorce* 1934, *Top Hat* 1935 and *Swing Time* 1936, to name the best) and several impressive solo outings (*Bachelor Mother* 1939, *Kitty Foyle* 1940, *Tom, Dick and Harry* 1941). Interviewed for British television in the late 1980s, Rogers did not waste time giving *Saleslady* the trashing it deserved. All Eastwood could hope for was that his creditable, if fleeting performance would get him noticed. Sadly, as he soon discovered, his biggest moment as a fresh-faced leading man in-waiting had already passed.

While Arthur Lubin negotiated another production deal with RKO, Eastwood took a trip back to ex-employers Universal-International, who were offering a one film contract for a bit part in the 'B' western *Star in the Dust* (1956). The title may have been an optimistic reference to the blockbuster western *High Noon* (1952), where disillusioned lawman Gary Cooper drops his sheriff's badge on the ground, disgusted by the cowardice of the townspeople who elected him when faced with four vengeful villains. If so, the magic touch didn't rub off. Produced by veteran exploitation king Albert Zugsmith, *Star in the Dust* exhibited all the care and money lavished on it: a first-time director (Charles Haas), a twelve day filming schedule and two dud stars: John Agar (yet again) and Mamie Van Doren. Cast in the almost invisible role of a ranch hand, Eastwood knew he was merely marking time and picking up a little cash (Some sources credit Eastwood with an additional split-second appearance during this brief return to U-I, cast as a marine in *Away All Boats* (1956), a workmanlike World War II actioner starring Jeff Chandler, George Nader, Lex Barker, Richard Boone and David Janssen.) It is unlikely he had much to say to Agar, who despite a severe drinking problem and zero acting ability could still pick up the parts no-one would even think of offering to him. In later years, Eastwood may have taken some grim satisfaction in the knowledge that Agar remained stuck in the 'B' movie rut, never able to rise above the likes of *The Mole People*

(1956), *Daughter of Dr Jekyll* (1957) and *Journey to the Seventh Planet* (1964). Agar's only (minor) salvation came in the shape of former co-star John Wayne, who eventually took pity on him, handing out bit parts in *The Undefeated* (1969), *Chisum* (1970) and *Big Jake* (1971). Agar finally had the good sense to leave the movie business, retiring to become an insurance salesman. It took Italian mogul Dino de Laurentiis to lure him back again, for a cameo in the supremely tacky (though expensive) remake of *King Kong* (1976). If nothing else, Agar still knew where his special talents belonged.

Eastwood's rather more impressive talents remained untapped. Once Lubin had closed the deal for his second (and last) RKO film, *Escapade in Japan* (1957), it became obvious that there was no suitable role in it for his friend and discovery. Shot largely on location in Japan, the film is a pleasant, if flimsy combination of travelogue and good relations propaganda, aimed at endorsing the post-World War II reconciliation between the two former enemy countries (between 1945 and 1952, Japan had been placed under Allied, mostly American occupation). The story has adulterous, Tokyo-based diplomat Cameron Mitchell and his estranged wife Teresa Wright on the verge of divorce when the plane bringing their small son to meet them (and hear the bad news) crashes in the sea. The boy is picked up by a Japanese fishing boat and befriended by the son of its owner. For contrived reasons, the two of them then go for a long trek around the more photogenic parts of the country. The family is eventually reunited, Mitchell and Wright forget their differences and the world is a better place. Filming in the widescreen format Technirama (a short-lived rival to Cinemascope), Lubin directed with his usual competence and the script made liberal use of untranslated Japanese dialogue.

As a favour to Eastwood, Lubin found him yet another bit part, paying $175 for a day's work. Cast as a US Air Force rescue pilot, Eastwood again got to prove he could fly a mock-up aeroplane interior with the best of them, this time not obscured by an oxygen mask. He is onscreen for no more than ten seconds, squeezing in just two lines of dialogue as Pilot Dumbo Victor. Some sources claim that Eastwood took a trip to Japan to film his role. Considering its studio-bound nature, this seems a little extravagant. Response to the film proved minimal and Lubin decided to branch into television, quickly scoring a hit with *Mr Ed* (1960-65), a series involving a talking horse (let no-one say this man couldn't handle variety). His would make only four more feature films, notably a French-Italian remake of *The Thief of Baghdad* (1960), with 'sword and sandal' superstar Steve Reeves, and *The Incredible Mr Limpet* (1964), a man-into-fish fantasy (part animated), starring the deeply unlovable Don Knotts. By the time this Warner release emerged, Eastwood had made his own trip to Italy. For now, he needed to pick up his dwindling career without relying on Lubin to back him up.

Surprisingly enough, Eastwood seemed to have found the desired upturn in his fortunes in a short space of time, winning a supporting role in the World War I flyers drama *Lafayette Escadrille* (1957, released in Britain as *Hell Bent for Glory*). Financed by Warner Bros, the project had possibilities, despite the wooden presence of 'teen rave Tab Hunter as the star. The partly autobiographical story derived from producer-director William Wellman's experiences as a pilot with the American Air Force during the 1914-18 war (William Wellman Jr appears in the film as his father's younger self). Responsible for such Hollywood classics as *The Public Enemy* (1931, with Eastwood favourite James Cagney), *A Star is Born* (1937), *Beau Geste* (1939) and *The Story of GI Joe* (1945), Wellman

● *The First Traveling Saleslady*: Molly Wade (Carol Channing) finds true love in the arms of Lieutenant Jack Rice.

was the first big-name director Eastwood had served under. Playing one of Hunter's fellow pilots, he also had another chance to compare career notes with flying comrade David Janssen. Unfortunately, Wellman appeared to experience a prolonged series of off-days, resulting in a disjointed and uninvolving film, redeemed only by its well achieved period setting (Eastwood blamed the script rather than the director, with whom he became friends). To make matters worse, Jack Warner decided that the downbeat ending, where Tab Hunter meets a tragic death, would be unacceptable to Hunter's fans. Wellman received the order to shoot a new, happy ending, his protests that the main character had died in real life falling on uninterested ears. Contractually obliged to produce the desired footage, Wellman acquiesced, feeling so embittered by the experience that he decided never to make another film (and didn't). While Eastwood could admire Wellman, both for his principles and his work (Eastwood cites Wellman's 1943 western *The Ox Bow Incident* as one of his favourite films), it is likely he also appreciated Warner Bros' side of things. He certainly had no problem returning to the studio for *Dirty Harry* fourteen years later, eventually making it his base of operations in 1975.

Even with its happy ending, *Lafayette Escadrille* made little box-office impact. Eastwood went unnoticed in his non-speaking part and, for the first time since *Revenge of the Creature*, he had no film work on the horizon. He auditioned for RKO's production of *The Naked and the Dead* (1958), director Raoul Walsh's sanitized version of Norman Mailer's controversial World War II novel, without any success (RKO went out of business the same year, taking a modest last bow with *The Girl Most Likely* 1958, a passable remake of *Tom, Dick and Harry*). Following Arthur Lubin's example, Eastwood turned to television for gainful employment, landing a few bit parts in the series *Highway Patrol*, *Navy Log* and *West Point*, on which he enjoyed a run of twelve episodes. Otherwise, he was once again earning a living from the swimming pool business. A film did finally come his way, a poverty row western called *Ambush at Cimarron Pass* (1957). Produced by Regal Pictures for distribution through Twentieth Century Fox, *Ambush* took a mere eight days to shoot, making the production on *Star in the Dust* look positively lavish. Painfully aware of this, Eastwood may not have been too flattered that producer Herbert E. Mendelson had chosen him for the first co-starring role of his career (third down the cast-list), playing an ex-Confederate cowboy fighting with his ex-Union boss (Scott Brady) in between clashes with marauding Apaches. This film couldn't even afford John Agar. It got worse. Director Jodie Coplain (never quite a household name) had been lumbered with a cheap widescreen process called Regalscope (no surprises there) which resulted in what Eastwood described as the worst looking film he ever saw. A combination of substandard technology, rushed filming and careless processing produced unfathomable murkiness in some scenes and blinding over-exposure in others. Regal were reputedly so embarrassed by the finished film (or possibly plain uninterested), that there was no screening for the cast and crew prior to its release, obliging Eastwood to take Maggie along to a regular cinema showing. At one of the lowest points in his career, Eastwood watched and despaired. Once the lights went up his response was directly to the point: 'I have got to get out of this business'. Straightforward enough, as the business seemed more than happy to let him go. Eastwood would not make another film in America for ten years.

His film career shot to hell (to coin a cliche), Clint Eastwood now found his fledgling television career approaching its last chance saloon. He knew that CBS were casting for their forthcoming western series, *Rawhide*. Feeling that he would be perfect (if a little overage) for the second lead, Eastwood asked his then agent, James Arthur, to try and get him an audition with *Rawhide* creator-producer Charles Marquis Warren. Apparently unaware that the series had more than one starring role, Arthur reported back that the part had already been given to an actor named Eric Fleming. Eastwood took a stroll down to the CBS production offices, ostensibly to visit Sonia Chernus and managed to talk his way into an audition with Warren (Chernus may well have played a part). Handed a script he had no time to learn all the way through, he decided to improvise a little, not realizing that the script was written by Warren, who didn't appreciate Eastwood's creative input. Informed of this later on, a dejected Eastwood became convinced he'd thrown his chance away. From Warren's point of view he was quite correct. The producer didn't want Eastwood in the role (which must have made relations a little tense once *Rawhide* got underway). Much to Warren's dismay, the CBS executives begged to differ, instructing him to offer Eastwood the part of Rowdy Yates. He had no trouble accepting it, taking Maggie out for a celebration the same evening.

Opting to produce thirteen sample episodes (roughly half a season's worth), rather than a single pilot show, Warren and his executive producer A.C. Lyles sent the *Rawhide* cast and crew on location to Nogales, Arizona in the summer of 1958. With a budget of $40,000 per episode, Warren planned to have the show ready to form part of the autumn season line-up, the traditional time for launching new series. Ten episodes into the filming, CBS got very cold feet, worried that the tv western market had reached saturation point. Potential sponsors already had at least ten to choose from and initial response to *Rawhide* suggested they wouldn't be fighting to put their names to it. Recalling the production team from Nogales, the executives announced an indefinite postponement for the series, at least until audience reaction could be gauged. Following on so soon from the fiasco of *Ambush at Cimarron Pass*, this development left

● *Ambush at Cimarron Pass*: an uncomfortable moment for Keith Williams (Eastwood in his least favourite role).

Eastwood feeling both wretched and cheated. The chance of fame and a regular pay-check had been tantalisingly offered, only to be snatched away and dumped in the CBS vaults. He looked around for any available work, gratefully taking a walk-on part in the popular western series *Maverick* (1957-61). Cast as a hostile cowboy with a grudge against star James Garner, Eastwood's performance must have carried an unusual sense of authenticity. Unable to kid himself that acting these occasional bit parts could produce a decent living, he began to reconsider his long-dropped business studies (no doubt encouraged by Maggie). During a not very merry Christmas vacation in late 1958, Eastwood received a telegram from agent James Arthur. One of CBS's new series had flopped with audiences and a mid-season replacement was needed. *Rawhide* would begin transmission at 8pm on Friday, the ninth of January, 1959.

2

Rawhide

You've got to want to try; win, lose or draw.
Rowdy Yates, *Incident of the Day of the Dead*

Keep movin', movin', movin'.
Frankie Laine, 434 times

Looked at nearly forty years on, the late fifties prime-time television western series (whether *Rawhide, Maverick, Gunsmoke* or *Wanted: Dead or Alive*) have little immediate appeal other than to the nostalgia market, appearing cheap (often studio bound), slow, predictable, stereotyped and dull. It is difficult to appreciate that these programmes were once both wildly popular (worldwide) and respectable entertainment for adults (while remaining suitable viewing for the whole family, naturally). Up until the mid-1950s, television westerns were invariably aimed at undemanding children, one of the most successful being *The Lone Ranger* (1952-56), with Clayton Moore and Jay Silverheels. In 1955 Warner television launched *Cheyenne*, the first 'adult' western series, promoting the largely despised genre from the Saturday morning 'kids only' slot to a place in the peak-time weekday evening schedules. 'Adult' in this context meant hour long episodes (as opposed to half hour instalments for restless children), slightly more elaborate storylines, marginally more developed characters (with a little history and social comment thrown in), a little more violence and a lot more talk (usually about what a man has to do in the name of righteous justice). Audiences were impressed and *Cheyenne* quickly found itself in competition with the likes of *Lawman, Have Gun Will Travel* and *Wagontrain*. Its biggest rival soon proved to be *Gunsmoke*, put into production the same year by shrewd creator-producer Charles Marquis Warren. Starring James Arness as Sheriff Matt Dillon (a marked improvement on being *The Thing* 1952), and Dennis Weaver as his nerdy sidekick Chester, *Gunsmoke* went on to enjoy a run of twenty years, making it the all-time small-screen western champion (*Bonanza* notched up a mere fourteen years by comparison). Not content with just the one western hit, Warren looked around for a format which provided a little variation on the standard lawman-on-the-beat set-up. His final choice, cattle drovers on the San Antonio (Texas) to Sedalia (Kansas) trail, did not immediately catch on with television executives and three years passed before Warren could begin casting for *Rawhide*. Not that the producer-writer-director needed to worry, as his career in big-screen westerns still had some life in it.

Never a close friend or influence for Eastwood, Warren still deserves his place in any history of the star. A respected novelist and historian of the Old/Wild West, he turned to the film industry in the late 1940s, churning out scripts for *Streets of Laredo* (1949), *Springfield Rifle* (1952) and *Pony Express* (1953), to name but a few. By 1951, Warren had made enough impression to merit promotion to writer-director, working on above-average low-to-medium budget westerns such as *Little Big Horn* (1951), *Arrowhead* (1953), with Jack Palance and a young Charlton Heston, and *Trooper Hook* (1957), with Barbara Stanwyck (another Eastwood favourite) and cowboy icon Joel McCrea. His inspiration for *Rawhide* appears to have been threefold. Howard Hawks' seminal *Red River* (1948)

5113

offered the archetypal cattle-drive western scenario, with John Wayne as a stern, author-itarian trail boss and Montgomery Clift as his rebellious, humanitarian adopted son (Eastwood claims to have met Hawks during location shooting on the film, earning the director's thanks when he helped rein in some runaway horses). The long trek scenario enabled writers Borden Chase and Charles Schnee to throw any number of perils at the drovers: Indian attack, natural disaster, desertion and mutiny. Warren also drew from the diary of a real trail boss, George C. Duffield, written in the 1870s. A more immediate influence (from a commercial point of view at least) was the success of his western *Cattle Empire* (1958), which cast Joel McCrea as a loner trail boss returning to the cattle drive business after five years wrongful imprisonment. Reworking the storyline for a television version presented few problems, the only essential change being to render the trail boss a little more sociable and give him a sidekick. Christopher Frayling suggests this came about simply because it was the fashion in television westerns (as with the Dillon/Chester combo in *Gunsmoke*). True up to a point, yet practical reasons also played a part. Television has always been a more dialogue dependent medium than the cinema (conversation being cheaper than action) and firm-but-fair boss Gil Favor needed some-one to talk to for most of the running time so that costly chases, punch-ups and shoot-outs could be kept to the bare minimum.

The regular cast line-up for *Rawhide* consisted of seven principal characters: Gil Favor (Eric Fleming), Rowdy Yates (Eastwood), dependable second-in-command Pete Nolan (Sheb Wooley), comedy-relief cook Wishbone (Paul Brinegar), his dimwitted assistant Mushie (James Murdock) and good-ole-boy drovers Jim Quince (Steve Raines) and Joe Scarlet (Rocky Shahan). Casting most of the supporting roles proved laughably easily for Warren, as Brinegar, Raines and Shahan had already played identical parts in *Cattle Empire*. The choice of Fleming for the senior lead role (Eastwood got equal billing) proved a good one. Though only six years older than his co-star, Fleming looked more, with his solid build, broad features and authoritative (yet kindly) voice. Like Eastwood, he had enjoyed the beginnings of a film career in the mid-fifties, taking co-starring roles and occasional leads in the minor league efforts *Conquest of Space* (1955), a rare failure for fantasy pro-ducer George Pal; *Fright* (1956), a reincarnation shocker directed by Billy Wilder's broth-er W. Lee; *Curse of the Undead* (1959), a vampire western, and *Queen of Outer Space* (1959), a dire science fiction comedy featuring Zsa Zsa Gabor and costumes left over from *Forbidden Planet* (1956). Viewed as a group (or one at a time) these efforts are even less impressive than Eastwood's 1950s movies, though Fleming did manage more than five minutes of screen time. Of the entire *Rawhide* cast, only Sheb Wooley had a particularly notable film credit to his name, playing one of the gunmen giving Gary Cooper a hard time in *High Noon*.

For the first season of *Rawhide* (the ten sample episodes plus thirteen new instalments filmed in 1959), Warren assembled a fairly constant production team. Regular writers included David Lang, John Dunkel, Les Crutchfield and Fred Freiburger, who later turned producer with shows such as *Star Trek* (the much debated third and final season) and *Space 1999*. Most of the striking, high contrast black and white photography came courtesy of Philip Lathrop, a talent quickly grabbed by the cinema for *Experiment in Terror* (1962), *The Pink Panther* (1963), *The Cincinnati Kid* (1965) and *Point Blank* (1968), among others. Despite extensive location shooting, *Rawhide* couldn't escape its share of stu-dio-bound open plains (filmed at the MGM studios), usually for scenes sensibly set at night-time. While these never looked very convincing, thanks to Lathrop and his col-leagues they at least looked good.

The various directors hired for the series provide an interesting indicator of the state of the film industry at the time. Apart from Warren himself, these included Richard Whorf, Ted Post, Andrew V. McLaglen, Jesse Hibbs, George Sherman, Buzz Kulik, Stuart Heisler and Eastwood's old friend Jack Arnold. Whorf started out as an actor (co-starring with James Cagney in *Yankee Doodle Dandy* 1942), turning director with moderate star vehicles such as *Champagne for Caesar* (1950), with Ronald Colman and Vincent Price, and *The Groom Wore Spurs* (1951), with Ginger Rogers, before finding a niche in series television (*Gunsmoke*, *Wagon Train*). Post had managed only two film credits, the 'B' westerns *The Peacemaker* (1956) and *The Legend of Tom Dooley* (1959), when the small screen beckoned. McLaglen was more impressively connected than most, being the son of actor Victor McLaglen and a former

● *Rawhide:* Trail boss Gil Favor (Eric Fleming), a good man in a harsh world.

assistant to John Ford and Budd Boetticher, yet couldn't manage any better than Post. Following two undistinguished westerns, *Gun the Man Down* (1956) and *The Abductors* (1957), starring his dad, McLaglen signed on with CBS as a contract director, working on *Have Gun Will Travel*, *Gunsmoke* and *Perry Mason*. He later got his break into big screen/big time westerns, directing *McLintock!* (1963), *The Undefeated* and *Chisum* for Big John Wayne, and *Shenandoah* (1965) for James Stewart. Apart from the latter, McLaglen's talent remained obstinately small time. Hibbs had worked for Universal-International ('B' division), turning out *Ride Clear of Diablo* (1954), with Audie Murphy; *Black Horse Canyon* (1954), with Joel McCrea; *Walk the Proud Land* (1956), with Murphy and a young Anne Bancroft, and *Ride a Crooked Trail* (1958), with Murphy and a young(ish) Walter Matthau. He lasted at the studio just a little longer than Eastwood and Arthur Lubin, but got fired anyway. RKO not being around anymore to offer alternative film employment, Hibbs went straight to television. Sherman could boast the longest career in cheap westerns, starting in the late 1930s with *Wild Horse Rodeo* (1937). By contrast, Kulik had only just got started and would remain a television director until the early 1960s. Of the group, only Heisler could be looked on as a director of the first rank. His output includes *The Biscuit Eater* (1940), a popular 'two boys and their dog' adventure; *The Glass Key* (1942), a Dashiell Hammett crime melodrama with Alan Ladd and Brian Donlevy (also Akira Kurosawa's inspiration for *Yojimbo*); *Along Came Jones* (1945), a Gary Cooper comedy western, and (moving a little downmarket) *The Lone Ranger* (1956), a spin-off from the television series. That just leaves Jack Arnold.

Unlike several of the *Rawhide* directors, Arnold (who worked on seasons 1, 2 and 7 of the series) had not yet waved goodbye to his film career. Following the inevitable departure from Universal-International, he took a trip to England to shoot *The Mouse That Roared* (1959), a successful comedy starring Peter Sellers in three roles (four years before he pulled a similar trick in *Dr Strangelove* 1963). This comedy trend continued with two below-par Bob Hope vehicles, *Bachelor in Paradise* (1961) and *A Global Affair* (1963), and *Hello Down There* (1968), an unbearably cute underwater caper. By the time of *Hello Down There*, Eastwood had established Malpaso, though there doesn't appear to have been any phone call offering work to the man who directed his film debut (not to mention *Tarantula*). Perhaps memories of Arnold's attempt to cut him out of *Revenge of the Creature* still rankled. By the time of *The Outlaw Josey Wales*, Arnold had sunk to dismal, end-of-the-cycle blaxploitation, directing the western *Boss Nigger* (1975, now known simply as *Boss*) for writer-star Fred Williamson. Twenty years can certainly make a difference.

If the directing talent employed on *Rawhide* had a decidedly grade 'B' flavour to it (more or less inevitable for a medium budget television show), Warren could not be accused of skimping when it came to hiring for the musical side of the production. Realizing that a rousing theme tune could immediately catch on with audiences even if the series and stars didn't, he called on the services of composer Dimitri Tiomkin, lyricist Ned Washington and singer Frankie Lane. An Academy Award winner from Hollywood's 'Golden Age', Tiomkin had produced scores for *The Lost Horizon* (1937), *Duel in the Sun* (1946), *Portrait of Jennie* (1948), *High Noon* (1952) and *Giant* (1956). Washington, a veteran of both the Marx Brothers (*A Night at the Opera* 1935) and Walt Disney (*Pinocchio* 1940, *Dumbo* 1941), worked with Tiomkin on *High Noon*, netting himself an Oscar in the process. Warren's decision to team them up with Laine certainly showed astuteness, if not originality. The previous year, all three had collaborated on John Sturges' *Gunfight at the OK Corral* (1957), a blockbuster western starring Burt Lancaster and Kirk Douglas as Wyatt Earp and Doc Holiday. The *Rawhide* lyrics, notably 'keep them dogies movin'/though they're disapprovin'', may not be among Washington's best, yet allied with Tiomkin's driving score and Laine's aggressive vocals (plus a little strategic whip-cracking), they have a way of lingering in the mind. Long after the series finished its first run (the final original episode aired on December 7 1965), the theme song (heard over the opening and closing credits of each episode) remains a part of the collective American consciousness. In the cult musical car-chase comedy *The Blues Brothers* (1980), writer-director John Landis paid homage by having his ultra-cool heroes sing *Rawhide* to placate the hostile patrons of a country and western bar. The kind of bar where several of Eastwood's then current screen incarnations (Philo Beddoe, 'Bronco' Billy McCoy) spent much of their time.

Once over the euphoria of landing his first worthwhile starring role, Eastwood got down to the arduous, often exhausting task of acting in the series. Filming on *Rawhide* took up six days a week, starting at 5.30 am and lasting until the scheduled scenes were completed. As this could entail working until close to midnight on some days, Eastwood must have been grateful for his long established routine of fitness and healthy eating. Apart from an occasional beer drinking binge, he looked after his body in a way most actors would have found positively puritanical: a daily workout at the gymnasium, no smoking and a diet consisting mostly of fresh vegetables, fish, regular vitamin supplements (the only drugs that ever passed Eastwood's lips), no carbohydrates and as little red meat as possible. Despite these measures, the ridiculously intensive work schedule soon took its toll (one hates to imagine its effects on the less fit members of the cast). Both behind and in front of the camera, the production team found the pace demanded intolerable. Fleming decided to take a stand, announcing one day that he would finish work at six o'clock in the evening, whether or not CBS's work quota had been met. The studio executives huffed and puffed and threatened to blow his career away (or fire him at any rate). Fleming stood his ground and CBS, faced with the prohibitive cost of replacing a series star midway through a season, backed down (for the time being) and the 6 pm finish became official. Eastwood's role in this confrontation (if any) is uncertain. He got on well with Fleming, who regarded their co-starring roles as complementary rather than the basis for rivalry, and it is likely that he would have quit if the threat to fire Fleming had become a reality.

The first of the 217 *Rawhide* episodes to hit the television screens of America laid out the basic formula of the series, albeit in slightly tentative style. *Incident of the Tumbleweed Wagon* (ninth of the trial run of ten), follows the theme song with traditional western incidental music (assertive brass, soaring strings) and a kind of drovers' homily delivered by Gil Favor (over shots of his cowboys at work), explaining the hardships of being on a cattle drive (harsh weather, poor pay, lousy food, stupid animals, trigger-happy rustlers etc). Educational if not exciting. The story involves a prison wagon transporting assorted thieves, murderers and general villains to be taken for sentencing at the distant Fort Gregg. There just aren't enough judges or unbiased juries to go round (liberal attitudes/social comment). The sheriff and deputy in charge of the wagon are injured during an attempted breakout (the deputy eventually dies) and Favor and Yates agree to take over, despite warnings that a female convict's gunfighter boyfriend is on his way to rescue her. Eager woman-chaser Yates has a run-in with the lady, Dallas (presumably named after the Claire Trevor character in John Ford's *Stagecoach* 1939), rolling around in the dust with her after she attempts to escape. Wise and fairminded Favor gets to know and understand Dallas as a person, accepting that she turned bad after the law failed to give her wronged family justice. By the time her pistol-packin' bad boy lover appears on the scene, Dallas has learned to trust and even like her new warders. In a climax that became an established *Rawhide* favourite, Dallas expires heroically, taking the bullets intended for Favor and Yates (who immediately avenge her by shooting her former boyfriend full of holes).

Aided by the extensive location shooting, Richard Whorf directs in a straightforward, sometimes rather static fashion. Fred Freiberger's script is adequate, if heavily padded out and the pace could best be described as unhurried. Favor and Yates have a clear father-son relationship, with the impetuous, eager-to-impress Yates not always appreciating his boss's good sense and experience (Eastwood already has his trademark hairstyle: backcombed/sideburns/serious hair gel). The performances are all competent, and Eastwood's soft spoken, understated style makes an effective contrast with Fleming's solid, deep-voiced no-nonsense acting. For all the limitations and constraints of *Rawhide*, the series did give Eastwood a valuable chance to develop as an actor. Later episodes reveal a growing confidence and charisma. Particularly noticeable is his assured handling of love scenes (Rowdy Yates had his share of romantic, if brief liaisons), a neat combination of bashfulness and smooth talking. *Incident of the Tumbleweed Wagon* also established the enduring policy of the *Rawhide* guest star. Unlike more recent American series, where the term appears to mean any actor not part of the regular cast, *Rawhide* often obtained the services of well known faces from both television and films. *Tumbleweed* features Tom Conway (brother of George Sanders), an actor best known for his films with producer Val Lewton (*Cat People* 1942, *I Walked With a Zombie* 1943, *The Seventh Victim* 1943), and Terry Moore (as Dallas), one-time Howard Hughes *protege* and the star of *Mighty Joe Young* (1949), an enjoyable giant gorilla fantasy from the makers of *King Kong* (1933). While these were not quite top-flight names, later episodes could boast the likes of Charles

Bronson, Leslie Nielsen, Brian Donlevy, Victor McLaglen (as a punch drunk boxer, his last role), Vera Miles, Peter Lorre, Frankie Laine (two years and 60 episodes on from recording the title song), Agnes Moorehead, Woody Strode, Mary Astor, John Cassavetes, Barbara Stanwyck, James Coburn, Claude Rains, Dean Martin, a pre *Hawaii Five-O* Jack Lord and Lee Van Cleef, with whom Eastwood would have further business. And John Agar, with whom he would not.

Rawhide continued its first season with a series of watchable, if unsurprising plotlines, notably a prodigal son returning home to shoot rather than embrace his father (*Incident of the Alabaster Plain*); a mysterious, guilt-stricken hired gun shadowing a stranded group of stagecoach passengers (*Incident with an Executioner*); an abused young wife running away from her psycho-sheriff husband (*Incident of the Widowed Dove*); a deranged ex-Confederate officer attempting to revive the fight for the South (*Incident on the Edge of Madness*); a suspected outbreak of anthrax among the cattle (*Incident of the Town in Terror*); a definite outbreak of gold fever among the drovers (*Incident of the Golden Calf*); a tangle with evil Mexican bandits (*Incident of the Coyote Weed*) and a small boy who appears to be a compulsive liar (*Incident of the Roman Candles*). As will be noted, each episode had to be some kind of Incident (a policy rigidly adhered to until the fourth season (1961/62), when it was gradually discontinued). Throughout these episodes, a number of recurring themes surfaced. Cowboys have to be businessmen. The days of the gunfighter are over (in any case, gunfighters are immature, death-obsessed gamblers). Drovers are as vulnerable to human frailties as anyone else. People treated badly can turn bad. Honest townspeople will succumb to blind, unthinking prejudice and cruelty when ruled by fear.

Amid the lessons in history and ethical behaviour, Favor and Yates were given a little room for character development. In *Widowed Dove*, an unusually cynical Favor harshly judges the lady who turns to Rowdy for help, warning his friend about 'a certain kind of woman'. Rowdy quits his job with the drive rather than abandon his damsel in distress, having first been soundly thrashed in a fistfight with his boss (a consistent motif in Eastwood's later feature films). Rowdy has to get beaten up all over again by the sheriff before Favor accepts that he may have been a little hasty. Pausing only to shoot the sheriff, he admits he was wrong about the lady. Even trail bosses have their flaws. This harsher side of Favor resurfaces in *Coyote Weed*, where he leaves a drover to die in a stampede rather than risk losing any of the 3000 strong herd (the property of various small-time owners, not one big company). Rowdy later takes up Favor's example, protecting the herd from rustlers while his boss faces a gang of bandits alone. The occasional background detail also emerged: Favor fought on the Confederate side during the Civil War (1861-65), leaving him with a hatred of all conflict; Rowdy spent time in a military prison during the same war. Both skilled gunmen, neither has any taste for violence (so they say). Not even the love of a good woman can deter Favor from his sense of duty to the cattle drive. In *Incident West of Lano*, he falls for Hannah (Martha Hyer), leader of an all-woman troupe of sharpshooters, knifethrowers and trick-ropers (the kind of act badly needed by third-rate Wild West showman Bronco Billy). Hannah's feelings for Favor can't be questioned ('You don't find his kind very often'), yet he is a man with a job to do. Luckily, his dilemma is solved when Hannah is shot dead by a rival cattleman. After her funeral and a quick helping of lead death for the murderer, a heartbroken Favor moves on.

● *Rawhide: Incident of the Red Wind.* Rowdy Yates in aggressive mode. Guest star Neville Brand looks suitably impressed.

Despite mixed reviews (one critic complained he couldn't tell who the stars of the series were), season one of *Rawhide* proved a solid success, with respectable ratings and no further production traumas. Eastwood took advantage of his new-found wealth, buying his first house, situated in north Los Angeles. He socialized regularly with the other members of the cast and crew, keeping in contact during the long summer break before production on season two commenced. Not everyone involved with the show felt quite the same enthusiasm. Interviewed by John Mitchum in the late 1980s, Ted Post (who worked on the first six seasons of *Rawhide*) expressed open contempt for Eric Fleming, complaining that he had no more than a superficial grasp of acting, over-relying on his imposing voice, with no sense of subtlety or understatement. Worse, he either could not or would not take direction (from Post, at any rate). Going by the evidence of the episodes themselves, this view seems a little harsh. Fleming may not have been a great actor (or even a particularly good one), but he could do his job.

Whether out of confidence in Eastwood's growing star quality or a less laudable desire to show Fleming that he was not indispensable, CBS opted to open season two with a solo outing for Rowdy Yates, *Incident of the Day of the Dead*. Under the firm control of Stuart Heisler, this episode proved to be the best so far, with a carefully developed script (by David Victor and Herbert Little Jr) and good performances. Riding into a small town to collect the drovers' mail, Rowdy gets a little drunk and loses badly at poker, amassing an unpayable debt. He is bailed out by a mysterious Mexican senorita (Viveca Lindfors, at one time Mrs Don Siegel), who demands that he pay her back by breaking in a dangerous wild stallion, unsubtly named La Muerta ('Death'). The lady's family includes a kindly, staid English husband and an unhappy step-daughter, apparently crippled when she attempted to ride the horse and got thrown (her injuries are purely psychological). Rowdy fails in his efforts to tame the horse (a sequence giving a lot of work to Eastwood's stunt double), yet his example inspires the daughter to get up and walk. She departs with her father, who has decided that mixed marriages don't work. The senorita sets La Muerta free, and a bemused Rowdy makes his excuses and leaves.

Set against the backdrop of the Day of the Dead festival (which adds a touch of macabre atmosphere), with a Juarista subplot (see Chapter 5) thrown in for a bit of action, *Day of the Dead* provides a useful vehicle for Eastwood's gentler side, especially in his scenes with the daughter. He is well matched by Swedish actress Lindfors, entirely convincing as the cruel, passionate Mexican aristocrat. None of the other regulars appear at all, except for a brief glimpse of Fleming yelling 'Head 'em up' at the end, hinting at some anxiety on CBS's part that audiences would think they had tuned into the wrong show (a ten week break between seasons can be a long time in television). Aside from *Day of the Dead*, season two of *Rawhide* made no great demands on Eastwood. He did get to do some serious rock climbing in *Incident at Jacob's Well* (which now looks like a dry run for *The Eiger Sanction*), albeit in the service of a contrived and preachy script. The more Eastwood showed what he could do in *Rawhide*, the clearer it became that the series had little left in the way of challenges to offer. There were still a few fringe benefits, one of them being actress and stuntwoman Roxanne Tunis, whom Eastwood met during filming in 1959. Their relationship would last until 1975, even longer than the much more public affair with Sondra Locke. Maggie dealt with this fling of her husband's in much the same way she would deal with all the others: by shutting it out of her mind. Eastwood has described his thirty-year relationship with Maggie as 'married bachelorhood', leaving him free to pursue other women (and be pursued himself). One wonders if he bothered discussing this with her back in 1953.

By 1960, *Rawhide* was a regular fixture in the weekly list of television's top ten programmes. Feeling he should take advantage of his position, Eastwood pressed CBS to let him perform a few more of his own stunts or play cameraman for some unusual action shots (such as on horseback in the middle of a cattle run). The executives responded that stars could not be allowed to expose themselves to physical peril (for insurance reasons); nor could they turn technician when it suited them (for union reasons). The latter explanation being tenuous at best, Eastwood continued to lobby for some behind-the-camera work, setting his sights on directing. CBS finally agreed, on the strict proviso that Eastwood first demonstrated his competence by filming a few trailers for the next season. Having completed these to the studio's satisfaction, Eastwood looked forward to his directorial debut on *Rawhide*. The anticipated day never arrived. CBS broke the agreement, ostensibly on the grounds that another series star-turned-director had gone way over schedule and budget when left in charge of his show (the identity of this particular actor/series appears elusive). By way of compensation, Eastwood did get the chance to sing 'Unknown Girl' in one episode, impressing enough people to convince CBS that the song merited release as a single (co-star Sheb Wooley had enjoyed unexpected chart success as the writer/performer of the 1959 hit 'Purple People Eater'). It didn't sell, and Eastwood had to wait until *Paint Your Wagon* before getting the chance to stun the world with his vocal flair.

If the above indicates an extremely inflexible attitude on the part of Columbia television (plus a desire to keep ambitious actors in their place), the studio did on occasion indulge the more modest whims of the *Rawhide* cast. Both Steve Raines and Sheb Wooley got the chance to co-write scripts for the third season (1960-61), *Incident at Roja Canyon* and *Incident of the Blackstorms*. Eric Fleming tried out his literary talents co-writing a fourth season (61-62) episode, *A Woman's Place*. CBS knew it had little to lose giving the actors a one-off break like this (their respective writing partners could help them out of any difficulties), and these occasions were too infrequent to cause any union friction with the regular series writers.

Not being particularly inclined towards script endeavours, Eastwood found himself getting increasingly restless after three years of *Rawhide*. The series had provided fame and relative fortune, both highly useful in any attempt to restart his film career. He certainly felt no great loyalty to CBS (Charles Marquis Warren left the series following season three), especially after the company had played on, then frustrated his film-making ambitions. Eastwood's contract did not allow him to take roles in other television shows, making the now undemanding part of Rowdy Yates seem all the more restricting (he did manage an appearance, as himself, in a 1962 episode of *Mr Ed*, presumably his way of paying off a little of his debt to Arthur Lubin). By 1961, Eastwood felt irritated enough to make his problems with CBS public knowledge, giving a bitter interview to *The Hollywood Reporter*, in which he announced his willingness to go on suspension if the studio didn't release him for other work. Film offers were coming in from Britain and Italy, roles which would pay a lot more than another season of *Rawhide*. All this sounding off contained a great deal of bluster (and bluffing). Eastwood knew perfectly well that his exclusive CBS contract only applied to television work. There were no restrictions on him making film appearances during the summer breaks in production. This being the case, either the touted European movies didn't appeal or were more hypothetical than actual. What seems likely is that Eastwood still felt nervous about retrying his luck in films. Quitting *Rawhide* meant saying goodbye to a substantial regular income, something movies would almost certainly never provide. However strong the yearning for big-screen success, Eastwood was still a married man with a mortgage to pay, responsibilities he took very seriously (he later cited his need for financial security as one of the reasons it took nearly fifteen years for him and Maggie to start a family). He knew that a mere handful of television stars had made the successful transition to films, Hollywood tending to look down on small-screen actors (arguing that audiences would not pay to see faces already available in their living rooms free of charge). His only real role models in this quest were Steve McQueen, star of *Wanted: Dead or Alive* (1958-61), and James Garner, star of *Maverick*. Like Eastwood, Garner had done his time in 'B' westerns, such as *Shootout at Medicine Bend* (1957), with Randolph Scott, and war movies, taking the lead in the World War II actioner *Darby's Rangers* (1958), the second-to-last film directed by William Wellman (like Wellman, Garner had actual combat experience, being a decorated Korea veteran). *Maverick* launched him into successful roles in serious drama (*The Children's Hour* 1962), block-buster adventure (*The Great Escape* 1963), and Doris Day comedies (*The Thrill of It All* 1963, *Move Over Darling* 1963). McQueen worked even faster, getting noticed in *The Blob* (1958), a lurid piece of science-fiction filmed in glorious DeLuxe colour, *The Great St Louis Bank Robbery* (1958) and *Never So Few* (1959), a World War II drama directed by John Sturges. He needed only a couple of seasons on *Wanted: Dead or Alive* to relaunch his film career, winning a pivotal co-starring role opposite Yul Brynner in Sturges' *The Magnificent Seven* (1960), a popular western remake of Akira Kurosawa's *Shichi-nin no Samurai / Seven Samurai* (1954), and leads in *Hell is for Heroes* (1962), directed by Don Siegel, and *The Great Escape*. Still stuck in *Rawhide* after five years (six season's worth), Eastwood could take little comfort in the knowledge that McQueen was the same age as him, and Garner only two years older. The old Rock Hudson/Tony Curtis syndrome seemed to have resurfaced. Eastwood's film career had gone nowhere in the 1950s because he didn't meet the requirements of the wholesome, clean cut style of leading man then in vogue. After appearing as a wholesome, clean cut (if slightly rugged) television cowboy for longer than he cared to contemplate, Eastwood now found he didn't match the qualities flaunted by Hollywood's new male stars. Rowdy Yates resembled neither McQueen's bold, insouciant rebel nor Garner's more urbane and sophisticated man-about-town (or cowboy-about-range). If this didn't depress him enough, he also knew that time had ceased to be on his side. Today's television phenomenon could rapidly become yesterday's has-been, good only for parts in other, less prestigious small-screen vehicles. At the age of 33, Eastwood couldn't continue as a bashful juvenile for much longer. Yet Hollywood still showed no interest. Not one studio had approached him for a role in a feature film.

By 1964, Eastwood would probably have accepted any film role, just to get away from *Rawhide* and the typecasting he knew could kill his career. At last the phone rang, with news of a slightly unusual offer from Italy. Two producers, Arrigo Colombo and Giorgio Papi, needed an American leading man, and their director, a relative newcomer named Sergio Leone, had chosen Eastwood for the honour. Based in Rome, Colombo and Papi ran their own production company, Jolly Film, which specialized in highly lucrative low-budget exploitation movies. Their more recent successes included a number of Hammer-inspired horror films, most notably *The Mask of Satan* (1960, aka *Black Sunday*), directed, photographed and co-written by Mario Bava. To convince audiences that these efforts were actually made in Britain (the real thing, so to speak), Colombo and Papi adopted a policy of anglicising the films' production credits. Bava, for example, became John M. Old or John Foam (a little known English surname). The producers now intended to pull a similar trick with the hallowed American western (always a very popular genre in Italy, not to mention the whole of Europe). Just as *The Mask of Satan* needed an English star (former J. Arthur Rank starlet Barbara Steele) for added authenticity, so their western, provisionally titled *The Magnificent Stranger*, required a genuine American. Jolly Film had already experimented with this formula, releasing *Gunfight at Red Sands* (1963, aka *Gringo*), with minor 'sword and sandal' star Richard Harrison in the lead. Faced with a mediocre film and modest box-office returns, Papi and Colombo realized that any follow-up would need a leading man with a little more experience in the saddle. Besides, Harrison had already turned *Magnificent Stranger* down.

Managing to contain his enthusiasm, Eastwood considered the offer very carefully. The budget for *Magnificent Stranger* ran to a mere $200,000, modest even for an Italian exploitation film. His own fee would be $15,000, derisory by Hollywood standards, yet comparing quite favourably with the going rate for *Rawhide*. The script presented more serious problems, giving away its origins as Italian badly translated into English on every page ('He is buried in the hill of boots'). Eastwood stayed interested, mainly because he recognized where the story had been swiped from. Colombo and Papi were offering him a faithful, if simplified remake of Kurosawa's *Yojimbo*, where wandering samurai Toshiro Mifune strolls into a one-gun, no-horse town controlled by two powerful factions. Mifune sells his services to both sides in turn, engineering a highly profitable all-out war which he finally draws to a bloody close (also netting himself the Best Actor award at the 1961 Venice Film Festival). Eastwood had seen the film and been highly impressed, as he recalled years later: 'I said it would make a great western, but no one would have the nerve to make it.' It certainly bore little similarity to any of the American westerns then in production, most of which Eastwood dismissed as tedious and uninspired. He showed the script for *Magnificent Stranger* to Maggie, who agreed that, clumsy dialogue aside, it offered an intriguing central character, 'Joe the Stranger', who would appeal to women as much as men. Eastwood's business manager refused to join in the excitement, pointing out the Italian film industry's reputation as the place where old American actors went to die (or appear in abysmal movies). Only sad has-beens or the never-weres currently employed in 'sword and sandal' epics worked there. Eastwood decided to ignore this advice, the final factor being that he and Maggie both wanted to see Europe, and this might be their only opportunity for a long time to come. He'd already signed up for yet another season of *Rawhide* (number seven), and in all likelihood a cheap Italian western shot with Spanish and German money wouldn't travel outside its continent of origin. The English-speaking world would never even hear of *The Magnificent Stranger*.

3

A man called Joe

In these parts, a man's life often depends on a mere scrap of information.
Don Miguel Rojo, *A Fistful of Dollars*

Two hundred thousand dollars is a lot of money. We're going to have to earn it.
Blondie, *The Good The Bad and The Ugly*

The spectacular rise of the Italian 'spaghetti' western can be traced back to three particular film-makers, only one of them a native of the land of pasta, chianti and overweight dictators. In the mid 1950s, Akira Kurosawa produced *Seven Samurai*, his homage to the American western. Distinguished by extraordinary style, bravura acting (notably Takashi Shimura and Toshiro Mifune), in-depth characterization, ferocious violence and a gripping storyline (a small band of expert fighters defends a village from marauding bandits), the film proved a worldwide hit. Not one to miss a trick, Hollywood producer-director John Sturges bought up the remake rights (Kurosawa admired Sturges' work), changed the setting to the nineteenth-century Mexican borderland, cast Yul Brynner and a group of charismatic, if not yet star actors (Steve McQueen, James Coburn, Charles Bronson, Robert Vaughan and Horst Buchholz), threw in a lot of dialogue about the nature of true manliness and shot a lot of Mexican extras. *The Magnificent Seven* may not live up to Kurosawa's original (it is a little too talkative, the talk often being overly 'significant'), yet it scores where it counts. The action sequences are impressively staged, Elmer Bernstein's music is unforgettable and there is no-one to touch Yul Brynner when it comes to bald star power (dressing in black helps). A further plus is the amusingly over-the-top presence of stage actor Eli Wallach as the chief villain, Calvera. After all the waffle about doing the right thing, his dying words to Brynner ('You came back. Why?'), have a striking (and commendable) brevity.

Released through United Artists, *The Magnificent Seven* enjoyed solid box-office success in the United States, without quite making it to blockbuster status. In Europe it became a huge hit, eventually prompting the production of three adequate, if unmemorable sequels (*Return of the Seven* 1966, with Brynner; *Guns of the Magnificent Seven* 1969, with George Kennedy; and *The Magnificent Seven Ride* 1972, with Lee Van Cleef). Sergio Leone hadn't called his western script *The Magnificent Stranger* for nothing. By the time United Artists showed enough sense to commission the first sequel for profitable export, various European producers had beaten them to it, reasoning that as their fellow countrymen were used to watching their American westerns dubbed into the native language (whether Italian, French, German or Spanish), it wouldn't matter if the films weren't in English to start with. As long as their ersatz versions looked vaguely American, with Americanized credits and (budget permitting) an American 'star', the films could be marketed, with production costs so low that a profit would be virtually guaranteed.

The race to produce the first smash-hit EuroWestern became a neck and neck contest between the Italians and the Germans. The latter had a slight head start, with scores of western novels by German writer Karl May just waiting for adaptation. Former *Tarzan* Lex Barker, his American career all but finished, agreed to star in the German-French-Yugoslavian co-production *Treasure of Silver Lake* (1962). Worse than mediocre, the film nevertheless made respectable money and Barker went on to enjoy something of a career renaissance in *Winnetou* (1963), a German-French-Yugoslavian-Italian co-production; *Old Shatterhand* (1964); *Winnetou II* (1964); *Winnetou III* (1965), with only the Germans and Yugoslavians still interested; *Dynamite Morgan* (1967); and the inevitable *Winnetou and Shatterhand* (1968), one of the last gasps of the 'Saurkraut' western mini-boom. British actor Stewart Granger, veteran of brooding (if occasionally laughable) Gainsborough melodramas (*The Man in Grey* 1943, *Madonna of the Seven Moons* 1944) and a rather unfulfilling spell in Hollywood (*Scaramouche* 1952 excepted), also signed on, appearing in *Rampage at Apache Wells* (1965) and *Old Surehand* (1965), both German-Yugoslavian co-productions. What exactly audiences made of an English actor in a German story pretending to be a grizzled Westerner is open to conjecture. Evidently not enough to sustain this dubious phase in Granger's career. Perhaps the Germans just didn't have the knack for turning out authentic fake westerns. In the event, the end results didn't travel well, largely because the increasingly intense Italian competition soon proved to be greatly superior.

Italy's slightly delayed start in the pseudo-western stakes probably resulted from the fact that exploitation producers were still doing very nicely out of the pseudo-mythical/historical 'sword and sandal' cycle, which kicked off in 1957 with Pietro Francisci's *Hercules*, starring American body-building champion Steve Reeves (later immortalized in the *Rocky Horror Show* song 'Sweet Transvestite'). Reeves' success in *Hercules* and its even more profitable sequel, *Hercules Unchained* (1959), made him a star (though he didn't enjoy making the films very much) and inspired a host of musclebound hopefuls to set sail for Italy, enabling Francisci's competitors/imitators to choose from the likes of Gordon Scott, Reg Park, Richard Harrison, Kirk Morris, Alan Steel and Dan Vadis (later a member of the Malpaso repertory company). A few of them could act a bit (check out former King-of-the-Jungle Scott in *Tarzan's Greatest Adventure* 1959), not that these films really demanded it, and cameramen such as Mario Bava supplied a little visual flair to enliven the standard flexing and fighting. When producers decided to give spaghetti westerns a go, they naturally looked to the ever-swelling ranks of 'sword and sandal' leading men, most of whom were American, if not yet big names back home. Which explains how Richard Harrison, star of *Invincible Gladiator* (1961); *Perseus Among the Monsters* (1962, aka *Medusa Against the Son of Hercules* aka *Perseus the Invincible*); *Gladiators Seven* (1962), an 's and s' rip-off of a western rip-off of a samurai film, and *Giants of Rome* (1963), came to be shooting it out with assorted bad guys in *Gunfight at Red Sands*.

A co-production between Jolly Film and the Spanish company Tecisa, *Gunfight at Red Sands* is of most interest today as an example of the Italian western before the genre found its own real style. Harrison stars as left-handed gunfighter Ricardo Martinez, nicknamed 'Gringo', the adopted white son of a poor-but-honest Mexican family. The setting is United States-Mexico borderland, around the Rio Grande river, a location which became a firm favourite with spaghetti westerns (most Italian actors look more plausible as Mexicans rather than Americans). After four years fighting with the Juaristas against the Mexican army, Gringo returns home in search of a more peaceful life. Luckily for the audience, he soon discovers that his father has been murdered and his brother badly injured by thieves after the family gold. While the brother (a hard-drinking and hard-gambling wastrel) recovers, Gringo and his tough, independently-minded sister attempt to bring the killers to justice. They suspect a local group of sneering, racist Americans, yet Sheriff Corbett, who sports a smart designer waistcoat and hairstyle, seems curiously apathetic with his investigation. In a plot 'twist' of staggering predictability, Corbett turns out to be the chief villain, and all three Martinez children face him (and his obligatory gang of mean hombres) for the inevitable showdown.

Filmed in a straightforward, reasonably lively fashion by director 'Richard Blasco', *Gunfight at Red Sands* has more in common with the old-style American 'B' westerns than the later spaghettis (which unfortunately includes a mediocre script and plodding pace). Harrison is a conventional, clean-cut hero, his only mild quirk being a questionable passion for his sister. His supporting cast, including 'G.R. Stuart', Mikaela and 'Dan Martin' (who later turned up in *A Fistful of Dollars*), is adequate, if a little anonymous. Aside from the mechanical dubbing, the only real hints that the film is not quite the genuine article are the violence, which is stronger than would be expected in a Hollywood family western, a pronounced anti-American slant, an assortment of sweating mediterranean faces (often in close-up), a particularly wicked henchman with a mad laugh, and the kind of mobile, hand-held camerawork that would send less adventurous American film-makers into a rage. The latter came courtesy of director of photography Massimo Dallamano, credited as 'Jack Dalmas'. The score, a traditional arrangement with occasional flourishes from the guitar, trumpet, oboe and drums, was by one 'Dan Savio', better known (in Italy at least) as pop composer/arranger Ennio Morricone, who thankfully cannot be blamed for the accompanying English lyrics ('Keep your hand on your gun/Don't you trust anyone'). When Jolly Film decided to produce *The Magnificent Stranger*, they retained the services of Dallamano and Morricone (plus their respective pseudonyms), not to mention a job lot of army uniforms and some exterior sets built in Almeria, Spain (where the landscape bore a passing resemblance to the wide open plains and deserts of the Old West). Director Roberto Sergio Leone now had his chance to give the spaghetti western the style, mood, pace and intensity it so badly needed.

The son of one of Italy's film industry pioneers (Vincenzo Leone), Leone had been involved in movies since the age of eighteen, working as a production assistant and occasional extra (he appears in Vittorio De Sica's *Bicycle Thieves* 1948). By the early 1950s, American companies were regularly filming productions in European locations (partly to take advantage of lower costs, partly to use up overseas revenues they couldn't export back to the United States), giving him the chance to work as an assistant director with film-makers he idolized (Leone loved American films, especially westerns). Over the space of ten years (and close on 60 films) as an assistant, Leone took orders from the likes of Mervyn LeRoy (*Quo Vadis* 1952), Raoul Walsh (second unit director on *Helen of Troy* 1955), Andrew Marton (second unit director on *Ben Hur* 1959) and Robert Aldrich (*Sodom and Gomorrah* 1961). Not a great fan of biblical or mythological epics (no gunfights), Leone eventually let his increasing boredom show. Aldrich fired him from *Sodom and Gomorrah* (effectively co-directed by Leone, according to some sources), when he discovered that the Italian had been taking two hour lunch breaks, along with his crew.

The rise of the home-grown (if cut-price) toga epic gave Leone the chance to diversify a little, though still constrained by the requirements of the genre. He co-wrote the scripts for the above-average efforts *Aphrodite, Goddess of Love* (1958) and *Sign of the Gladiator* (1959), then helped out Mario Bonnard with the direction on the 1960 Steve Reeves vehicle *The Last Days of Pompeii* (Bonnard took sole credit on the English-language version). Leone finally made his official directing debut with *The Colossus of Rhodes* (1961), a Spanish-Italian co-production starring exiled American Rory Calhoun (born Francis Timothy Durgin) and sultry Lea Massari. Again working as a co-writer, Leone found himself lumbered (or lumbered himself) with a typically flimsy and cliched script, involving the adventures of a dimwitted Greek on the island state of Rhodes, where various traitorous elements plan to assist the evil Phoenicians with their invasion. Apart from a few moments of visual flair, well staged (if overlong) action sequences and some inventive torture scenes (a Leone trademark), the film is slow and tedious, a very average 'sword and sandal' epic. Calhoun, star of numerous minor league westerns (*Massacre River* 1949, *Rogue River* 1950, *Powder River* 1953), looks ill-at-ease in his tunic and his performance consists mainly of assorted grins, smirks and grimaces. Leone directs with competence but no real enthusiasm (torture aside), as if fully aware that any real effort on his part would be wasted (any film which resorts to a man in a sub-standard gorilla suit is in trouble). The only memorable element in *The Colossus of Rhodes* is the Colossus itself, a giant hollow statue of a man bestriding the entrance to Rhodes harbour. Doubling as a defence against invaders (it can pour molten lead onto people below and catapult fireballs from its head), the statue is the real star of the film, also providing the offbeat location for a swordfight, as Calhoun and assorted enemy soldiers climb out of its right ear and run along its arms, lunging and riposting as they go. Leone's working relationship with Calhoun doesn't appear to have been notably successful. Despite his extensive western experience, the latter never made it onto the director's shortlist for *The Magnificent Stranger* (Eastwood claims that Colombo and Papi considered Calhoun for the title role, only to be deterred by the actor's price tag).

For all its faults, *The Colossus of Rhodes* scored well enough at the international box-office (with English-language distribution through Metro-Goldwyn-Mayer) for Leone to wave goodbye to togas and chariots and concentrate his attentions on his western project. By the end of 1963, he had a finished script (co-written with Duccio Tessari) and a co-production deal. Following John Sturges' example, Leone took his inspiration from a Kurosawa film, *Yojimbo*, the Japanese director's biggest ever box-office hit. This way, he would be cashing in on the success of an American remake of a Japanese film with an Italian remake of a Japanese film, itself inspired by an American crime movie. Leone later claimed (perhaps with legal considerations in mind) that both *Yojimbo* and *A Fistful of Dollars* were based on Carlo Goldoni's eighteenth-century comedy *The Servant of Two Masters*. While this assertion might win points for sheer nerve, it is entirely unconvincing. Kurosawa's influence is at work through virtually every aspect of *A Fistful of Dollars*, which even re-uses some of the same compositions and camera angles. Toshiro Mifune's bodyguard-for-hire (a Yojimbo) refers to himself only as 'Sanjuro'. As this means 'thirty years old', he qualifies as a mysterious (not to say magnificent) stranger, or even a man with no name. Moving through an amoral world, Mifune relies on his intelligence, cunning, strength and phenomenal fighting skills to bring him financial gain, the only achievement that others will respect. His one serious opponent is Unosuke (Tatsuya Nakadai, later Kurosawa's King Lear in *Ran* 1985), a cocky, slightly camp gunslinger who owns the one firearm in the town. The plot is played out with much black

● *A Fistful of Dollars:* Joe the Stranger and Marisol (Marianne Koch). A rather misleading publicity still, more rawhide than spaghetti.

humour and stylised violence, embroidered with snappy dialogue ('The smell of blood attracts the hungry dogs') and a great deal of rain and mud. Kurosawa's direction makes spectacular use of landscape and space, emphasized with deep compositions and long, fluid takes. Leone cannot be blamed for becoming so enamoured of *Yojimbo* (both its content and style) that he just had to rework it as a western. Oddly enough, his one major change to the original script (by Kurosawa and Ryuzo Kikushima) proved a mistake. Perhaps concerned that audiences might find Joe the Stranger just a little too strange, Leone and Tessari wrote in a great deal of background information and motivation for the character. This may well have been the right thing to do when it came to attracting backers. Producers Arrigo Colombo and Giorgio Papi picked up the script and went looking for business partners. At no point did anyone think of actually purchasing the *Yojimbo* story rights from Kurosawa.

Typical of its time, the co-production deal for *The Magnificent Stranger* (which remained the official title all the way through shooting) involved Jolly Film, the West German company Constantin and the Spanish company Ocean. As the $200,000 budget did not stretch to building any sets from scratch, Leone and his art director, Giancarlo Simi, would have to make use of the western town set already standing in Almeria. This could incorporate both exteriors and interiors, greatly simplifying the ten week shooting schedule. Any outstanding interior filming would be completed at the Cinecitta Studios, near Rome. Leone had no objections to Jolly Film's choice of Massimo Dallamano as cameraman, and Ennio Morricone had been a friend of his since childhood. When it came to selecting the supporting cast, the requirements of the various co-producers dictated that Leone use an Italian leading man for the chief villain, Ramon Rojo, and a higher-billed German leading lady for the rather marginal heroine, Marisol. For the former he selected Gian Maria Volonte, an intense, aggressive actor whose much professed left-wing politics (shared by Leone) did not deter him from accepting roles in such capitalist fodder as *Hercules and the Captive Women* (1961, aka *Hercules Conquers Atlantis*), with Reg Park and Fay Spain (a *Rawhide* guest star twice over). Despite criminally poor dubbing and some surreally risible dialogue ('Today is dedicated to Uranus'), the film is not at all bad, with imaginative story elements and art direction. More to the point, Volonte, cast in a brief role as a Greek king, gets to look imposing in his cloak-draped toga and throw a mean spear. Holding 'sword and sandal' epics and spaghetti westerns in equal contempt, Volonte managed nevertheless to grit his teeth and take the cheque proffered by Colombo and Papi, who insisted he humiliate himself even further by assuming the name Johnny Wels for the credits. Marianne Koch, the actress chosen for Marisol, got to keep her own name, either because it sounded like it might be American or because German audiences would recognise her straight away from previous efforts such as *Monster of London City* (1964), an Edgar Wallace-derived thriller shot in her native country. Koch had previously appeared in some real American films, though with negligible results. Active in German movies since 1950, she was cast in the Twentieth Century Fox production *Night People* (1954), shot on location in Berlin. This appearance prompted interest from Universal-International, who imported Koch for two co-starring roles in the minor efforts *Four Girls in Town* (1956), with George Nader, and *Interlude* (1957, first anglicizing her name to 'Cook' (a literal translation). Having just missed her chance for an earlier encounter with former U-I employee Eastwood (unless he ran into her on his return visit), Koch/Cook found her US film career meeting with a similar lack of success. By 1963 she was back in low-budget fodder such as the British Edgar Wallace adaptation *Death Drums Along the River* (1963), co-written by a young Nicolas Roeg, and it is unlikely that she would have regarded *The Magnificent Stranger* as any kind of step upmarket. The remaining roles were divided between Italian, German and Spanish actors, several of whom underwent a change in identity (Benito Stefanelli became Benny Reeves, for example). Leone decided on Bob Robertson as a suitable *nom de film*. Colombo and Papi, evidently less imaginative (or less confident of their identity) assumed the names Harry Colombo and George Papi, fooling absolutely no-one. If Leone felt this to be a little unfair, he had the good sense not to say so. Besides, he still had to deal with the more pressing matter of an American leading man. $15,000 wouldn't bring the big western stars running.

It certainly couldn't get him veteran star Henry Fonda, Leone's dream choice for Joe the Stranger. Far more versatile and wide-ranging than the likes of John Wayne, Randolph Scott and Audie Murphy, Fonda had notched up an impressive run of western roles, appearing in the John Ford classics *Drums Along the Mohawk* (1939), *My Darling Clementine* (1946) and *Fort Apache* (1948) and a host of others, notably *Jesse James* (1939), *The Return of Frank James* (1940), *The Ox-Bow Incident* and *Warlock* (1959). Lowering his sights a little, Leone offered the *Magnificent Stranger* script to Charles Bronson, who, apart from the box-office appeal of *The Magnificent Seven*, had paid his western dues with distinction in the likes of *Apache* (1954), *Vera Cruz* (1954) and *Run of the Arrow* (1957). Bronson hated the script so much that he didn't even bother to negotiate for more money before rejecting it ('What I didn't appreciate was what Leone would do with it'). Still determined to get himself a legitimate *Seven* connection, Leone then approached James Coburn, who'd enjoyed an early career break with the Sturges western (he made his film debut in 1959 in the Budd Boetticher-Randolph Scott western *Ride Lonesome*). Second time round, Leone got lucky, finding Coburn both available and interested. Unfortunately for both Leone and Coburn (not so unfortunate for Eastwood), the latter didn't feel able to accept less than $25,000, his absolute minimum fee. Colombo and Papi couldn't negotiate an increase in the overall budget and paying out an extra $10,000 for the star would hurt the rest of the production. Leone reluctantly discarded all thoughts of a legitimate Hollywood star. It is likely that his producers suggested *Gunfight* star Richard Harrison, who certainly wasn't the director's idea of a lean, laidback gunman. Running out of options, Leone made a formal offer to Harrison, who declined (no

doubt to Leone's extreme relief), preferring to diversify a little into James Bond rip-offs (*Spy Killers* 1965) and Bengal Lancer movies (*Adventures of the Bengal Lancers* 1965). While one might question Harrison's career plan (he ended up back in spaghetti westerns, including the interesting *Vengeance* 1968), he can take part credit for one of the modern cinema's most important casting decisions. Harrison knew Eastwood from his television work (i.e. *Rawhide*) and, obviously feeling benevolent, recommended the actor to Leone. Leone had never even heard of Clint Eastwood (though *Rawhide* played regularly on Italian television) and decided to do a little research, viewing a fourth season episode of his cowboy series (*Incident of the Black Sheep*). Impressed by the actor's charisma and good (though not bland) looks, Leone also found himself intrigued by Eastwood's ability to dominate scenes without appearing to do anything. Moving in a way that seemed both graceful and lazy, then blazing into action, the actor would be ideal for Joe, alternating stillness with split second carnage. Leone had found his leading man and Eastwood the luckiest break of his career, not that he appreciated it just yet. One can hope that he later found the time to thank Richard Harrison.

Appreciating that his first film as a star (his first of any kind for seven years) didn't boast no-expense-spared production values, Eastwood decided to do a little shopping for Joe's wardrobe before climbing on a jetplane bound for sunny Spain. The exact extent of this is disputed, though it seems likely that the pistol and gunbelt were courtesy of CBS property department (Eastwood could return them when shooting on season seven of *Rawhide* commenced), while the famed hat and sheepskin waistcoat came from a costume store situated in Santa Monica Boulevard, Los Angeles (Eastwood later claimed that providing his own costume was a condition of getting the job). The poncho, which Leone claimed to have added to broaden Eastwood's shoulders a little (lean but not scrawny), joined the icon-making ensemble on location in Spain. According to biographer Minty Clinch, this durable garment lasted throughout the filming of the entire *Dollars* trilogy without a replacement or even a wash. If so, this is a fine tribute to the quality of Spanish workmanship, though after three years' use in sweltering locations it must have smelled a bit. (That said, Eastwood only wore it for the opening and closing sequences of *A Fistful of Dollars*.) Joe's unshaved look (long before the thankfully brief days of designer stubble) and unsavoury smoking habit almost certainly originated with Leone. No-one else had his flair for close-ups of sweat-drenched facial hair and non-smoker Eastwood wouldn't have offered to stick foul-smelling cigarillos in his mouth without prompting. He later claimed that they helped his character, putting him in the appropriate mean mood ('One drag and I was right there'). It is noticeable in *A Fistful of Dollars* that Eastwood's dialogue is sometimes delivered in a markedly slurred manner, as if the actor was either very drunk or about to lose consciousness (or both). Perhaps the cigarillos were a little stronger than he realized.

Arriving on location in Almeria, Eastwood soon learned the eccentricities (and hazards) of low budget European co-productions. The language barrier raised its awkward (if predictable) head straight away. Eastwood spoke virtually no Italian (or Spanish) and Leone seemed to have little grasp of English (he used a multi-lingual Polish interpreter), which would explain the dialogue in the script (though one wonders how he managed to work as an assistant to American directors for ten years,

● *Yojimbo.*

unless there were no English-speaking assistant directors available). During shooting (which began in May 1964), the actors would speak their lines in their own language, leaving the dubbing editor to sort out the standardised dialogue tracks in post-production (this might explain why actors such as Steve Reeves seem a little perplexed in their movies). Marianne Koch aside, only a few of the supporting cast spoke more than basic English, with Gian Maria Volonte fluent enough to redub himself for the English language version of the film. It is not known if he found time to talk politics with the decidedly right-wing Eastwood.

Facilities during location filming were basic in a way that American unions would not have permitted. Eastwood didn't have to worry about not knowing the Italian for 'Where is the lavatory, please?' as there weren't any. If this caused the star more than a little discomfort, he gamely clenched his teeth and soldiered on (the alternative being endless *Rawhide*s). In any case, there were more serious matters to contend with. The financial deal between Jolly Film, Constantin and Ocean turned out to be less than airtight, resulting in regular cash-flow problems (not even enough cash for a modest trickle). The film crew (mostly Spanish) found themselves working without pay for weeks on end, a situation not conducive to a happy on-set atmosphere. Tiring of Leone's arguments and appeals to their better nature, the crew opted to go on strike. Eastwood's lack of education in mediterranean languages meant that while he heard the arguments, he could only determine their precise meaning the hard way. After a lengthy session in the make-up chair for the scene where a badly beaten-up Joe crawls along under the boardwalks of the town street to escape the Rojo gang, Eastwood made his way to the set and found it utterly deserted. Standing alone under the Spanish sun with quantities of uncomfortable latex cuts and bruises glued to his face (closing one eye completely), he decided that even *Rawhide* wasn't this bad. Eastwood walked off the set and back to his hotel, leaving a message for Leone that he could be found at the airport. Leone caught up with his star in the hotel lobby, apologized for not telling him (or the make-up artist) about the production difficulties and promised that everything would be sorted out when Eastwood returned to the set. Accepting that Leone could not be blamed for Colombo and Papi's accounting problems, Eastwood graciously agreed to resume filming. Shooting on *The Magnificent Stranger* recommenced without any serious further incident, drawing to a close on budget and schedule. Star and director found they worked well together (Eastwood later described the western-mad Leone as 'like a little kid'), especially when it came to paring down Joe's dialogue, restoring the ambiguous/mysterious aspect of the character that made Sanjuro so intriguing. His role completed, Eastwood said goodbye to Leone and headed for home, reasoning that, if nothing else, he'd picked up a relatively easy $15,000 and given Maggie a free holiday. Now the time had come for another batch of *Rawhide*s, still a fair audience puller after six seasons. In the meantime, Colombo, Papi and Leone agreed that *A Fistful of Dollars/Per un pugno di dollari* might be a catchier title than *The Magnificent Stranger*, four years having passed since the Sturges film.

Essentially a simplified version of *Yojimbo* (with fewer characters), the plot of *A Fistful of Dollars* is as audacious as it is straightforward. A mysterious stranger rides into the border town of San Miguel, seated on a mule. He quickly learns that the town is controlled by two powerful families, the American Baxters, who deal in guns, and the Mexican Rojos, who deal in liquor. John Baxter, the nominal sheriff of San Miguel (he hides his badge in a jacket pocket), is dominated by his Mexican wife, Consuela. The Rojos, three sadistic brothers, are led by Ramon, the best shot in the town and the proud owner of a repeating rifle. A borderline psychotic, Ramon is infatuated with Marisol, wife of a poor farmer he beat at cards (by cheating). Ramon keeps Marisol as his prisoner, claiming her as payment for her husband's debt. The latter is regularly beaten up by the Rojos' henchmen to keep Marisol compliant. Lodging with the town innkeeper, Silvanito (Pepe Calvo), Joe the Stranger decides to play the two factions against eachother, netting a good profit for himself. Having gunned down four of Baxter's men (for shooting at the ground under his mule's hooves), Joe offers his services to Don Miguel Rojo, charging $100. He then sides with the Baxters, offering Consuela information about Ramon's nefarious activities (he machine guns a Mexican Army platoon and steals the gold they are carrying) for $500. The Rojos get to hear what the Baxters know about them for another $500. Things are progressing well until Joe takes pity on Marisol and her family, helping them escape and giving her his various earnings to start a new life elsewhere. Caught and tortured by the Rojos, Joe is saved from death by Silvanito and Piripero (Josef Egger), the gainfully employed town coffin-maker. After witnessing the massacre of the Baxters by the Rojos (who think the Americans are shielding him), Joe is then taken to an abandoned mine-shaft, where he slowly recovers. Realizing that Ramon's rifle will always out-perform his Colt .45 pistol, he fashions a crude breastplate out of a sheet of iron. Piripero brings news that Silvanito is being tortured to make him reveal Joe's hiding place. Joe strides back into town to take on the Rojo gang, knowing that Ramon likes to aim for the heart.

Aside from a few technical imperfections inevitable on a low budget film, *A Fistful of Dollars* holds up remarkably well, appearing as fresh and innovative as it did thirty years ago. The film's ambition is evident from frame one, with an elaborate credits sequence (designed by Luigi Lardani) surprising for such a modest production. Along with the title shot ('Fistful of Dollars'), various animated figures appear, including a man on a galloping horse and numerous gunmen, all rendered in stark black, red and white (this animation is based on live action footage from the film, a process known as rotoscoping). On the soundtrack, Ennio Morricone's driving score incorporates a mix of guitars, drums, whistles, whips and bells, along with the repeated lyrics 'We can fight' and 'We can hang' (the background percussion was largely lifted from Morricone's earlier hit single, 'Pastures of Plenty'). Leone opens the film proper with a shot of desert terrain and walking mule's legs, tilting his camera up to reveal its rider, Joe, as he arrives in San Miguel. Stopping at a well, Joe looks up (accompanied by a musical trill) to show his face for the first time, with squinting eyes and a week's worth of beard. As he drinks, Joe observes a small boy and his father being knocked around by Rojo henchman Chico (Leone regular Mario Brega) after the child attempts to see his mother, Marisol. At this point, any self-respecting cowboy of the John Wayne school would reach for his gun ('A man ought to do what he thinks is right'.) Joe merely looks on. Also watching is Marisol, imprisoned behind a barred window. She sees Joe and catches his eye. This seems to bond them and when the time is right, Joe will answer her look. Leone evidently felt this exchange to be crucial. While there is an equivalent abused family in *Yojimbo*, it is far more peripheral, not even appearing until an hour into the film. Joe continues his ride into the town, passing under a noose dangling from a tree branch (an image used in the film's Italian advertising). As a grand total of four townspeople clear the

● *Yojimbo:* **Mean hombres – Japanese style.**

street, a horseman approaches at a slow trot, his face a little pale. Riding nearer, Joe sees that the man is extremely dead, held in his saddle by a forked stick. Pinned to his back is a notice bearing the legend 'Adios amigo'. Joe touches his hat (a gesture of respect ?). This is a town with problems.

A greeting from the overly cheerful town bellringer ('Welcome to you stranger') does little to reassure us. In San Miguel a man will either get rich or dead; the town exists only to sell guns and liquor (socialist Leone always liked to include an anti-capitalist theme or two in his movies). After his mule bolts, Joe ends up hanging from a lamp-post (which resembles a mini-gallows) outside Silvanito's inn. He speaks his first line to the latter ('Hello'), drops down to the ground and delivers his verdict on San Miguel: 'I never saw a town as dead as this one.' Once Joe has set his various machinations in motion, Silvanito acts as a kind of confidant to him (they also share a bedroom), asking the questions the audience wants answered (not that Joe is forthcoming). In this respect, the innkeeper resembles a more moral version of the Eli Wallach character, Tuco in *The Good The Bad and The Ugly*. When the Mexican soldiers pull into town and then head off to the Rio Grande, Joe follows with Silvanito in tow. A group of men in American Army uniform approach from the opposite direction, leading an intrigued Silvanito to comment that it's 'like playing cowboys and Indians' (a sentiment Leone could surely agree with; if any character in the film acts as a surrogate for the director, it is the short, stocky Silvanito). The men in blue are revealed as Ramon and his gang, the former first glimpsed firing away with a gattling gun, laughing maniacally. Silvanito doesn't always approve of Joe's methods (such as using two dead soldiers to lure both the Baxters and the Rojos to the town cemetery), yet stays by his side. When the Rojos capture Baxter's son, they find that Marisol has been delivered to Consuela Baxter (no prizes for guessing who by). During the exchange of prisoners the next day, Silvanito pulls a shotgun on a Rojo henchman intent on killing Marisol's husband, Julio. It isn't clear if it is this action which prompts Joe to help the family out. His explanation is vague ('I knew someone like you once. There was no-one to help'), one of only two allusions to a past that is otherwise unexplored (the first is a mere throwaway: 'I never found home that great'). In *Yojimbo*, Sanjuro refuses to reveal why he helps the family, other than some feeling that the way of life they represent is worth protecting. Both Sanjuro and Joe pay for their humanity, enduring beatings savage enough to kill a normal man.

Following Joe's recovery (a 'resurrection' that Eastwood later made a cliche in his own films), he prepares for the inevitable battle, a sequence where Leone's Kurosawa-influenced style comes into its own. Making impressive use of panoramic long shots (severely diminished in the cropped television/video version of the film), striking close-ups of faces and feet (the latter usually incorporating a distant figure in the background) and a lot of swirling dust, the director takes his story into the realm of myth. So effective is his style that it makes no difference if at least one shot (Silvanito suspended on a rope in the foreground, the villains in the middleground, Joe in the background) is a direct lift from *Yojimbo*. As Joe predicted, Ramon aims for his heart each time, making a series of precise dents in the iron-plating (he's a little slow on the uptake, but what the hell). Joe shoots Ramon, first giving him a sporting chance to reload his rifle. Silvanito, cut down from the rope, gets the last Rojo henchman with his shotgun, saving Joe's life again (by implication at least). A showdown which an American western would get over and done with in under a minute is beautifully sustained over at least five minutes here. As the crane-mounted camera rises in the air for a last high angle shot of the town, Joe rides off into the distance while Piripero measures up. Eastwood's persona, Leone's style and Morricone's music aside, the most striking thing about *A Fistful of Dollars* is the level of violence depicted, very strong for the time and by no means mild today. A small boy is kicked around by a giant-sized thug. Joe impales one of the Rojo gang on a machete (seen sticking out of the man's back). The Rojos beat Joe to a pulp, stomping on his hands as he crawls on the ground. The most protracted and sadistic episode is the massacre of the Baxters, where the Rojos torch their house and then shoot the survivors as they run out begging for mercy (the British censor cut this scene, leaving a number of noticeable jumps). Eastwood felt the violence in the film to be particularly effective because Leone was not constrained by (or even aware of) the requirements of the 1930 Hays Code, an industry-sponsored rulebook dictating what Hollywood film-makers could and couldn't show. One of the code's more ridiculous rulings stated that during scenes of violence a gun being fired and a victim falling to the ground could not be shown in the same shot. Leone, on the other hand, could happily show multitudes of guns and bullet-ridden victims in the one camera set-up. Eastwood may have been slightly sweeping in this generalization (American films had become increasingly violent in the 1950s, *The Big Heat* (1952) and *Kiss Me Deadly* (1955) being good examples), yet it is certainly true that *A Fistful of Dollars* took western brutality into new realms.

The flaws evident in the film are minor, the result of insufficient funds rather than carelessness or a lack of imagination. The dialogue sounds very post-synched (recorded after, not during shooting), with a noticeable studio-bound acoustic (a slightly flat, hollow sound that wouldn't be present out-of-doors). Several scenes set at night (such as the graveyard shootout) have obviously been shot in normal daylight, the 'darkness' simulated by a not very convincing use of filters and shadowy lighting. Apparently sensitive to such deficiencies, Colombo and Papi expressed no great enthusiasm for the film during production (when the footage was only available for viewing in unflattering black and white, according to Eastwood). They changed their minds (a little) on seeing Leone's final edit of *A Fistful of Dollars*, accepting that it might be just a little out of the ordinary. Extraordinary or not, it still fell into the category of cheap western, and as such merited no more than a low key initial release to gauge audience reaction. The film premiered in a modest cinema in Naples, attracting little response from local critics other than a few derisory comments. Audiences felt differently and word-of-mouth praise soon produced queues around the block and an impressive box-office take (the cinema retained *A Fistful of Dollars* for over a year). A local surprise hit rapidly became a national, then an international phenomenon, enjoying huge popularity in European and South American countries. The blockbuster success of *A Fistful of Dollars* in its native Italy merited mention in the Hollywood tradepaper *Variety* (not that this meant anything to Eastwood; the last time he looked the film still bore the title *The Magnificent Stranger*). Faced with such a response, Colombo and Papi realised that their western deserved a full worldwide release, especially to the highly lucrative US market (where a rather less impressive Kurosawa remake, the *Rashomon*-inspired western melodrama *The Outrage* (1964), was currently doing the rounds). The only factor holding them back was the small matter of copyright. To protect their investment, the producers had to secure full international copyright on *A Fistful of Dollars*. As the film clearly breached the copyright on another film, this might prove tricky. Kurosawa had heard about the runaway success of an Italian *Yojimbo* rip-off and felt entitled to a little compensation. Any legal action on his part could bring the success of *A Fistful of Dollars* to a screeching halt.

Basing a film on someone else's original work without first seeking their permission always carries a certain amount of risk. The most famous example of

● *A Fistful of Dollars:* Joe and Silvanito (Pepe Calvo).

big-screen plagiarism is F.W. Murnau's horror movie *Nosferatu* (1922), an unautho-
rised German version of Bram Stoker's novel *Dracula*. Murnau made a token attempt
or two at covering his tracks (such as changing the vampire's name to Graf Orlock),
without success. Stoker's widow sued for breach of copyright and won her case. The
court ordered that the film be withdrawn from circulation and all copies (plus the
original negative) destroyed. Luckily for Murnau and film enthusiasts, *Nosferatu* survived (tracking down every single print of a film for destruction would be very difficult) and today is rivalled only by the 1958 *Dracula* as the best film adaptation of
the Stoker original. Equally luckily for Colombo, Papi, Leone and Eastwood, attitudes to copyright theft had become less puritanical by the early 1960s. The *Fistful
of Dollars* problem amounted to a simple matter of profit sharing and a deal with
Kurosawa and Toho (the studio which backed *Yojimbo*) soon followed, with the
Yojimbo copyright owners granted sole distribution rights for Leone's film in Japan,
South Korea and Taiwan (then called Formosa). In addition to this highly profitable
market, they would also receive 15% of the total worldwide box-office gross. Not
only had Colombo and Papi bought themselves out of a potentially disastrous situation, they had secured a Far East distributor for any sequels. Little did they know
that when Leone got around to a follow-up, they would no longer have a part to
play. The *Yojimbo* problem and later legal maneouverings prevented *A Fistful of Dollars*
(and its sequels) from getting an American (and British) release until 1967. By this
time, Eastwood would be more than ready to cash-in on their success.

The seventh season of *Rawhide* (1964-65) proved a sad disappointment. If the
previous run had netted adequate rather than impressive audience response, the
reception given the new season rated no higher than mediocre to poor. It might be
argued that five years is a respectable run for any series (especially one with such a
rigid formula), and a slide into predictable tedium inevitable if the show outstays its

● *A Fistful of Dollars:* **Joe takes on the Rojo gang.**

natural lifespan. CBS decided otherwise, announcing that *Rawhide* would
return for an eighth season once a
few minor adjustments had been
made. Looking for a handy scapegoat
to hang a little blame on, the network fired Eric Fleming, claiming
that he had breached his contract by
accepting a supporting role in a
Doris Day comedy, *The Glass Bottom
Boat* (1966). Considering Eastwood's
recent film activities, this explanation rings a little false. It seems more
likely that CBS still resented
Fleming's victory over working hours
back in the late 1950s, and now they
had a pretext for getting rid of him.
Losing a lead actor while the ratings
were still top of the league would
be bad business. Now that the show
no longer commanded a place in the
viewer's top ten, there could be a
little more room for personal resent-

● *A Fistful of Dollars:* **Ramon Rojo (Gian Maria
Volonte) and some very dead henchmen.**

ments. Fleming probably wanted a way out, anyway, as his sixth-billed role in the
film, a frenetic spoof of the then popular spy genre, hardly provided the best career
stepping stone. Cast as a CIA agent, he did little other than look on as Doris Day and
leading man Rod Taylor tangled with various hostile factions. *The Glass Bottom Boat*
proved a solid success, prompting the production of another Day spy spoof, *Caprice*
(1967), with Richard Harris in support. By this time, Fleming's film career had
reached an abrupt end. Working on location in Peru in 1966, he drowned in the
rapids of the Amazon River.

The news that he would be promoted to trail boss for *Rawhide*'s eighth season did
little to inspire Eastwood. His new solo star billing came at Fleming's expense and
the series couldn't last much longer anyway. In any case, his work on the ill-fated seventh season took second place to a more pressing (and unexpected) matter awaiting
him on his return from Italy in 1964. After a little hesitation, Roxanne Tunis
informed Eastwood that she had given birth to their daughter, Kimber. He had
already seen the baby at Roxanne's house when she broke the news, but thought
nothing of it, assuming the child to be her sister's. Ever the businessman, Eastwood
quickly recovered from his shock and worked out the best plan of damage limitation.
If the news agencies discovered that the star of television's *Rawhide* had fathered a
child without bothering to bring his wife into the process, Eastwood's career could
suffer, in America at least. The much vaunted 'swinging sixties' had yet to get into
motion and an illegitimate child (or even an extra-marital affair) still bore a social
stigma. Neither Eastwood nor Roxanne wanted to end their relationship and they
agreed on a deal that brought mutual benefit. Eastwood would look after Roxanne
and Kimber financially for the rest of their lives in return for a guarantee of silence.
A slightly devious arrangement on the star's part, perhaps (surely his girlfriend and

baby deserved his support whether or not the affair became public), yet the bargain held for twenty five years. Maggie's reaction to the news proved typically stoical. Eastwood promised that their marriage was still secure and she accepted his word. If she felt threatened by the idea that her husband now had a 'family' relationship with Roxanne, while their official union remained childless, Maggie didn't let it show.

Compared with this drama, exciting events during filming on *Rawhide* #7 were few and far between. When jobbing (often unemployed) character actor Lee Van Cleef turned up as a guest star for the intriguingly titled episode *Incident of the Enormous Fist* (broadcast on October 2 1964), Eastwood little realized that they were soon to meet again for a film which would confirm his new status as Euro-superstar and give Van Cleef a career as one the cinema's least likely leading men. Still not entirely aware of *A Fistful of Dollars'* box-office impact, Eastwood received a call from Sergio Leone, who now had a sequel in preproduction, this time not involving either Akira Kurosawa or the Colombo-Papi team. Kurosawa had in fact made a semi-sequel to *Yojimbo*, the equally striking *Sanjuro* (1962), again with Toshiro Mifune (an inferior third instalment, the non-Kurosawa *Zatoichi meets Yojimbo*, arrived in 1970). While the Japanese director would doubtless have been happy to lease his *Sanjuro* script to Leone, the latter prudently decided not to tempt fate twice. He set to work with new collaborator Luciano Vincenzoni on an original storyline for the aptly titled *For a Few Dollars More/Per qualche dollari in piu*, developing the result into a screenplay with Fulvio Morsella (Vincenzoni got to write the dialogue). The break with Colombo and Papi also had an air of inevitability. Jolly Film worked on a strictly small-time scale and Leone had serious ambitions for his sequel. He also had a few scores to settle with his erstwhile producers. They had let him down with the finance on *A Fistful of Dollars* (nearly losing their star in the process), insisted on using puerile pseudonyms for the credits and coerced him into a change of title (Leone seems to have had a fixation on the word *Magnificent*: *For a Few Dollars More* originally bore the title *Two Magnificent Strangers*, while *The Good The Bad and The Ugly* started life as *The Magnificent Rogues*). Of the three production companies involved on *A Fistful of Dollars*, only one, the German outfit Constantin, survived for the sequel. Leone formed a partnership with Italian lawyer turned producer Alberto Grimaldi, who'd been in the movie business since 1962 with his own company, PEA (Produzioni Europee Associate). Director and producer agreed on a budget of $600,000, a 200% improvement on the funding for the previous film. This bold move upmarket necessitated a third production partner, the Spanish company Arturo Gonzales (when filming on location in Spain, a native co-producer always came in handy). Offered $50,000 plus a percentage of the box-office gross *plus* a brand new Ferrari, Eastwood had no hesitation in accepting the starring role. Now renamed 'Manco' (Italian for 'not even' or 'less'), his character was still effectively Joe the Stranger. Leone recast Gian Maria Volonte as the completely psycho villain Indio, giving him many of the same henchman (notably Mario Brega) he'd used in *Fistful* (this stock company of tough hombres, regularly employed by Leone and other spaghetti directors throughout the 1960s, became one the genre's most distinctive hallmarks). Useful additions to the villain's gallery were Luigi Pistilli, cast as Indio's shrewder-than-average colleague Graghi, and German actor Klaus Kinski, playing a hunchbacked killer appropriately named Wild.

Leone's only major difficulty during casting involved the choice of Eastwood's co-star. The script for *For a Few Dollars More* required an actor who could pass as

American with no difficulty. Commercial considerations required that they be not only a genuine American but an actor with a well known face (even a box-office name). Not one to give up easily, Leone reapproached Charles Bronson, who turned his offer down flat, claiming that the script did not show any improvement on *Fistful*. The director then contacted hard-as-very-hard-nails leading man Lee Marvin, an experienced screen villain (*The Big Heat*, *The Wild One* 1954, *The Man Who Shot Liberty Valance* 1962) now working his way into more heroic, if still ultra-violent roles. His recent success in Don Siegel's *The Killers* (1964) proved that even woman-beating psychopaths could somehow earn audience sympathy. More canny than Bronson, Marvin expressed interest in the role of Colonel Douglas Mortimer, a soldier turned bounty hunter by a family trauma. Alas, he had already committed to *Cat Ballou* (1965), a comedy western co-starring Jane Fonda. This turned out to be a very smart move, as Marvin later won an Academy Award for his performance in the dual role of alcoholic gunfighter Kid Sheleen and his evil tin-nosed brother, ruthless killer Tim Strawn. Nevertheless, it is a pity that Eastwood never got to act with Marvin in a solid vehicle. Their joint appearance in *Paint Your Wagon* would prove a low point in both actors' careers. Feeling that the name 'Lee' might still be lucky for him, Leone set his sights on the only suitable candidate, Lee Van Cleef.

Usually cast as a sneaky, malicious cowboy, gangster or army sergeant, accountant-turned actor Lee Van Cleef had notched up memorable (if brief) roles in *High Noon* (stalking Gary Cooper with Sheb Wooley), *The Big Combo* (1955), *Gunfight at the OK Corral*, *Ride Lonesome*, *Posse from Hell* (1961) and *The Man Who Shot Liberty Valance*, a film now regarded as director John Ford's last masterpiece. He'd had less luck with good-guy roles, aside from a bit part as the army sniper who shoots *The Beast from 20,000 Fathoms* (1954). Blessed with a face resembling a particularly untrustworthy rat's, Van Cleef's career progressed well enough until 1962, when a heart attack put him out of work for a while. By the mid-sixties, his only income came from occasional television work (plus any repeat fees), unemployment benefit and the salary brought home by Mrs Van Cleef, who worked for IBM. For all this (plus an injured leg), Van Cleef did not immediately respond to Leone's offer of a starring role with too much enthusiasm. Five years older than Eastwood, he may have been more sensitive to Italy's reputation as a workplace for American no-hopers. Whatever the case, Van Cleef had no other offers of work coming in, his phone bill needed paying, and the $17,000 fee for *For a Few Dollars More* ($2000 more than Eastwood got for *Fistful*) could not be sneered at. He accepted the part and flew out to Italy, where filming would commence at Cinecitta Studios before the production team made the return trip to Almeria.

Generally regarded as a marked improvement on *A Fistful of Dollars*, *For a Few Dollars More* certainly looks (and sounds) like a more lavish and confident production. Leone's direction develops the highly ritualized style (vast panoramas, lingering close-ups, precision editing, measured pacing, black humour, prolonged shootouts, ingenious sadism) of the first film, adding a few touches of religious/anti-religious imagery (Indio's gang hides out in an abandoned church). Morricone's score is even more eccentric, incorporating a whistled main theme, a church organ for a shootout, the tinkling of two musical watches and reducing the lyrics used in *Fistful* to a series of unintelligible growls. The camerawork (again by Massimo Dallamano) exhibits all the advantages of generous funding (more lights), including one scene (Joe's encounter with a mad old man living next to a railway) lit to resemble a Rembrandt painting. Where the film falls down slightly is in the script department. Alternating between a large scale reworking of *Fistful* and a dry run for some ideas better employed in *The Good The Bad and The Ugly*, the screenplay isn't a successful whole, relying too much on plot contrivances to get to the final show-down. One of its most puzzling elements is the way it deliberately reduces Eastwood's character to a secondary role, making Van Cleef's more experienced (and more intelligent) Colonel Mortimer the undisputed hero of the film.

Opening on a train (a Leone motif much used in later films), *For a Few Dollars More* first introduces the pipe-smoking Colonel (his face initially hidden behind a bible) taking a ride into the town of Tucumcari to hunt down a wanted killer named Guy Calloway (as the written prologue puts it: 'In a world where life had no value, death, sometimes, had its price. That is why the bounty killers appeared.'). The train isn't actually scheduled to stop at this destination, so Mortimer pulls the emergency cord, bringing it to a halt with the wagon holding his horse conveniently positioned beside a loading ramp. Having easily located Calloway at a local hotel, Mortimer lets the man ride away as far as the end of the street before shooting his horse from under him. As Calloway returns fire, Mortimer stands his ground, knowing that the out-law's gun lacks the range to hit him from any distance. Once the killer is close enough to be a danger, Mortimer selects a weapon from the assortment attached to his saddle (accompanied by a musical twang), takes aim and shoots Calloway in the head. This man is cool.

Slightly less cool is Joe, first seen walking into town just as a downpour of rain gets going. Pausing only to light a cigarillo under the shelter of his hat brim, Joe goes after Red Cavanaugh, a bandit protected by the corrupt local sheriff. Attempting to take Cavanaugh alive, he has to resort to some undignified fistfighting, eventually shooting the man after three friends arrive for an unsuccessful rescue attempt. Alternating between coolness and giggling mania, Indio lingers in prison, calmly waiting for his gang to break him out. They soon oblige, shooting a lot of guards in the process, and Indio wastes no time going after the bounty hunter who turned him in. Discovering that the man now has a wife and baby, Indio has the father tortured and his family shot (a scene hated by chief British film censor John Trevelyan), before killing him in an unfair shootout. Very mad and very bad.

A reward of $10,000 is announced for Indio's capture (or execution). As Mortimer stares at the details on the wanted poster, Leone cuts between increasing-ly brief shots of the man's face and a line drawing of the killer (accompanied by gun-shots on the soundtrack). Clearly there is more to Mortimer's pursuit of Indio than mere business. Deducing that the latter plans to hit the bank at El Paso (Indio shared his prison cell with a carpenter who worked for the bank, building the fake cabinet that houses the real safe), Mortimer establishes a stakeout from a hotel window over-looking the bank. When three of Indio's gang ride into town for a little reconnais-sance, he strikes a match on Wild's face, gaining much amusement from the sight of the other two restraining the hunchback in order to protect their cover.

Mortimer is not, of course, the only bounty killer after Indio. Joe is also watch-ing, from another hotel window across the street. After a mutual test of nerve, the two men agree to work together, splitting the reward for the whole gang 50/50. As Mortimer puts it, 'When two hunters go after the same prey, they usually end up shooting eachother in the back' (which would actually be very difficult). Aiming to use his share of the money to buy a farm and retire (an ambition achieved by bounty hunter William Munny in *Unforgiven*), Joe agrees to infiltrate the gang, winning Indio's trust (or so it seems) by springing an old friend of his from prison (Mortimer's idea). The robbery goes ahead, with the gang making a clean getaway. Having argued over who messed up their scheme, Mortimer and Joe warily agree to continue with the partnership, neither trusting the other. Joe catches up with Indio and attempts to lead him away from the place of ambush agreed with Mortimer. Indio prefers a third destination, the town of Agua Caliente (Spanish for 'hot water', which Joe soon finds himself in). Seeing through his partner's attempts at double cross, Mortimer beats the gang to their destination and offers his services as a safe cracker (using a small drill and a bottle of acid rather than destructive and wasteful dynamite).

The plot gets a little too twisty and schematic from here on. Mortimer and Joe decide to take the money for themselves (their original bounty-hunting scheme apparently forgotten). They are captured and beaten up, though Indio mysteriously allows them to live. It transpires that the not-so loco killer wants all the money for himself. He orders left hand man Nino (Mario Brega) to release his two prisoners, intending that his other men will be killed in the resulting shootout with Mortimer and Joe. Only one gang member, Graghi, sees through this, killing Nino and forcibly allying himself with Indio, who now seems mainly interested in smoking marijuana. The bounty hunters emerge from their battle unscathed (Eastwood gets to do some neat firing from a spinning chair, a trick he later reused in *High Plains Drifter*) and Mortimer calls on Indio to join him for a showdown. Watched over by Joe, the two men face eachother within a marked-out circle/arena (a device re-employed on a much bigger scale in *The Good The Bad and The Ugly*). Indio is gunned down and Mortimer finally reveals the reason for his pursuit of the killer: many years before, Indio raped the Colonel's sister on her wedding night (first shooting her husband); the sister then shot herself with the outlaw's pistol. The older man tells Joe to keep all the money (both the reward bounty and the bank takings) and rides off into the desert. Joe loads up the numerous corpses on a handy wagon (Leone's comment on the destructive nature of a capitalist society ?) and goes his own way.

Even with the flaws, *For a Few Dollars More* offers a lot of entertainment, especially in the humour department. The pre-credits sequence, a vast hill-top longshot of arid desert, is accompanied by the sound of an unseen bounty hunter humming to himself as he prepares to shoot an approaching rider (a tiny figure in the distance). Leone provided the voiceover himself, in a style very similar to the sound effects used by animator (now director) Terry Gilliam for his *Monty Python* cartoons. The prissy manager at Joe's hotel resembles Benny Hill's more prudish younger brother. The scene where Mortimer and Joe check out eachother's hard-man credentials is played mainly for laughs (they shoot eachother's hats off). Eastwood provides a lot of the humour, through dialogue and well-judged reactions. Some of the underlining comedy music is a little heavy-handed, as is the scene with the old man Prophet (Josef Egger), where an approaching train shakes his house and fills it with smoke, indicating that Leone still needed to fine-tune his style a bit.

The most interesting aspect of *For a Few Dollars More* is its use of flashbacks, as a drugged out Indio recalls seeing the Colonel's sister show off her brother's gift of a musical watch to her husband, then breaking into their home to wreak havoc. He stole the watch, using its chime to time his shootouts. Mortimer has an identical watch, bearing a portrait of his dead sister inside the case lid. Indio's final flashback,

● *For a Few Dollars More:* Colonel Douglas Mortimer (Lee Van Cleef).

depicting his rape of the sister and her subsequent suicide (a scene cut from some English-language prints of the film), reveals why he must die at Mortimer's hands. The Colonel's personal reason for hunting down Indio (vengeance) is shown to be more worthy than Joe's purely financial interest. Unlike *Fistful* and *The Good The Bad and The Ugly*, Eastwood's character displays no trace of humanity here (Leone later perfected his flashback device in *Once Upon a Time in the West* 1968, where the hero and villain are linked by a harmonica, signifying joint memories of the cold-blooded murder of the former's brother).

Unperturbed by such details, audiences turned *For a Few Dollars More* into an even bigger hit than its predecessor. Van Cleef found himself a sudden star attraction in Italy, later commenting that 'being born with a beady-eyed sneer was the luckiest thing that ever happened to me' (initially perplexed by Leone's film-making style, Van Cleef quickly realized he was on to something big). Confident that he would soon be called back by Leone for a third movie, Eastwood returned to the United States to work on season eight of *Rawhide*. He knew it could only be a matter of time before the show rolled over and died, making his new status as trail boss more of an ordeal than a pleasure. Aside from the ousted Eric Fleming, the series had lost Sheb Wooley, James Murdock and Rocky Shahan, reinforcing the feeling that the rollin' cattle drive was now more of a sinking ship. In the event, Eastwood's discomfort proved mercifully brief. Unimpressed by the new cast line-up (including television's first black cowboy, played by Raymond St Jacques) and the miracle of colour film, audiences turned over/off in their own droves, prompting CBS to cancel the show after just thirteen episodes. This decision appears to have been an abrupt one, as the network found itself with a four week gap to fill between the last original transmitted episode (shown on December 7 1965) and the start of the mid-season replacement series. Not inclined to waste useful material, CBS repeated four old *Rawhide* episodes, bringing the series to an official close on January 4 1966 (fifteen years on, the show would find new popularity as American television's most requested repeat). Eastwood received a $119,000 payoff, walking away from the series with much relief. *Rawhide* had played an important part in his career and Eastwood remained on good terms with several members of the production team. Sheb Wooley and Paul Brinegar later played supporting roles in Malpaso films (Brinegar in *High Plains Drifter*, Wooley in *The Outlaw Josey Wales*). Glenn Wright, a costume designer employed on the show, ended up on the Malpaso staff, as did script reader Sonia Chernus (to whom Eastwood owed a favour or two), who got a writing break on *Rawhide* with the original story for the fourth season episode *Grandma's Money*. Of all the *Rawhide* collaborators, the biggest influence on Eastwood's future film work could be claimed by writer Dean Riesner, whose scripts for the show included a fifth season episode entitled *Incident of the Pale Rider*. Not a great friend of the actor, Riesner can take credit for salvaging the scripts for the films which established Eastwood's reputation as a 'genuine' Hollywood star: *Coogan's Bluff* and *Dirty Harry*. (The son of comedy film director Charles Riesner, Riesner Jr's main non-Eastwood claim to fame is directing the offbeat drama *Bill and Coo* 1948, notable chiefly for a cast made up entirely of trained birds).

For the time being, Hollywood continued to regard Eastwood as a television actor, now unemployed. Only the American release of his *Dollars* films could change this view. Eastwood knew his immediate future still lay in Europe, where he now attracted such plaudits as serious film-artist (France) and western icon (Italy). A boost to his ego (if not his bank balance) arrived in the form of an offer from acclaimed director Vittorio De Sica (best known for *Bicycle Thieves*). De Sica had signed on with producer-mogul Dino de Laurentiis to direct an episode of the compendium film *The Witches/Le Streghe* (1966), essentially a glossy showcase for Silvana Mangano, de Laurentiis' actress wife. A big admirer of the director, Eastwood took the unlikely role of Mario, husband of Giovanna (Mangano), in a 19-minute dream sequence entitled *A Night Like Any Other/Una sera come le altra*. Having secured his first 'art' film credit, he got down to the serious business of making his third and final appearance as Joe/Manco/No Name in *The Good The Bad and The Ugly/Il buono il brutto il cattivo* (the Italian title literally translates as 'The Good The Ugly and The Bad', but the English rearrangement scans better).

The success of *For a Few Dollars More* meant that Leone and Grimaldi no longer had any need of co-production deals. *The Good The Bad and The Ugly* would be one of the first spaghetti westerns made with entirely Italian finance. It would also be the first of Leone's epic westerns, lasting nearly three hours, with an intricate, large-scale story and hundreds of extras running about (at 130 minutes, *For a Few Dollars More* was merely long, overplotted and in need of a little editorial tightening). Epic scripts require epic money and Grimaldi came up with a production budget of $1.2 million, double that of the previous film. Eastwood's salary rose to $250,000, a 400% raise on his last outing, plus 10% of the net profits from western territories (no car this time round). Filming would commence in the spring of 1966, with the usual spells at Cinecitta and Almeria, plus a trip to Burgos, an area north of Almeria with a slightly greener landscape. Replacing Massimo Dallamano as cameraman was top Italian director of photography Tonino Delli Colli, who would be Leone's cinematographer of choice for the rest of the director's career (Delli Colli also photographed Lubin's *Thief of Bagdad*). If Eastwood felt that *For a Few Dollars More* had worked out better for Lee Van Cleef than himself, his massive pay increase for the new film provided ample consolation. Van Cleef would be appearing in *The Good The Bad and The Ugly* (Leone didn't intend to let his new star go just yet), this time playing the villain. Eastwood didn't have to worry about competition in the cool hero stakes. Unless, of course, Leone persuaded Charles Bronson to take the third starring role, a Mexican bandit named Tuco.

One of the problems with the second *Dollars* film stemmed from the lack of a more volatile co-star interacting with Eastwood. The characters of Joe and Mortimer are very similar, with the latter clearly intended as an older, wiser version of his accomplice/apprentice (they regularly refer to eachother as "old man" and "boy"). In *Fistful*, the shorter, more emotional and excitable Silvanito provided an effective contrast to Joe, emphasizing the latter's laid-back, apparently cold persona. Leone doesn't seem to have entirely appreciated this, as casting Bronson for *The Good The Bad and The Ugly* would play off one very tight-lipped, inexpressive star with another. As (bad) luck would have it, Bronson proved to be unavailable once more, though this time he actually wanted the part. Evidently impressed by the script (by Leone, Luciano Vincenzoni and Age Scarpelli), he declined only because he had already committed to Robert Aldrich's production of *The Dirty Dozen* (1967), playing one of the hardened (yet sensitive) death-row convicts recruited by Army major Lee Marvin for a daring mission behind enemy lines. Playing his *Magnificent Seven* card one more time, Leone changed tack, offering the role to Eli Wallach, a respected New York stage actor whose style was anything but understated. Aside from his grinning, laughing, arm-round-the-shoulder-bullet-in-the-head bandit chief in the Sturges film, Wallach's notable screen credits included Elia Kazan's self-consciously sleazy *Baby Doll* (1956) and Don Siegel's *The Line-up* (1958), a movie spin-off from the television series *San Francisco Beat*. Wallach's performance in *The Good The Bad and The Ugly* would get him arrested for criminal overacting in any other film, yet here it blends perfectly with Eastwood's taciturn understatement, Van Cleef's leering cruelty and the overall style. Once Wallach was cast, Leone had all the ingredients he needed for the finest film of the trilogy.

The plot of *The Good The Bad and The Ugly* is essentially an eight-month three man treasure hunt where the American Civil War keeps getting in the way. A Confederate platoon escorting an army payroll of $200,000 in gold is mysteriously ambushed (offscreen). There are only three survivors: Jackson, Baker and Stevens. A court hearing clears the men of any blame for the loss of the money, which has vanished without a trace. Jackson then disappears, leaving his former partners in crime with nothing. Baker hires the infamous killer Setenza aka Angel Eyes (Van Cleef) to track Jackson down, neglecting to tell him the reason why. Setenza learns about the missing cashbox from Stevens (before killing him) and decides to go after it (pausing only to shoot Baker four times in the head). He finds Jackson's girlfriend, Maria, and tortures her for information about her lover. Jackson has changed his name to Bill Carson and rejoined his old regiment, first hiding the money somewhere very safe. Jackson, meanwhile, is running out of luck. His troop suffers another ambush (a real one this time) and the hospital wagon he gets loaded on ends up lost in the desert without a driver. Dying of thirst, Jackson encounters a scruffy bandit named Tuco, currently taking his former partner Blondie (Eastwood, who is fair-haired by Italian standards) on a long walk under the burning sun to teach him a lesson about loyalty

● *For a Few Dollars More:* A wagonload of bounty. Chief villain Indio (Gian Maria Volonte) gets to lie at the top of the pile.

in business. Jackson begs for water, telling Tuco that there is $200,000 in gold buried in Sad Hill cemetery, just waiting to be collected. Tuco reluctantly goes to fetch water, only to find that Jackson has died before he can learn the name on the grave containing the money. Crouching next to the corpse is Blondie, nearly dead through dehydration, exhaustion and exposure to the sun. Blondie whispers to Tuco that Jackson told him the name (and then passes out). Their partnership is back on.

Opening with the most elaborate title sequence of the trilogy, *The Good The Bad and the Ugly* starts with incredible confidence and style and continues that way. Accompanied by Morricone's justly famous score (dominated by shrieking vocals and electric guitar), credits specialist Luigi Lardani reintroduces the man on the galloping horse, plus swirling Civil War scenes (stills from the film), close-ups of the three stars and an animated cannon which shoots the words of the title onto the screen. Not one to take a back seat, Sergio Leone's name is also shot onto the screen to replace the horseman (bit by bit). The first scene shows his unique style at full strength, with the uncertainties of *For a Few Dollars More* nowhere in evidence. Presenting us with the standard introductory long shot of western desert terrain, Leone then has the extraordinarily ugly face of a bounty hunter swing into close-up (the face belongs to Canadian actor Albert Mulloch, also seen in *Tarzan's Greatest Adventure, Dr Terror's House of Horrors* (1964) and *Once Upon a Time in the West*). The setting is a windswept ghost town, with rolling tumbleweed and a lone dog (a Leone motif). The bounty hunter waits with his horse at one end of town, while two other men appear on the far side, dismounting from their horses and striding towards him with clear purpose. The lone man walks towards the approaching strangers, a gun-fight seeming inevitable. They meet up with eachother outside the door of a hotel, nod in agreement, then break the door down, guns blazing. The camera fast tracks to an adjacent window through which the figure of Tuco Benedicto Pacifico Juan Maria Ramirez comes crashing, a chicken leg in one hand, a gun in the other. The picture freezes and a superimposed title formally identifies the man: Il brutto/The Ugly (Eastwood's Good and Van Cleef's Bad get their own introductory titles later on.) Unfrozen, Tuco looks about him, snarls, then gallops off on a convenient horse. Leone cuts back to the three hunters, two of them now dead. The Mulloch character, shot in the right arm, attempts to fire his gun one last time before fainting.

In no great hurry to bring Blondie/Joe back into the picture, Leone then introduces us to Setenza, first seen as a distant figure on horseback, before dismounting and walking into striking close-up. Visiting Jackson, Setenza enjoys a meal with the man before getting down to business (food before killing) and accepts a commission to shoot Baker. Jackson dead (along with his foolishly brave older son), Setenza calls on Baker (bedridden by tuberculosis), delivers the information he wanted and then sticks a pillow on the man's face, through which he fires his gun, allowing himself a laugh or two. Death is merely business and all services paid for will be rendered. It can only be a good thing if a man's job is also his hobby.

When Eastwood finally shows up, it is to 'rescue' Tuco from another trio of bounty killers (why do gunmen always come in groups of three ?) Dispensing with the sheepskin waistcoat, poncho and standard cowboy hat, Blondie is stylishly attired in a long, narrow coat and wide-brimmed hat. Though a lightning quick shot, he isn't just another bounty hunter, operating an equally profitable (and much safer) scam. Blondie delivers Tuco to the nearest sheriff, collecting a $2000 reward and some choice insults from his prisoner: 'You're the son of thousand fathers, all of them bastards like you'. While Tuco's numerous crimes are fully cited according to due process of law (murder, robbing post offices, receiving stolen goods, selling stolen goods, statutory rape of a minor of the black race etc), the bandit sits on horseback under a gallows tree, the noose placed around his neck. At the moment a deputy drives the horse from under him, a strategically positioned Blondie shoots the rope above Tuco's head, cutting him free (he then diverts the assembled lawmen and townspeople by shooting their hats off). This scheme is repeated with success, until Blondie decides that Tuco will never be worth more than the current going rate of $3000. Tired of the bandit's greed (Tuco wants more than a half share in the reward money) and constant chatter, he leaves the trussed Tuco in the middle of a dry wasteland, hanging on to the reward money (Tuco gets to keep the rope).

So far, we have a blackly amusing partners-in-confidence-trickery plot, with two small time hustlers (for all Blondie's elegance, the man is still a petty crook). Mickey Knox's English dialogue is sharp, ranging from Tuco's picturesque 'When that rope starts to pull tight, you can feel the devil bite your ass', to Tuco's plain abusive 'hijo de una gran puta' ('son of a big whore'). Wallach's performance as the treacherous, deceitful, superstitious, foul smelling Tuco runs along in impressive maximum overdrive, while Eastwood underplays the black humour with great skill ('We cut down on my percentage, it's liable to interfere with my aim'.) The subplot, where Setenza chases after much bigger pickings, is far less humorous, with frequent bursts of brutality (as when he beats up Maria). The film moves into a different gear when the two storylines merge after the desert scene and the Civil War starts to play a more prominent part.

There is still much humour in the second half of the film (an amoral, profiteering hotel manager who switches allegiances in the middle of a sentence; Tuco greeting a division of grey soldiers with shouts of 'Hooray for General Lee' only to discover that they are Union troops covered in dust) but it has more of an edge. The tone becomes more sombre (and poignant), especially in three pivotal sequences: Tuco and Blondie's visit to a religious mission turned military hospital (both dressed in Confederate uniforms), their internment at a Union camp for Confederate prisoners of war and a pitched battle for control of a bridge. The monastery, where Blondie recovers after his desert ordeal, is run by Father Pablo Ramirez (Luigi Pistilli), Tuco's brother. Apart from humanising Tuco with a little family background, their confrontation allows him to explain why he became the way he did: 'Where we came from, if one did not want to die of poverty, one became a priest or a bandit'. Despite Pablo's expressed contempt for his brother, it is clear he accepts this. (During this scene, a watching Blondie is framed through the arms of a statue of Christ, underlining his 'resurrected' status).

The prison camp, where Blondie and Tuco end up after their encounter with the dusty Union troops, is a vivid hell on earth, rendered in utterly convincing (if not necessarily accurate) period detail, with strong overtones of World War II concentration camps (such as the band of prisoners forced to play music to cover the screams of men under torture). Through an unexplained plot device, Setenza has installed himself in the camp disguised as a Union officer, and now runs a sideline in robbing and murdering prisoners while he waits for any news of Jackson/Carson. Recognizing Blondie and Tuco (presently going under Jackson's alias), Setenza calls in the latter for some food and a talk, then has his strongarm thug, the one-eyed Sergeant Wallace (Mario Brega), beat Tuco up for information regarding the gold's whereabouts (a harrowing scene even by today's standards). Armed with the name of the cemetery, Setenza attempts to make a deal with Blondie, even handing over some

● *The Good The Bad and The Ugly*: Tuco (Eli Wallach) renews his acquaintance with Blondie.

civilian clothes (long coat, jeans, sheepskin waistcoat, cowboy hat) for the journey to the money.

The battle scene, where Tuco enlists himself and Blondie into the Union army to avoid becoming prisoners again, is a vast setpiece involving hundreds of extras, as the two sides mow eachother down over a wooden bridge (which leads to Sad Hill cemetery). As Blondie comments 'I've never seen so many men wasted so badly.' His new commanding officer, a drunken captain (Aldo Giuffre) tells the new recruits about his dream of blowing up the bridge, leaving the two sides with nothing to fight over. When he is badly injured in a skirmish, Blondie hands the dying man a bottle of whisky and a parting piece of advice: 'Keep your ears open'. Accompanied by a montage of firing cannons, Blondie and Tuco dynamite the bridge (the captain lives to hear it), leaving themselves free to continue over to the other side without interruption. Blondie makes just one more diversion, encountering a dying teenage Confederate recruit in the ruins of a burned-out church. Hit in the stomach, the soldier is shivering pitifully. Blondie drapes his coat over the boy and gives him his cigarillo to smoke, taking his mind off the pain. The soldier at least dies with a measure of peace. This is a genuinely moving moment and Leone does not attempt to lighten the mood by having Blondie or Tuco then rob the body. The former notices a folded poncho lying near the dead soldier and takes it, completing his mysterious stranger 'uniform'. Blondie now has the persona (humanity and all) of *Fistful*'s Joe (this transformation hints that the events in *The Good The Bad and The Ugly* are set before the stories told in *A Fistful of Dollars* and *For a Few Dollars More*, though it is unlikely Leone intended the idea as anything more than a pleasing narrative twist).

Arriving first at the huge, circular graveyard, Tuco performs an impressive runaround (backed by the soaring vocals of Edda Dell'Orso) in search of the name given him by Blondie just before the bridge went up: Arch Stanton. Tuco finds the grave, quickly joined by Blondie (who throws him a shovel), and then Setenza (who throws Blondie a shovel). Blondie produces his trump card, revealing that Stanton's grave is empty (except for Stanton). Anyone who wants the money will have to beat him in a gunfight. The legendary three-way shootout now follows, staged in a large circle set in the centre of the cemetery. Blondie, Tuco and Setenza take their places in this arena and for minutes the protagonists stand and stare at eachother, while Morricone's trumpet, drum, piano, choir and glockenspiel earn their overtime (the string section does its bit as well). Leone cuts between long shots taking in two or three of the combatants and close-ups of anxious faces (Blondie looks as calm as ever) and hands hovering over weapons, slowly increasing the editing tempo and moving in on the trio's eyes. (Leone shot and edited the showdown to fit Morricone's pre-recorded score, resulting in one of the cinema's most perfect fusions of music and image.) Setenza finally goes for his gun, only to be beaten by Blondie, while Tuco quickly discovers that his weapon has been unloaded. Blondie puts a second bullet in a still moving (and still aiming) Setenza, sending the bad man tumbling into an open grave, where he is quickly joined by his hat and gun. Tuco is obliged to dig up the gold (from the grave marked 'unknown' next to Arch Stanton) and then finds himself staring up at a noose dangling from a tree over a grave marker. His head placed in the tightened noose, the precariously balanced bandit is forced to look on as Blondie collects his share of the money (a fair 50/50 split), loads it up on a waiting horse, and rides off, eventually pausing to shoot the rope from above Tuco's head (just like old times). The bandit falls to the ground for another captioned freeze frame, followed by one each for Setenza (in his grave) and Blondie (on his horse). Tuco gets the last word ('Hey blonde. You wanna know what you are. Just a dirty son of a...'), and audiences get their last glimpse of Joe the Stranger, galloping off in the far distance a rich man.

Along with *Once Upon a Time in the West* and the underrated (if flawed) *Duck You Sucker/Giu la testa* (1971, aka *A Fistful of Dynamite*), *The Good The Bad and The Ugly* stands as one of Leone's best films. Of Eastwood's later output, only *The Beguiled*, *Dirty Harry* and *The Outlaw Josey Wales* come close to equalling it. The title has become a part of the language and the style subject to countless parodies/homages (two by Eastwood, in *Kelly's Heroes* and *Every Which Way But Loose*). Released to ecstatic audience response, the film confirmed beyond a doubt that the spaghetti western had become a genre to be reckoned with (for another eight years or so). By 1966, a few serious rivals were appearing to challenge Leone/Joe, most notably *Django* (1966), a spirited *Fistful* rip-off (a rip-off of a rip-off, in fact) directed by Sergio Corbucci. Imaginatively designed by Leone regular Giancarlo Simi, *Django* boldly dispenses with the standard American leading man, casting Italian actor Franco Nero as the Civil War veteran turned machinegun-toting avenger (he carries his firearm around in a coffin). Obviously approving of the hero's anti Ku Klux Klan battles, Italian audiences turned *Django* into an even bigger hit than *A Fistful of Dollars* (over 25 sequels/imitations followed). Corbucci certainly took the *Fistful* story elements to extremes, throwing in more mud, more violence, far more corpses and touches of inventive sadism even Leone would balk at (including a man forced to eat his own severed ear). Impressed, Eastwood took notice of Corbucci's work (see Chapter 7).

● *The Good The Bad and The Ugly*: Setenza aka Angel Eyes (Lee Van Cleef) picks up a little information.

Realizing they were on to a good thing, several of the *Dollars* veterans stayed with the genre for a little while. Gian Maria Volonte appeared in the avowedly political westerns *Quien Sabe ?* (1966 aka *A Bullet for the General*), co-starring Klaus Kinski, and *Face to Face* (1967), directed by the gifted Sergio Solima (being called 'Sergio' appears to have been an advantage for any budding spaghetti film-maker). Eli Wallach accepted a role in the modest *Ace High* (1968), most notable now as an early vehicle for the emerging action-comedy team of 'Terence Hill' (Mario Girotti) and 'Bud Spencer' (Carlo Pedersoli), later popular in the *Trinity* films. Lee Van Cleef decided to base most of his career in Italy, capitalizing on a level of success he'd never dreamed of back home. His later westerns didn't live up the standards of *The Good The Bad and The Ugly*, though at least a couple (Solima's *The Big Gundown* 1967, Gianfranco Parolini's *Sabata* 1969) came within a respectful distance. Eastwood felt he had more than done his time in Italian westerns, returning home to await the belated American release of the *Dollars* trilogy and the impact the films would have on his still moribund Hollywood career.

Purchasing the rights to *Fistful* from Colombo and Papi, Alberto Grimaldi approached Hollywood giant United Artists with a three-film distribution deal. The company showed interest, though initially only in *For a Few Dollars More* and *The Good The Bad and The Ugly*. Not about to waste his money, Grimaldi refused to drop the first of the trilogy from any negotiations and United Artists eventually gave in (The company also bought the distribution rights for *The Witches*, decided the film didn't suit Eastwood's image and buried it in their vaults). Settling on early 1967 for *Fistful*'s release date, United Artists set about devising a suitable marketing campaign, with questionable results. Aside from the 'Man with No Name' tag, their trailers featured such feeble slogans as 'The first motion picture of its kind. It won't be the last' and 'Danger fits him like a tight black glove', an ad-line better suited to James Bond, another film series distributed by United Artists (perhaps their advertising copy got put in the wrong file). The only smart move the company made with their *Fistful* advertising was to identify No Name by his various props (cigar, gun, poncho). Asking audiences to take an interest in a character who didn't even have a real identity could easily backfire. At least they might remember the poncho. Whatever Leone made of the American promotion, he could at least take heart in the knowledge that he'd achieved sufficient recognition to merit billing under his own name ('Dan Savio', 'Jack Dalmas' and 'Johnny Wels' weren't so lucky).

A Fistful of Dollars premiered in 80 New York cinemas on 2 February 1967. Reviews proved mostly damning, as United Artists had probably expected. As the company had certainly hoped, audiences turned up in impressive numbers, generating box-office receipts of around $5 million (it has been suggested that the film's cynicism and dark humour matched the prevailing mood in America at the time — Vietnam, Kennedy *et al*). *For a Few Dollars More* followed in May of the same year ('The Man with No Name is Back'), promoting Lee Van Cleef as 'The Man in Black' and giving Gian Maria Volonte back his real name. Both films also received their first screenings in Britain, once the prudish censor had taken a few bites out of each one. *For a Few Dollars More* suffered similar liberties in the United States, where United Artists felt obliged to remove a few bullet wounds (including the fatal shot self-inflicted by the Colonel's sister) and tone down one of Indio's more frenzied killings.

These minor snips were as nothing compared to the damage inflicted on *The Good The Bad and The Ugly* before it opened in 1968. Feeling the film to be too long at 175 minutes (some sources quote 180 minutes), United Artists removed nearly fifteen minutes of footage. Several scenes were cut entirely (Setenza questioning some Confederate soldiers about Jackson's whereabouts; Tuco taking the hospital wagon to a Confederate encampment where he is advised to head for the monastery), while others were truncated to push the story along, losing some intriguing detail (Tuco washing his feet in the desert while a parched Blondie crawls on his hands and knees; the two men travelling down a road lined with dead soldiers and abandoned weapons before meeting the dust-caked Union troops). Adding insult to grievous bodily harm, United Artists then botched the trailer, misidentifying Eli Wallach as The Bad and Lee Van Cleef as The Ugly. It got even worse when the film reached England. The distributor's London office chopped the already abbreviated print down to 148 minutes, losing a major scene where Tuco drops in on a storekeeper, checks out the man's supply of revolvers, takes several apart to produce a customised model, tests it on three target dummies (displaying considerable shooting prowess), then robs his host of $200. The censor insisted on making his usual cuts, toning down Setenza's attack on Maria, Wallace's torture of Tuco, and Tuco's subsequent revenge on his tormentor (he bashes Wallace's head in on a pointed rock). The more respectable 161 minute print is now in circulation in Britain (both on television and video), though it is a pity that Leone's original cut of the film remains unseen by English speaking audiences (that said, France is still stuck with the 148 minute version).

Despite this hacksaw treatment, *The Good The Bad and The Ugly* scored a big success in both America and Britain (making the UK top ten general release chart for 1968), benefiting its star and its director (a less expected beneficiary was American composer Hugo Montenegro, who enjoyed a hit record with an abysmal cover version of the theme tune). Leone now had the opportunity to work with both Henry Fonda and Charles Bronson on the Paramount financed *Once Upon a Time in the West* (partly shot in the United States). James Coburn turned down the role offered to him, yet he couldn't escape Leone forever, starring in *Duck You Sucker* three years later as a reformed IRA explosives expert aiding the revolution in 1913 Mexico. By the time Eastwood's final Leone collaboration premiered in his native country, he already had an American-shot follow-up awaiting release. No more than a standard revenge western, *Hang 'Em High* could nevertheless be regarded as a milestone in his career: the first film produced through Eastwood's own company, Malpaso. The television actor from the failed cowboy series had turned movie producer with a vengeance.

4

Return of the Native

Every gun makes its own tune and it's perfect timing, large one.
Blondie, *The Good The Bad and The Ugly*

You can be the best there is if you remember this... You work for justice.
Judge Adam Fenton, *Hang 'Em High*

The colour of pity is red.
Deputy Sheriff Walt Coogan, *Coogan's Bluff*

Arriving back home in 1966, Eastwood could feel justified in a little self-congratulation. The *Dollars* trilogy had made him a relatively wealthy man (he used some of his earnings to buy property in Carmel, the first step in establishing himself as a fully fledged resident) and audiences the world over looked on him as a film superstar. American moviegoers might not yet appreciate this fact, yet the imminent release of *A Fistful of Dollars* would surely convince them. A more complacent actor might well have sat back, enjoyed his new financial status and waited for studio executives to start knocking on his door. Eastwood's reluctance to take this easy option probably stemmed from two major factors: his experience of Hollywood producers gave him little faith in their ability to appreciate his talent and he felt little inclination to just sign on the dotted line as a contracted star-for-hire, surrendering control of both his films and his career. For all the American reports of *Fistful*'s huge international success, the film had barely registered in Hollywood. The oft-repeated story of Italian star Sophia Loren visiting Los Angeles, asking to meet hot new star Clint Eastwood and being met with blank looks ('the guy in that failing television series ?') illustrates this all too clearly. There may well have been an element of snobbery in Hollywood's attitude to Eastwood's spaghetti westerns. If the films were merely crude and bloody imitations of the hallowed American originals, he was an imitation star, with no more claim to their attention than the likes of Steve Reeves or Gordon Scott. Importing European stars for roles in American films might be seen as adding a touch of exoticism (such as Sophia Loren in the Cary Grant vehicle *Houseboat* 1958) or prestige (such as Swedish actor Max Von Sydow starring as Jesus Christ in *The Greatest Story Ever Told* 1965). Hiring an American obliged to work in Europe for want of any offers back home seemed to have little point (Frayling suggests that Hollywood also felt uneasy about Eastwood's amoral, profit-motivated No Name persona, yet the ethically dubious anti-hero had long been a staple of American movies, notably in the *film noir* which influenced Kurosawa's *Yojimbo* in the first place). While Eastwood could count on favourable box-office response to the *Dollars* films, he had no way of predicting industry reaction. With this in mind, he opted to take full control of his still tentative star career, its ultimate success or failure resting entirely on his own decisions: he would set up his own, independent production company; he needed to find the right vehicle to ease the transition from spaghetti superstar to respectable (and bankable) American player, and he wanted to continue working with Sergio Leone, without whom Eastwood's career would still be in limbo.

Much has been made of Eastwood's decision to found his own company, perhaps because it reinforces his image as a Hollywood 'loner' determined to choose his film projects without interference from philistine money men. There is certainly some truth to this, though his late sixties work made through Malpaso reflects the canny business-man side of Eastwood as much as the creative talent. The multiple attractions of picking the films, controlling the costs and taking a larger share of any profits had proved irre-sistible to a number of Hollywood stars before Eastwood. United Artists, the distribu-tor for the *Dollars* films, was founded in 1919 by director D.W. Griffith and actors Mary Pickford, Douglas Fairbanks (senior) and Charles 'Charlie' Chaplin in the hope of wrest-ing control of their careers from insensitive (and greedy) studio moguls. James Cagney founded the unimaginatively named Cagney Productions in 1942, followed by Humphrey Bogart's company Santana (named after his boat) in 1947. John Wayne dab-bled in independent production from the early 1950s onwards, forming Batjac the same decade. In 1948, Burt Lancaster combined forces with his agent Harold Hecht to launch the straightforward Hecht-Lancaster partnership (they were later joined by producer James Hill, making it Hecht-Hill-Lancaster). Kirk Douglas followed suit in 1955 with Bryna productions (named after his mother). A number of Eastwood's contemporaries had got in on the act, with Steve McQueen establishing Solar in 1963 and James Garner forming Cherokee in 1964. In most cases, the stars found the business of independent production deals (usually with distribution through a major studio) more difficult than anticipated, with their companies swallowing up revenue which might otherwise have boosted their bank balances. Many quit the production business fairly rapidly, often with only financial losses to show for their efforts (Hecht-Hill-Lancaster, for example, went into liquidation in 1959). Eastwood differed from his predecessors in production in two important respects. While the others had founded their companies when they were established stars with proven box-office track records, he had no real commercial mus-cle in Hollywood. Studios uninterested in the spaghetti star would not care either way that he came with his own company in tow, while those prepared to take a chance on Eastwood might be impressed that he appeared ready to share the risks of feature film production. More important, Eastwood would make his company work.

Establishing Malpaso proved straightforward, if only because the company consist-ed of a mere four employees and no fixed base of operations (for the time being). Eastwood naturally held a controlling interest in the company as the majority stock-holder, but decided against taking an official position. The vacancy for President of the Board went to old friend Irving Leonard, who would also serve as an associate produc-er on the first two Malpaso productions. It took a few years for the company to become a fully effective force in Eastwood's career, yet by the early 1970s and the start of his long association with Warner, Malpaso occupied a unique and highly enviable position in the industry. To date, nearly 20 per cent of Warner's all-time total revenue has been grossed by the company's productions.

Choosing a suitable script for his first starring role in an American film proved a big-ger headache for Eastwood. By the time *For a Few Dollars More* opened in US cinemas in the summer of 1967, he had still not found the right vehicle to follow *The Good The Bad and The Ugly* when it premiered early in 1968. However impressive the latter's box-office take, Eastwood could not afford to leave any significant gap before releasing a follow-up. Even an indifferent film would be better than no film at all, which might explain how he came to make *Hang 'Em High*. While it is not surprising that the spaghet-ti westerns would be followed by the genuine article, this awkward attempt to combine the liberal/historical approach of *Rawhide* with Leone-inspired brutality made for uneasy entertainment.

Obviously in need of a little assistance, Eastwood joined forces with former Universal-International colleague Leonard Freeman, now an independent producer active mainly in television (scoring his biggest success with *Hawaii Five O* 1968-79). Freeman agreed to both co-produce *Hang 'Em High* with Eastwood (the former taking sole screen credit) and co-write the script, which Eastwood described as an examination of the pros and cons of capital punishment (perhaps influenced by *The Ox-Bow Incident*). No doubt eager to capitalize on their newly acquired 'star', United Artists agreed to act as the film's distributor, arranging a three-way deal with Malpaso and Leonard Freeman Productions. The budget of $1.6 million made the film Eastwood's most expensive to date, and his fee of $400,000 (plus 25% of the box-office gross) reflected his new status behind the camera. Filming would take place at the MGM studios (enabling Eastwood to relive his *Rawhide* days if he so chose) and on location at White Sands National Park in Las Cruces, New Mexico, with the production commencing in the late summer-early autumn of 1967. Around the same time, Maggie Eastwood announced that she was pregnant, giving her husband's personal life the same sense of fundamental change (with the accompanying excitements and trepidations) as he now found in his professional world. An earlier pregnancy had ended in a miscarriage, adding an extra element of concern to an already stressful time in any relationship. Miscarriages aside, Eastwood's official reason for the lengthy delay in starting a family (nearly fifteen years) had been that he felt it would be irresponsible for a couple to bring a child into the world until they had the domestic stability, financial means and personal commitment necessary to raise it properly. Bearing in mind the star's not inconsiderable income since the late 1950s, and the birth of Kimber Tunis three years earlier, another factor may have been Eastwood's reluctance to cope with two young children (and two mothers) growing up at the same time.

Freeman's script for *Hang 'Em High* gave Eastwood the tailor-made role of Jed Cooper, a former lawman turned cattle farmer who picks up a badge and reaches for a gun after being unjustly (and unsuccessfully) lynched for murder. Determined to take revenge on the men who strung him up, Cooper's quest gives him a few lessons in the nature of justice and retribution, both personal and legal. As with many of Eastwood's later vehicles, the supporting roles did not call for star names, not that the budget (modest by American standards, if not Italian) could have run to any. The only other significant part in the film is self-righteous, politically ambitious hanging judge Adam Fenton, who recruits a wary Cooper after the latter is rescued from his hanging tree. The role went to character actor Pat Hingle, who'd appeared with credit in *On the Waterfront* (1954), *Splendor in the Grass* (1961) and *The Ugly American* (1963), and the above-average westerns *Invitation to a Gunfighter* (1964), with Yul Brynner, and *Nevada Smith* (1966), with Steve McQueen. Highly effective as the ruthless, slightly eccentric Fenton, Hingle later rejoined the Malpaso organization for supporting roles in *The Gauntlet* and *Sudden Impact*, though neither film did his talent justice. Freeman also wrote in some love interest for Eastwood, without any great success. Cooper has a brief, unfulfilling relationship with a prostitute, Jennifer (Arlene Golonka), who simply disappears from the film. This is followed by a liaison with Rachel (Inger Stevens), a widowed storekeeper with a tragic past. Blonde, pale and fragile in appearance (and more sympathetic than Sondra Locke, who possesses similar attributes), Stevens gives her poorly conceived, tissue thin role a lot more than it deserves. A number of the smaller speaking roles are filled out by well-known (if not star) faces, notably Ed Begley, Bruce Dern, Alan Hale Jr., Ben Johnson, Dennis Hopper and L.Q. Jones, giving the film a 'guest star' feel more typical of a television movie.

With *Hang 'Em High* ready for shooting, Eastwood and Freeman only needed a director in place for all the production positions to be filled. Eastwood decided to offer the job to Sergio Leone, despite the fact that the erstwhile director-star team had not been on the best of terms since completing *The Good The Bad and The Ugly*. The reasons for this falling out do not appear to have been anything very major, possibly no more than the inevitable result of two strongwilled talents finding that their mutual success gave them less room for manoeuvre in their dealings with one another. In interviews, Leone felt no obligation to hide his not entirely favourable opinion of Eastwood's acting ability (questioned sixteen years later by Christopher Frayling on the set of *Once Upon a Time in America* 1984, he compared the star to a block of marble and a suit of armour with the visor firmly shut). Not inclined to do any favours for Leone, Eastwood refused the director's request that he play a cameo role in *Once Upon a Time in the West* (he later gave the same response re *Once Upon a Time in America*). Leone wanted to begin the film with Eastwood, Lee Van Cleef and Eli Wallach as three gunfighters mown down in a shootout with hero Charles Bronson. Van Cleef and Wallach agreed, but Eastwood declined (some sources state that he also turned down the lead in the film, though this casting is at odds with Leone's claim that he wanted to break from the *Dollars* style of western). From a career point of view, Eastwood's decision proved a wise one. Released in the United States in a heavily edited print which rendered several key plot points unintelligible, *Once Upon a Time in the West* did disappointing business (though it subsequently acquired cult status once the complete print became available). Though Leone needed an American success if he wanted to exploit the opportunities created by the *Dollars* films, he turned down Eastwood's offer of *Hang 'Em High*, possibly because he knew a mediocre script when he saw one (not that the director's judgement always did him credit: a few years later Leone would reject an offer from Paramount to direct *The Godfather* (1971), a decision he regretted when his career declined into a decade-long slump). For the record, Eastwood explained his split with Leone as a simple matter of film-making style. The latter wanted to make epics on a grandiose scale, while he increasingly favoured smaller, more personal films which did not demand vast budgets. Their subsequent careers bear this theory out, though Eastwood would have been happy to continue his working relationship with Leone if the latter had felt able to accept a shift in the balance of power. Throughout the *Dollars* films, star and director had functioned as equal partners (more or less). For Leone to direct *Hang 'Em High*, he would have to sign on as a Malpaso employee, with Eastwood the undisputed (if benevolent) boss. As the star later found with Don Siegel, strong directors rarely feel comfortable working under the thumb of their lead actors. Not yet ready to make his own move into the director's chair, Eastwood had to make a choice between genuine talent (with the possibility of creative clashes) and mere efficiency (with guaranteed compliance to his wishes). He chose Ted Post.

As Post's work on *Rawhide* had demonstrated, he knew a thing or two about film-making (Post has regularly taught masterclasses in directing at the University of California, Los Angeles) without having ever developed a distinctive style or vision. Eastwood knew he could depend on his old colleague and friend to deliver a

● *Hang 'Em High:* Marshal Jed Cooper.

professional product. United Artists were not so convinced, arguing that the director's lack of feature film experience made him a poor choice. Post had not directed for the cinema in nearly ten years and head of production David Picker asked Eastwood to think again. Recently promoted from United Artists' London office (where he'd made the deal with producers Harry Saltzman and Albert Broccoli that gave UA the distribution rights to the James Bond series), Picker evidently felt that Eastwood was drawing too heavily on his television connections, a retrograde step for an actor wishing to consolidate his big screen success (aside from Freeman and Post, Pat Hingle had appeared as a guest star on *Rawhide*). Eastwood did not care to have his choices as co-producer questioned. Not only would he refuse to consider another director (Leone's spurning may have rankled), he would shut down production rather than fire Post. Realizing that Eastwood meant business (in more ways than one), Picker relented. More charitable observers might read this episode as another instance of Eastwood's unswaying loyalty to old friends, yet there must also have been a strong element of power play at work. Eastwood's company. Eastwood's project. Eastwood's choices.

Following these preproduction traumas, the actual filming of *Hang 'Em High* should have been straightforward. Instead, Eastwood received a valuable, if irritating lesson in the risks of taking on a co-producer, especially one also responsible for the script (written with Mel Goldberg). Leonard Freeman decided to flex his executive muscle, making regular visits to the set in an attempt to dominate (and interfere with) the production. Described by Post as an 'arrogant egomaniac', Freeman slowed down the pace of filming, pestering the cast and crew with unhelpful suggestions and instructions. The working atmosphere grew steadily worse and Eastwood finally took drastic action, ordering Freeman off the set with the threat of a complete production shutdown if he showed his face again during shooting. Allowing the businessman in him to win out over the control freak, Freeman kept away and *Hang 'Em High* was finished on time and on budget.

The precredits sequence in *Hang 'Em High* demonstrates some uncertainty on Eastwood's part as to how he should blend his old *Rawhide*-Rowdy Yates image (still reasonably fresh in the viewing public's memory) with the tougher, less moral 'No Name' persona. For all his publicly expressed boredom and frustration with the role of Yates, Eastwood draws on the character throughout the film. The opening shots of Jed Cooper leading his newly acquired herd of cattle through a river could have been lifted intact from an old *Rawhide* episode. Clean cut and clean shaven, the leather chaps clad Cooper is immediately established as an honest, kind cowboy, rescuing a stranded calf stuck in the river ('I'm gonna have to carry you, huh ?'). A group of horsemen appear in the distance on the far side of the river. They surround Cooper and the leader, Captain Wilson (Ed Begley) accuses him of murdering a cattle farmer named Johanssen and stealing his herd. Cooper protests that he bought the cattle from the farmer for $800 (he has a receipt), only to discover that the man he describes bears no resemblance to Johanssen (we later discover that the real killer sold an unsuspecting Cooper the cows before making his getaway). Cooper's former lawman credentials cut no ice with the lynchers and he is roped and dragged back through the river to be strung up from a convenient tree. As Cooper is left to die, lurid red letters appear to announce 'Clint Eastwood starring in', accompanied by the sound of a gallows trap door opening and a body falling through. The title words 'Hang 'Em High' appear in the distance to zoom into close-up (inspired, perhaps, by Luigi Lardani's credits for the *Dollars* films). Aside from an effective overhead shot of Cooper hanging, Ted Post's direction is no more than competent,

falling back on some awkward zooms for dramatic emphasis. The bloody beating inflicted on Cooper before he is strung up seems gratuitous, as do the close-ups of his battered face. This level of violence may be no stronger than that found in the Leone films,
yet here it is included merely for box office reasons, imitating the Italian's style only on
the most superficial level. Post himself had little time for Leone's film-making, dismissing it in a later interview as ponderous, self-conscious and full of meaningless close-ups.
Whether or not one accepts this view, it cannot be disputed that his ritualized, almost
operatic staging of violence bears no more resemblance to the brutalities of the real
world than the cruelties of a fairy tale (Stuart M. Kaminsky describes Leone's films as
'comic nightmares about existence'). Post's indifferent, rather clinical treatment of
human nastiness borders on the tasteless. It has been claimed that Eastwood took effective control of *Hang 'Em High*'s direction, with Post serving as little more than a glori-
fied assistant. If so, the star had a lot to learn about being a director (bearing in mind
the style of Eastwood's later work, the likely truth is that Post helmed the film with only
occasional suggestions from his producer-star).

If Post reluctantly threw a few pseudo-spaghetti touches into his otherwise conventional direction, much the same can be said for the score by composer Dominic
Frontiere (best known for his television work, such as *The Outer Limits* 1963, and *The
Invaders* 1967). Frontiere incorporates some Morricone-style flourishes (including a
church organ) into a fairly standard, sometimes overemphatic western arrangement.
Just as half-hearted is Eastwood's own attempt to toughen up Cooper. The lynching
scene appears to signal a transformation from Rowdy Yates type to No Name type but
this doesn't happen. The injury to Cooper's neck leaves him with a temporary spaghet-
ti-style whisper-growl ('When you hang a man you better look at him'), and he shows
an interest in cigars. Otherwise, he remains a defiantly stereotyped cowboy hero out for
justice, with an identity, a past, an interest in women and a clear moral code. Typical of
this timidity is Cooper's dress sense. He may wear a dark shirt and jeans, yet his hat
always stays white.

The most interesting aspect of *Hang 'Em High* is its rather fumbled attempt to deal
fairly with all views on the death penalty. Judge Fenton represents the law's point of
view, with a few political undertones. Operating from Fort Grant in the territory of
Oklahoma, Fenton has to cover 70,000 square miles with less than twenty marshals,
who are paid a paltry $250 a month plus expenses. If Oklahoma is to be granted state-
hood, Fenton must be seen to take a hard line against all transgressors. At first concerned only with legally sanctioned vengeance against his would-be lynchers, Cooper
soon realizes that the law can be as harsh and unfair as any bloodthirsty mob. Two
teenage rustlers whose partner-in-crime murdered a rancher are sentenced to join him
on the gallows. Cooper's attempt to argue for clemency at their trial fails dismally, as he
is out-smarted by the smooth-talking prosecution lawyer (Mark Lenard, revered by *Star
Trek* cultists for his role as Sarek, Mr Spock's dad). To underline Cooper's revulsion, the
mechanics of execution are dwelled on in detail. The six-man gallows at Fort Grant is
freshly painted; the top grade hemp used for the nooses will snap a neck 'like a dried-out
twig'. A mass hanging is a big public event, with a carnival atmosphere. Caught between
hot-blooded lynch law and cold-blooded legal execution, Cooper opts to stick with the
latter, if only because he has still not tracked down all the original lynching party when
the film ends (Captain Wilson hangs himself rather than face Cooper's justice, a predictable piece of irony). *Hang 'Em High* never takes a very clear attitude to these amateur hangmen. Only two are depicted as out-and-out villains (notably Miller, played by

Bruce Dern in familiar edgy, sneering mode). The rest are respectable, public-spirited citizens who just happened to make a bad judgement.

The biggest failing of *Hang 'Em High* is its misuse of leading lady Inger Stevens. Eastwood's films have seldom provided half-decent roles for women (the exceptions, such as *The Beguiled* and *Tightrope*, are few and far between) and this movie is a major offender. Though Rachel appears during the opening sequence (she looks into the prison wagon that brings Cooper into Fort Grant for the first time), the character is given only fleeting screentime and a few enigmatic lines ('we all have our ghosts, Marshal'). Ninety minutes pass before she is properly brought into the story, tending to Cooper's gunshot wounds after a murder attempt by Wilson and two other members of the lynch party. Rachel takes Cooper out for a picnic in the countryside, where she gets to order him around ('Don't drink your milk so fast') and tell her tragic story (she was brutally raped and her husband murdered by two outlaws; she still looks out for the men when a new consignment of prisoners arrives in town). Touching as this story is, the scene is badly incorporated into the overall script (we are just waiting for Cooper to go after Wilson), ultimately seeming like a contrived way of padding out the running time. At the conclusion, it is not clear if Cooper and Rachel are meant to have any future together, as the film ends with a high-angled long shot of the Marshall leaving town in pursuit of the remaining members of the lynch mob. It is a pity that Eastwood never got the chance to work with Inger Stevens again. After a few more film appearances (*House of Cards* 1969, *A Dream of Kings* 1969), the actress killed herself with a barbiturate overdose in 1970.

United Artists opened *Hang 'Em High* close on the heels of *The Good The Bad and The Ugly* in early 1968, publicising the film with an appropriately snappy ad-line: 'They made two mistakes -they hanged the wrong man, and they didn't finish the job !'. Evidently impressed by the vigorous, if unexceptional action scenes (and undeterred by the lack of style or any sense of humour), cinemagoers turned *Hang 'Em High* into an instant hit. The film is reputed to have broken even on its opening weekend, earning more money than any of the *Dollars* films. Critics were still doubtful about Eastwood, yet he had now proved that he didn't need Sergio Leone to sustain his commercial success. What he did need was a vehicle to demonstrate that he amounted to more than a cowboy star with drive-in appeal. Waving goodbye to United Artists (until 1973), Eastwood took himself and Malpaso over to Universal Studios, happy to forgive and forget that a decade earlier this same company had unceremoniously fired him.

Universal had seen a few changes since Eastwood's brief stint as a contract bit player. In 1962 the studio underwent a takeover by the vast agency MCA (Music Corporation of America), which dropped the 'International' tag from the name. Still flourishing in both film and television production, Universal offered a sound base of operations. The studio also offered Eastwood a promising project, a contemporary 'fish out of water' action movie involving an Arizona sheriff who takes a trip to New York to pick up a prisoner wanted for an offence back home. *Coogan's Bluff* began life as a treatment by proficient screenwriter Herman Miller. Miller had developed the basic story into a script, though both executive producer Richard Lyons and vice president in charge of film production Jennings Lang felt it needed a few rewrites. Unconcerned with this minor hitch, Eastwood agreed to make the film as a Universal-Malpaso co-production, and set up an office for his company on the Universal backlot. No doubt hoping for a less fraught period of preproduction than he'd endured on *Hang 'Em High*, Eastwood found himself disappointed. The script difficulties persisted. Miller soon departed, making way for Roland Kibbee, who rapidly gave way to Jack Laird. Two new writers and numerous script drafts did not make anyone happier with the screenplay. Matters were further complicated by the lack of a director. Eastwood, Lyons and Lang could not agree on a suitable candidate and by the time veteran director-producer Don Siegel arrived on the scene, *Coogan's Bluff* appeared to heading nowhere very slowly.

The story of how Clint Eastwood and Donald Siegel came together to form one of the cinema's most effective actor-director partnerships has taken on the status of myth. Siegel's own version of events, recounted in his autobiography *A Siegel Film*, is the most amusing (and probably the least accurate). He claimed that Universal had reduced their shortlist of directors for *Coogan's Bluff* down to a couple of names: Alex Segal and Don Taylor. Unable to decide between these two, the executives fed the directors' details into the studio computer, which promptly resolved their dilemma by answering with the name 'Don Siegel' (or possibly 'Don Segal'). No doubt a little nonplussed by this decision, the Universal management nevertheless resolved that expensive modern technology could not be wrong and offered Siegel the job. This may not be quite as ridiculous as it sounds (Siegel was under contract to Universal at the time), yet the actual circumstances were a little more banal, if equally complicated.

It is the case that Universal wanted Alex Segal to direct the film. This choice is a little puzzling, as the New York-based director worked mainly in television and theatre, with a mere three feature films to his credit. His debut movie, *Ransom* (1956), a suspense drama starring Glenn Ford and Leslie Nielsen, might have been felt to be a sufficient qualification for a cops-and-robbers storyline. The subsequent films, *All the Way Home* (1963), a nostalgic small-town drama with Robert Preston, Jean Simmons and Pat Hingle, and *Joy in the Morning* (1965), a romantic drama with Richard Chamberlain and Yvette Mimieux, suggest that Segal's real talents lay with less macho themes. Whatever the case, Alex Segal got the job, only to quit shortly afterwards, either because he disliked the script(s) (standard version of events) or for personal reasons (Eastwood's version of events). In need of a swift replacement, Eastwood suggested Don Taylor, an actor turned director with a handful of unassuming films: *Everything's Ducky* (1961), a comedy featuring Mickey Rooney, Buddy Hackett and the aforementioned duck, *Ride the Wild Surf* (1964), a beach movie with Fabian Forte Bonaparte and Eastwood's old co-star Tab Hunter, and *Jack of Diamonds* (1967), a dull 'caper' movie that wasted both George Hamilton and Joseph Cotten. Even allowing for *Coogan's Bluff*'s modest budget, this choice of (inexpensive) director reflects a desire for extreme economy on Eastwood's part which could have hurt the finished film. Unimpressed with Taylor's body of work to date, Universal rejected their star's choice, suggesting actor-turned-television-director Mark Rydell as an alternative. Rydell was not interested, opting instead to make his feature film debut with *The Fox* (1968), an adaptation of D.H. Lawrence's tale of lesbian love and betrayal starring Anne Heywood and Sandy Dennis (not too much common ground with *Coogan's Bluff*, though both films feature scores by Lalo Schifrin). Evidently feeling that the Universal executives needed a little guidance, Rydell recommended Don Siegel, with whom he'd worked (as an actor) on the above-average 'teen angst drama *Crime in the Streets* (1956). Lang and Lyons were enthusiastic and put the choice to a dubious Eastwood, who, having never heard of Siegel, suspected he was about to be fobbed off with one of Alex Segal's less talented relatives (who just happened to spell his name differently). Reassured, the star agreed to look at some of Siegel's films and found himself impressed by the director's ability to produce outstanding work with limited resources (many of Siegel's earlier pictures were shot on 'B' budgets). Siegel, in turn, knew little about Eastwood and watched the *Dollars* films before agreeing to take up Eastwood's offer to direct *Coogan's Bluff*. Impressed by Eastwood's onscreen charisma, business sense and film-making know-how, Siegel accepted the assignment.

One of the American cinema's finest (if erratic) directors of thrillers, westerns and science-fiction, Don Siegel excelled with Eastwood's style of character: an outcast or loner (whether gunfighter, policeman or criminal), infusing his storylines with a careful blend of violence and humour. Originally trained as an actor (at London's Royal Academy of Dramatic Art), Siegel broke into films in 1934, when an uncle secured him a job at Warner Brothers as an assistant in the studio film library. After spells as an assistant editor and special effects man, Siegel found his niche in the montage department, specializing in time lapse and transition sequences. In this capacity, Siegel got his name onto some major productions, such as *Confessions of a Nazi Spy* (1939), *The Roaring Twenties* (1939), with James Cagney, *Blues in the Night* (1941), co-starring *Rawhide* director-to-be Richard Whorf, and *They Died With Their Boots On* (1941). On the latter he also served as a second-unit director, continuing to work in this dual capacity on *Mission to Moscow* (1943) and *Passage to Marseilles* (1944). In a fairer world, Siegel would have graduated to the director's chair with no difficulty. As Eastwood discovered ten years later, however, studios seldom made life too easy for their employees. Siegel received the expected offer to make his directing debut on the film *The Conspirators* (1944), only to discover that it would tie him to a laughably unfair seven year contract. His rejection of the deal incurred studio wrath, and Siegel found himself assigned to the film anyway, in the humble role of assistant director. Frustrating as this demotion must have been, it subsequently gave him the opportunity to work with Howard Hawks on the Humphrey Bogart-Lauren Bacall vehicle *To Have and Have Not* (1944). Warner finally relented, and after cutting his teeth on two short films, *Star in the Night* (1945), a modern retelling of the Nativity story which won an Academy Award, and *Hitler Lives* (1946), Siegel got to direct his first feature film, *The Verdict* (1946), a curious Victorian murder mystery starring Sidney Greenstreet and Peter Lorre. In 1948, Warner decided to terminate Siegel's

● **Don Siegel.**

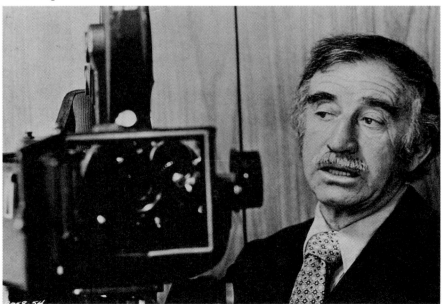

contract and for the next fifteen years he worked on a more or less freelance basis, making films for RKO (*The Big Steal* 1949), Univeral-International (*Duel at Silver Creek* 1953), United Artists (*Baby Face Nelson* 1957), Twentieth Century Fox (*Flaming Star* 1960, one of the few worthwhile Elvis Presley movies) and Paramount (*Hell is for Heroes*, a strong anti-war movie). Siegel's most fruitful collaboration in his pre-Eastwood days was with independent producer Walter Wanger. Working through Allied Artists, a modest outfit specialising in second features, they produced *Riot in Cell Block 11* (1954), a potent prison melodrama, and *Invasion of the Body Snatchers* (1956), an unsurpassed nightmare fantasy shot in 19 days for less than $300,000 (with a little help in the script and acting departments from Siegel's then assistant Sam Peckinpah).

By the mid 1960s, Siegel's career had suffered something of a slump. After signing an exclusive contract with Universal in 1963 (which limited his non-Universal work to television episodes), he found himself confined to television movies. His one big success, *The Killers*, only made it to the cinema because the studio regarded the level of violence as too strong for the small screen (they could have opted to cut it instead, so Siegel had some reason to feel grateful). Four years passed before Siegel made a fully fledged big-screen comeback with *Madigan* (1968), an effective renegade-cop-versus-psycho-villain police drama starring Richard Widmark and Henry Fonda. Similar to both *Coogan's Bluff* and *Dirty Harry*, the film makes good use of its New York setting (partly shot in Los Angeles) and provides a sympathetic hero in the form of Detective Dan Madigan (Widmark), a man whose ruthless skill in the pursuit of criminals is contrasted with his inability to lead a normal life off the streets, alienating both his boss (Fonda) and his wife (Inger Stevens). Considering the film's box-office success, it is surprising that Siegel did not make the original running for *Coogan's Bluff*. He knew both Richard Lyons, who'd produced his 1967 television movie *Stranger on the Run*, and Jennings Lang, who'd numbered the director among his clients in his former role as an agent. The parallels between *Madigan* and the Eastwood project must have been obvious to even the most thick-headed Universal executive.

Hiring Siegel to work on *Coogan's Bluff* (both as director and producer) did not immediately resolve its preproduction difficulties. Discarding the existing scripts, he recruited writer Howard Rodman to piece together a workable screenplay before filming commenced in November 1967. Anxious that Rodman should make full use of the New York setting, Siegel took him on his location scouting trips (the opening sequence would be shot in the Mojave Desert in Southern California). Despite this precaution, Rodman's rewrite didn't please Siegel, who felt it lacked humour. Eastwood's response proved to be a little stronger, the star announcing he detested the new script and wouldn't make the film until he saw a complete rewrite (number seven or thereabouts). At this point, the already tense relations between star and director broke down, and Siegel seriously considered resigning from the project (Eastwood subsequently explained that, in his view, Rodman's draft emphasized locations over story development to a harmful degree). Using Eastwood's new agent, Lennie Hirshan, as an intermediary, the two made peace and agreed to work together on a new script, taking bits and pieces from the earlier versions. This approach proved viable, if a little slow and with the impending start date in mind, Dean Riesner was recruited to finish the final draft, taking a mere two weeks. The decision to call for Riesner appears to have been entirely Siegel's. Eastwood has never mentioned the writer in his own account of events and, if Siegel is to be believed, showed some reluctance to recruit him. Riesner's *Rawhide* scripts need not have brought him into direct contact with Eastwood, whereas Siegel had worked closely with Riesner on the screenplay for *Stranger on the Run*. Eastwood's wariness towards recruiting another writer may have stemmed from the fact that the film had already got through four with little to show for their efforts. Whatever the case, Riesner's work gave Eastwood more than a little reason to be grateful.

The plot of *Coogan's Bluff* is so straightforward that the prolonged script agonies now seem a little mysterious (no doubt a fine tribute to the writing skills of Dean Riesner). Deputy sheriff Walt Coogan of Piute County, Arizona, is ordered by his sheriff to travel to New York to extradite aggressive hippie James Ringerman (Don Stroud, promoted by Siegel to a co-starring role after playing a police informer in *Madigan*). A native New Yorker, Ringerman is wanted for an offence committed in Coogan's home state and as the original arresting officer, the deputy gets the job of bringing him in. Once in New York, Coogan discovers that Ringerman is not going anywhere. After taking some poor quality LSD, he suffered a bad acid trip and is now confined to a prison hospital. Coogan's New York contact, Detective McElroy (Lee J. Cobb) advises the deputy to wait patiently until Ringerman can be discharged into his custody. Not overly concerned with official procedure, red tape or prisoner's rights (an attitude heartily endorsed by Harry Callahan), Coogan bluffs his way into the hospital, intimidates the officer in charge into handing over Ringerman and heads for the heliport with his prisoner in tow. Waiting for the flight, Coogan is ambushed by Ringerman's girlfriend and drug dealer, losing both his captive and his gun in the process. After various adventures in a disco and pool hall, Coogan corners the fugitive Ringerman in Fort Tryon Park, chases him on a motorbike and hands him over to McElroy until a judge can sign the relevant extradition papers (rendering Coogan's violent escapades a little pointless).

Opening with the familiar long shot of a barren landscape, *Coogan's Bluff* neatly transposes Eastwood the Cowboy into Eastwood the displaced Urban Cop. Siegel's camera pans across the desert to bring the figure of a watching Indian fugitive into medium close-up, this warrior clutching a telescopic rifle in place of the standard bow and arrow. A dust trail appears on the horizon, soon revealed as Coogan in his jeep (the modern cowboy's horse). Coogan's attitude to his Indian prisoner seems very much of the old west, as he strikes the man with a rifle butt before putting on the handcuffs. For his trip to New York, Coogan adopts an extreme cowboy-style wardrobe (ten gallon hat, long boots, string tie), leading all the urban dwellers to take him for a Texan (apparently not a compliment for a native of Arizona). The small town/big city culture clash is well drawn, with Coogan experiencing run-ins with taxi drivers, punks, thieving whores, hippies, uptight city cops and liberal social workers. Siegel directs with a good eye for background detail and his handling of the action scenes is impressive. The undoubted highlight of the film is a fight sequence in the pool hall where Coogan takes on a gang of Ringerman's friends, killing at least one before receiving the bloody beating virtually compulsory in any Eastwood film. Siegel's use of staging, framing and editing in this scene is a model of its kind, in marked contrast to Ted Post's clumsy treatment of violence in *Hang 'Em High*. Eastwood later cited Siegel's careful preproduction planning and 'cut in the camera' style (shooting only the footage needed for the final edit) as the main influences on his own directing. He also learned a great deal about the filming of action scenes. During the production of *Coogan's Bluff*, Eastwood continued his policy of making a few creative suggestions to his director, Siegel being only too happy to listen to his cine-literate star when the ideas were good.

• *Coogan's Bluff*: **Coogan and Ringerman (Don Stroud) take a trip.**

Apart from the rather noticeable rushed plotting in the latter stages (as if the film-makers realized they were running out of screen time), the only drawback to *Coogan's Bluff* is its romantic subplot(s). Coogan enjoys liaisons with both Ringerman's spaced-out girlfriend, Linny Raven (Tisha Sterling), and Julie (Susan Clark, Henry Fonda's lover in *Madigan*), a social worker in charge of Linny's case. Eastwood does his standard awkward/smooth loverboy act to good effect, but the women's roles are ill-conceived. Priding herself on being a caring professional who understands the 'kids', Julie serves mainly as a source of information to advance the story. Her scenes with Coogan are a little tiresome and, as with Rachel in *Hang 'Em High*, the film seems unsure what to do with the relationship. Julie's appearance at the conclusion to wave Coogan (and Ringerman) off at the heliport looks tacked on. Similarly, Coogan's seduction of the diminutive, childlike Linny is uncomfortable to watch (though he only does it to learn Ringerman's whereabouts). Dean Riesner hated the scene (dismissing it as 'stupid') and argued for its removal from the script. For reasons best known to himself, Eastwood refused to lose it and his decision remained in force. No-one has ever been fool enough to suggest that the star really does have a dubious interest in teenage girls a fraction of his age (Eastwood has made use of the libel laws more than once), yet a number of his film scripts skate on thin ice. When Coogan responds to Julie's line: 'I only handle young single girls' with the quip 'Yuh, me too', Eastwood is asking for at least a few raised eyebrows. On balance, women get a raw deal in *Coogan's Bluff*. A battered wife won't press charges against her violent husband; an old lady fantasizes about rape; Ringerman's mother is a sozzled old witch. In fairness, this element seems as much to do with Siegel as Eastwood. The director's recollections of his dealings with Tisha Sterling (who went into a sulk when her location expenses were stolen) and Susan Clark (who threatened to ruin the continuity in a sequence by changing clothes halfway through) are not very favourable.

The only source of contention between Eastwood and Siegel during shooting stemmed from the star's persistently macho attitude to doing his own stunts. For the climactic motorbike chase, Siegel naturally hired two stunt riders. The late autumn-early winter weather had left the ground in Fort Tryon Park covered in frost and wet leaves, increasing the risk of accidents during shooting. Don Stroud had never ridden a motorbike before and so had no objections to being doubled. Unconcerned by the poor conditions or the risk of production delays should he be injured, experienced biker Eastwood wanted to do all his own riding. Siegel refused to give way on the trickier shots and his star walked off the location in protest. It is unlikely that Eastwood really felt that using a double made him less of a man, yet this desire to perform his own stunts has remained a constant in his career. As it is, the motorbike chase in *Coogan's Bluff* is not entirely successful, mainly because it goes on too long and makes use of some speeded up footage that fails to convince.

For all these drawbacks, *Coogan's Bluff* remains a pivotal film in Eastwood's career. Aside from being his first collaboration with Siegel, it introduced him to several production personnel who would take key positions in later Malpaso films. Art director Alexander Golitzen (an Academy Award winner for his work on Lubin's *Phantom*) had first encountered the star during his Universal-International days (Golitzen worked on Eastwood's first five films for the studio). Eastwood used him again for *The Beguiled*, *Play Misty for Me*, *Joe Kidd* and *Breezy*. Composer Lalo Schifrin already had a good movie track record, writing the scores for *The Cincinnati Kid* (1964), *Cool Hand Luke* (1967), *Who's Minding the Mint ?* (1967) and *Bullitt* (1968), among others. His lively score for *Coogan's Bluff* impressed both Eastwood and Siegel, and Schifrin became the former's composer of choice, providing the music for *Kelly's Heroes*, *The Beguiled*, *Dirty Harry*, *Joe Kidd*, *Magnum Force*, *Sudden Impact* and *The Dead Pool*. Stuntman Wayne 'Buddy' Van Horn, who doubled for Eastwood in the opening scene (where Coogan swerves his jeep to avoid the Indian's gunfire) has remained on the Malpaso team to this day. Further down the credits, camera operator Bruce Surtees worked beyond the call of duty (sitting on the handle-bars of speeding motorbikes to film shots of the riders), earning his place in Eastwood's organization. Son of Academy Award winning cameraman Robert Surtees (director of photography on *Intruder in the Dust* (1949), *Quo Vadis* (1951), *The Bad and the Beautiful* (1952), *Ben Hur* (1959), *The Graduate* (1967) and *Sweet Charity* (1968), among many others), Bruce Surtees took one more Eastwood-Siegel credit as an assistant (*Two Mules for Sister Sara*) before the star-director team promoted him to director of photography on *The Beguiled*. Surtees would remain the principal Malpaso cameraman until the mid 1980s, photographing *Play Misty for Me*, *Dirty Harry*, *Joe Kidd*, *High Plains Drifter*, *The Outlaw Josey Wales*, *Escape from Alcatraz*, *Honkytonk Man*, *Firefox*, *Sudden Impact*, *Tightrope* and *Pale Rider*.

Of the *Coogan's Bluff* cast, only two worked with Eastwood again. Don Stroud got a supporting role as a hired gun in *Joe Kidd*. More interesting is the subsequent Eastwood-related career of black actor Albert Popwell, cast here as Wonderful Digby, a switchblade wielding hippie who forces Coogan to get tough in the Pigeon Toed Orange Peel disco sequence ('You better drop that blade or you won't believe what happens next'). Popwell later appeared as a shotgun-toting bank robber in *Dirty Harry*, a drain-cleaner squirting pimp in *Magnum Force* and a kleptomaniac political activist (non-violent) in *The Enforcer*, before finally getting on the right side of the law as a fellow policeman in *Sudden Impact*. The first three of these parts may not seem terribly progressive casting in more politically correct times, yet the choice of Popwell seems related more to the actor's flair for coolly threatening characters than any suspect racial motives on Eastwood's part (see Chapter 6). It must count for something that the star's action movies have been consistently popular with multi-ethnic audiences.

Released in 1968 to favourable reviews and solid box-office, *Coogan's Bluff* marked a successful move away from the westerns which had dominated Eastwood's career for nearly a decade (The film also inspired the popular television series *McCloud* (1970-76), though ex-*Gunsmoke* co-star Dennis Weaver made an unlikely substitute for Eastwood). The only source of disappointment for the star lay with the film industry, which still seemed unsure of his talents (not helped by some fairly malicious critics). When the offer of a role in a big budget film arrived during shooting on *Coogan's Bluff*, it was for a production based in Britain, to be filmed at Elstree Studios (near London) and on location in Austria. Considering whether or not to accept the proffered part in *Where Eagles Dare*, Eastwood found three drawbacks: he didn't like the existing script (by thriller writer Alistair MacLean); he wouldn't be the top-billed star, taking second place to Richard Burton, and producer Elliott Kastner's deal with backer MGM didn't allow him to involve Malpaso, placing Eastwood's production plans on hold. Against this, the film would be Eastwood's first 'A' budget vehicle ($7 million), and the $750,000 pay-check on offer his highest ever fee. Having completed the shooting for *Coogan's Bluff* on December 31st 1967, Eastwood flew out to London the same day, starting work on his classic comic strip World War II shoot-em-up just 48 hours later.

5

Jerry gets a Kicking

If I could climb up on my own, why can't he ?
Major John Smith, *Where Eagles Dare.*

Everybody's got a right to be a sucker once.
Hogan, *Two Mules for Sister Sara.*

We're just a private enterprise operation.
Kelly, *Kelly's Heroes.*

Where Eagles Dare began life as a concept rather than a script or even a story outline. Elliott Kastner, a London-based independent producer, wanted to put together a vehicle for star Richard Burton, who by the mid-1960s enjoyed the Hollywood equivalent of regal status despite a highly variable box-office track record. A major British theatre star since the late 1940s, Burton's early film career (*My Cousin Rachel* 1952, *The Robe* 1953, *Alexander the Great* 1956) had not brought him the same level of success, and it took his much publicised affair with (and subsequent marriage to) Elizabeth Taylor during the filming of *Cleopatra* (1963) to secure him both the roles and the media attention befitting a superstar. In fairness, Burton went on to demonstrate his considerable talent (specialising in brooding, self-mocking introspection) in John Huston's *The Night of the Iguana* (1964), *The Spy Who Came in from the Cold* (1965), *Who's Afraid of Virginia Woolf ?* (1966) and *The Taming of the Shrew* (1967), the last two co-starring an on-form Taylor. Sadly, laziness and poor judgement soon became evident, with the successes quickly outnumbered by the flops (*The Sandpiper* 1965, *Dr Faustus* 1967, *The Comedians* 1967, *Boom !* 1968), all co-starring an off-form Taylor. By 1967, Burton had suffered three box-office duds in a row and let it be known that he wanted a straightforward action-adventure vehicle to restore his increasingly doubtful commercial status. As a model for this proposed career booster, he cited *The Guns of Navarone* (1961), Columbia Pictures' hugely successful World War II adventure, starring Gregory Peck, David Niven and Anthony Quinn, based on a bestselling novel by Alistair MacLean.

Though he'd only been in film production for little over a year, Kastner (who worked with business partner Jerry Gershwin) already had three films to his credit: *Harper* (1966), with Paul Newman, *Kaleidoscope* (1966), with Warren Beatty, and *Sol Madrid* (1967), starring David McCallum and Telly Savalas. An astute operator, Kastner decided to snare Burton with the offer of a $1 million dollar fee (plus a share of the box-office gross) and an original Alistair MacLean screenplay written especially for the star. As he recounted in a recent interview with Philip Masheter, Kastner tracked down MacLean and made a deal with the initially reluctant author for a script (MacLean had no previous screenwriting experience), asking for nothing more specific than a World War II 'caper' movie with 4-5 main characters. Looking for a studio to buy his production 'package', Kastner took advantage of the knowledge that MGM currently had another MacLean adaptation, *Ice Station Zebra* (1968), in production, starring Rock Hudson. Confident of a box-office hit with the latter (wrongly as it turned out), the

MGM executives were naturally interested in a new MacLean script, named *Where Eagles Dare* by Kastner (a quote from William Shakespeare's *Richard III*). With a deal in the bag, Kastner set about recruiting his production team and Burton's co-stars, the latter to be chosen in consultation with Burton.

Kastner's choice of director, Brian G. Hutton, proved to be a fortunate one for Eastwood. An actor turned television director (he appears as a young hoodlum in the above-average Elvis Presley vehicle *King Creole* 1958), Hutton had made his film debut with *Fargo* (1965, aka *The Wild Seed*), a 'teen romance, followed by *The Pad (...And How to Use it)* (1966), a 'swinging' comedy, before teaming up with Kastner to make *Sol Madrid*, a modest secret agent thriller. As with United Artists and Ted Post a year or so earlier, MGM felt that Hutton lacked the necessary experience for a big-budget action movie, and Kastner had to exert his weight as producer to get Hutton accepted by the studio executives. In this he was aided by Burton, who apparently decided that the director's Welsh ancestry (shared by the star) made him the ideal choice.

In deciding on the co-stars for *Where Eagles Dare*, Hutton found himself at odds with Burton. Hutton wanted French actress Leslie Caron for the female lead, and Eastwood, whom he'd met during the early 1960s, for the role of Lieutenant Morris Schaffer, a United States Ranger specializing in assassination. His star preferred the choices of old friend Mary Ure, with whom he'd appeared in the unsuccessful film version of John Osborne's *Look Back in Anger* (1959), and American actor Richard Egan, an might-have-been leading man whose career never really got into gear. Egan hadn't made a good film since 1962's *The 300 Spartans*, and Hutton had little difficulty persuading MGM that Eastwood was a far better option. Somewhat concerned about Burton's box-office standing (rapidly slumping after the disastrous performance of *Boom !*, a pretentious fantasy based on a Tennessee Williams play), the studio readily agreed. Eastwood might not yet be a star of the first rank, but he could certainly draw the crowds. Not being a spaghetti western devotee, Burton had never heard of Eastwood, obliging Hutton to hard-sell his choice of co-star as the most dynamic, charismatic and generally wonderful new leading man in Hollywood (bearing in mind that Burton would not be happy with anyone who might try to upstage him). The final choices of Eastwood and Mary Ure proved highly satisfactory. A respected stage actress, Ure had no box-office name, but lent a touch of class to the proceedings. Eastwood provided raw, tight-lipped machismo that less sophisticated audiences could respond to. The remaining roles went to dependable character actors, notably Michael Hordern, Patrick Wymark, Peter Barkworth and Donald Houston (as Burton's not entirely trustworthy allies), and, in the German corner, Anton Diffring, Ferdy Mayne and Derren Nesbitt. Perhaps concerned that Ure alone did not provide sufficient glamour, Hutton cast the more blatantly sensual actress Ingrid Pitt as a British agent.

While Eastwood might have bemoaned the lack of any Malpaso personnel on the production team, he could still appreciate Kastner's choices. Prominent among these were cameraman Arthur Ibbetson, editor John Jympson (whose previous credits included *Zulu*, another top-flight action movie), composer Ron Goodwin and veteran stunt arranger Yakima Canutt. Best remembered as John Wayne's double for the Indian chase sequence in *Stagecoach*, Canutt now worked mainly as a second unit director, handling large scale action sequences in epics such as *Ben Hur* (where he staged the famous chariot race with fellow second unit specialist Andrew Marton).

The 300 strong production team arrived on location in Austria at the beginning of January 1968, setting up shop in the town of Salzburg. The script called for extensive use of a genuine castle, the Schloss Hohenwerfen, and the cable cars outside the town of Ebensee. Though far too long for Eastwood's liking, the five month shoot proved fairly disaster free, marred only by bad weather, Burton's over-enthusiastic alcohol intake, Mary Ure's near blindness when working without her glasses and a serious injury suffered by Derren Nesbitt when the detonation of a blood squib on his chest sent fragments into his eye. As with *Coogan's Bluff*, Eastwood found that his requests to perform his own stunts fell on deaf ears, leading him to nickname the film 'Where Doubles Dare'. Bearing in mind that his own double, British stuntman Eddie Powell, had to indulge in such antics as hanging off a moving cable car (intercut with studio shots of Eastwood gritting his teeth in front of back-projected Alpine scenery), one wonders just how far an unrestrained Eastwood would have gone in his pursuit of on-screen realism. Six years later, *The Eiger Sanction* went some way to answering this, resulting in the most disastrous production of the star's entire career.

As written by MacLean (and rewritten by Hutton), the plot of *Where Eagles Dare* is a satisfying mix of suspense, espionage and spectacular action. The British Intelligence department MI6 is believed to have been infiltrated by German agents. To root out the traitors, a fake rescue mission is put into operation, on which all the chief suspects will be sent. It is announced that a plane carrying a top American general has crashed in the Bavarian Alps. The general, one of the architects behind the impending Second Front in Europe, is being held prisoner in the Schloss Adler, the 'Castle of Eagles'. The only trustworthy MI6 agents are Major John Smith (Burton), and his partner/lover Mary Ellison (Ure). To improve their chances against the unknown double agents, they are joined by Lieutenant Schaffer, whose outsider status makes him dependable. After numerous shootouts, explosions, crashes and plot twists, the traitors are uncovered (and eliminated) and the fake general (an actor) rescued.

Virtually silent for the first twenty five minutes of the film, Eastwood's main function in *Where Eagles Dare* is as ruthless killing machine, despatching Germans too numerous to count (he even shoots a woman in the back). One of the film's most memorable images is Eastwood defending one of the castle corridors, holding off an entire battalion single-handed, firing off two sub-machine guns at once. In contrast to the verbose, slightly overwritten Burton character, his lines are brief and to the point, usually expressing utter bewilderment, ranging from 'I don't even know why the hell I'm here' to 'Major, right now you've got me about as confused as I ever hope to be'. Obviously respecting Eastwood's traditions, the script gives his character a brief beating scene, where Schaffer is kicked in the stomach by the diminutive double agent Berkeley (Peter Barkworth). That said, *Where Eagles Dare* is Burton's show most of the way, with Eastwood (and Ure) merely lending a hand. Hutton's direction is vigorous, if straightforward (making limited use of the widescreen Panavision frame), well supported by Ron Goodwin's famous score (heavy on the brass and drums) and Canutt's stuntwork. What is seldom remarked upon is the level of violence (with much spurting blood and a memorably wincemaking icepick through an arm), unusually strong for a family film.

Once location shooting was completed, the production team finished off at the Elstree-based MGM-British studios (soon to close down for financial reasons), where Eastwood also completed the post-production dubbing for *Coogan's Bluff*. Four days before filming drew to a close in May 1968, Maggie gave birth to Kyle Eastwood. All things considered, Eastwood had good reason to feel pleased with himself. The film had

● *Where Eagles Dare:* **Major John Smith (Richard Burton) and Lieutenant Morris Schaffer.**

turned out well (Hutton's rewrites allayed his doubts about the script), he was now the proud father of a son (who, unlike Kimber, didn't have to be hidden from the press), and his good working relationship with Richard Burton could only help his career. While making *Where Eagles Dare*, Eastwood had become friendly with both Burton and Elizabeth Taylor, who now expressed serious interest in working with him. She even presented him with a script, a western entitled *Two Mules for Sister Sara*, concerning the adventures of a wandering cowboy and a rather dubious nun.

Sold on the backs of both *The Guns of Navarone* and *The Dirty Dozen* (another MGM 'presentation'), *Where Eagles Dare* enjoyed considerable box-office success worldwide, grossing over $20 million on its original release (though Burton quickly cancelled out his success in the film by appearing in the likes of *Candy* 1968, and *Staircase* 1969). American producers could no longer afford to regard Eastwood as a transient, fluke star and by the time *Eagles* hit the cinemas he had two offers on his desk, one of which he wisely declined, the other he foolishly accepted. Columbia offered him the lead in the western *MacKenna's Gold* (1969), co-produced and written by Carl Foreman, whose impressive credits included *High Noon* and *Bridge on the River Kwai* (1957). Despite Foreman's recent success with *Guns of Navarone*, Eastwood declined the role, citing the cliched script as the reason (the part went to Gregory Peck). He then agreed to co-star in a film with an equally clumsy and stereotyped western screenplay, signing on for *Paint Your Wagon*, a late runner in the mega-budget open air musical stakes.

Perhaps the most implausible credit in Eastwood's filmography, *Paint Your Wagon* started life in 1951 as a modest Broadway musical, with lyrics by Alan J. Lerner and a score by his regular collaborator Frederick Loewe. The show made little impression and Hollywood studios expressed only token interest in turning it into a film. By 1967 the situation had altered a little. Film versions of *West Side Story* (1961), *My Fair Lady* (1962) and *The Sound of Music* (1965) had netted both vast profits and Academy Awards, convincing studio heads that just about any musical could become a smash hit movie. The resounding failures of the likes of *Dr Dolittle* (1967), *Camelot* (1967) and *Star !* (1968) quickly proved them wrong, but by the time the verdicts came in on these efforts, Paramount had already committed to filming *Paint Your Wagon* in association with Alan J. Lerner Productions. While Lerner had never actually produced a film before, he'd worked as a scriptwriter on screen versions of various Lerner-Loewe musicals (*An American in Paris* 1951, *Gigi* 1958, *My Fair Lady*) and Paramount evidently felt confident that he would learn as he went along. Armed with a $10 million budget (which eventually rose to at least double that), Lerner quickly proved the studio wrong, making several bad decisions in a row. Having decided to shoot *Paint Your Wagon* on location in the Cascade Mountains, Oregon (starting at the height of summer), he chose old friend Joshua Logan to direct. A stage director by inclination, Logan's few films (*Bus Stop* 1956, *South Pacific* 1958, *Fanny* 1961) exhibited little cinematic flair, remaining obstinately theatrical. Having recently been responsible for the failed *Camelot* (another Lerner-Loewe musical), Logan did not meet with Paramount's approval, leading to a dispute between the studio and Lerner which the latter won. Lerner also decided to dump the original *Paint Your Wagon* plot, retaining only the songs, and hired playwright Paddy Chayefsky to come up with a new storyline which also had to incorporate additional tunes by Lerner and Andre Previn (Loewe wasn't interested). Established during the 1950s as one of American television's top writers, Chayefsky had launched his film career with movie versions of some of his best known small screen hits (*Marty* 1955, *The Bachelor Party* 1957), none of which really qualified him to work on an all-singing, some-dancing

● *Where Eagles Dare:* Smith and Schaffer enjoy a beer with fellow agents Mary Ellison (Mary Ure) and Heidi (Ingrid Pitt). Schaffer's apparent interest in the latter is not borne out by anything in the finished film, their tentative relationship unceremoniously discarded on the cutting room floor.

western musical. Considering the finished product, Chayefsky was probably only too happy to let Lerner take official credit for the script.

When it came to casting the principal roles of a grizzled gold prospector, his good-natured partner and their shared wife (bought from a Mormon), Lerner exhibited the same unerring instinct for disaster. Having failed to interest either Mickey Rooney or James Cagney in the lead, he settled for Lee Marvin, agreeing on a $1 million fee (plus a share in the profits). Marvin had an undoubted flair for comic westerners (as in *The Comancheros* 1961, and *Cat Ballou*) but couldn't sing a note, as he memorably demonstrated in his bestselling rendition of 'Wanderin' Star', *Paint Your Wagon's* undoubted highlight. For his leading lady, Lerner approached Julie Andrews, still a hot item after *The Sound of Music.* Andrews' boyfriend, writer-director Blake Edwards, had shown some interest in directing the film. Despite Logan's offer to step down, Lerner rejected Edwards' approach, and Andrews opted to work with her husband-to-be on another Paramount-backed musical, *Darling Lili* (1970). Lerner replaced her with the non-singing Jean Seberg, who after a disastrous debut in Otto Preminger's *St Joan* (1957), had doggedly sustained her career in Europe in films such as *The Mouse That Roared* and Jean Luc Godard's *A Bout de Souffle* (1960). Doubtless aware of her questionable casting, Seberg hoped nevertheless that *Paint Your Wagon* might revive her moribund American career.

Aside from his $750,000 paycheck, it is now difficult to see why Eastwood got involved with such an obviously precarious production. His longstanding musical enthusiasms may have played a part, perhaps spurred by a desire for a slight change in screen image, showing off his versatility to previously sceptical critics. Another factor may have been Lerner's and Paramount's agreement to involve the Malpaso Company, albeit in a very minor capacity (the company's credit in the opening titles is virtually invisible). Interviewed at the time, Eastwood admitted a slight sense of reservation, only to dismiss it without pausing for breath, 'I'm not exactly Howard Keel, but I think it'll work.' He soon had good reason to regret his rather reckless optimism, as the production of *Paint Your Wagon* rapidly became a nightmare. Eastwood's working relationship with Lerner and Paramount got off to a less than ideal start when he was reputedly turned away from the studio gate by an overzealous guard, and things didn't improve once shooting commenced. Stuck on location nearly fifty miles from the nearest town (Baker, Oregon), various members of the cast and crew became increasingly difficult to work with. Logan found himself in continuous conflict with Lerner, who liked to issue his own directions to the actors and technicians, often contradicting Logan's instructions in a less than helpful way. Eastwood had already witnessed this kind of behaviour from an over keen producer/co-writer when working with Leonard Freeman on *Hang 'Em High*, only this time round he was not in a position to put Lerner in his place. Lee Marvin expressed his own dissatisfaction with Logan, demanding that he be replaced with either Don Siegel or Richard Brooks (who'd directed Marvin in *The Professionals* 1966). As Marvin spent much of the filming extremely drunk (vodka being his drink of choice), his problems with the director may have been entirely imaginary. Siegel visited the location (where a huge mining town set had been built) as a courtesy to Marvin, only to lose his temper with the inebriated star. Eastwood had no time for his boozing co-star's behaviour, which he regarded as highly unprofessional (and often violent), and informed Lerner that he would drop out of filming if Logan was fired midway through production. If this wasn't enough, the local hippies recruited as extras went on strike over pay and conditions. Shooting dragged on over six months, leaving Eastwood sick of big studio-big budget film-making. His mood didn't improve when Paramount decided to re-edit Logan's final cut of the film (which Eastwood thought acceptable), resulting in a messy release version that satisfied no-one.

During the frequent delays in production (often the result of Marvin's drinking) Eastwood played golf and got to know leading lady Jean Seberg. With his usual tact, the star has always declined to expand on the exact nature of their relationship, though the rumours prevalent at the time openly hinted at an affair. Seberg's then husband, novelist Romain Gary, took the stories seriously enough to fly out to the location and offer to rearrange Eastwood's face. Maggie, as usual, kept quiet. Rarely joining her husband on his film locations, and then only for a few days when it best suited him, she appeared content to stay at home, occasionally liaising with agent Lennie Hirshan over scripts, and taking news of Eastwood's alleged flings as par for the course.

As overblown, megabudget musical disasters go, *Paint Your Wagon* is a reasonably amiable misfire, an inoffensive curiosity at worst. Set against the backdrop of the nineteenth-century California goldrush, the story amounts to little more than two prospectors, Ben Rumsen (Marvin) and 'Pardner' (Eastwood), finding gold and founding a new mining town on the spot ('No Name City', presumably an Eastwood injoke). Their diggings eventually go all the way under the town's foundations, leading to its collapse at the film's climax (trashing a $2.4 million set). The subplot involves the chronic shortage of women in the area. A passing mormon (John Mitchum) is persuaded to auction off one of his wives, Elizabeth (Seberg), bought by Ben and Pardner for $800. Officially married to Ben, she and Pardner eventually fall in love, leaving together at the fade-out.

Anxious to appease the other miners, Ben appropriates six French prostitutes destined for another town (the emphasis on prostitution, with much talk of 'tarts', 'whores' and 'bawds', strikes an odd note for a family musical). Burdened with mediocre songs, a very slow pace, disjointed plot development, self-consciously 'quaint' dialogue, uncertain direction (varying from the static to the frenetic) and a sombre visual style (with much mud and rain) *Paint Your Wagon* never stands much chance of succeeding. The choreography consists mainly of miners stomping, whooping and waving their hats in the air, while Marvin spends much of his time lying in puddles dead drunk. Eastwood looks ill at ease for most of the film and his singing voice, though adequate, is too light and thin for a supposedly rousing musical (as well as being very obviously redubbed during post-production). Upstaged by Marvin, who despite his offscreen antagonisms gives a good-natured performance, he ultimately appears to have given up on *Paint Your Wagon*, simply walking through many of his scenes on autopilot. This approach works better than Seberg's valiant attempt to treat the script as serious drama. Similar in appearance to Inger Stevens (pale, blonde, intense), Seberg's straightfaced attempt to explain why she wants a threesome with Eastwood and Marvin ('a humane, practical, beautiful solution') is risible and her one song ('A Million Miles Away Behind the Door') had to be redubbed by a professional vocalist, Rita Gordon.

Hoping to appeal to the more permissive climate prevalent in the late 1960s, Paramount tried to market *Paint Your Wagon* as a 'hip' musical ('Ben and Pardner shared everything – even their wife !'). Aside from Lee Marvin's chart-topping success with 'Wanderin' Star', the film failed to catch on with any kind of audience, though the studio later announced a worldwide gross of nearly $15 million (still far short of recouping the production costs). Both Marvin and Eastwood escaped any real damage to their careers (by the end of 1968, Eastwood had made it to number five in America's top ten of male film stars). Lacking their box-office clout, Seberg didn't survive the failure of her intended comeback film. Apart from a supporting role in the Universal blockbuster *Airport* (1969), playing Burt Lancaster's mistress, her career rapidly plummeted to the depths of *Macho Callahan* (1970), an imitation spaghetti western starring Eastwood's old friend David Janssen, and *Kill!* (1971, aka *Kill, Kill, Kill*), a daft political thriller written and directed by Romain Gary. Logan never directed another film, leaving him a little time to contemplate what might have been if Lerner and Paramount had followed his suggestion that *Paint Your Wagon* be filmed entirely on the studio backlot. Amazingly, Lerner remained on good enough terms with Paramount to work (as a writer only) on two further musicals for the studio, *On a Clear Day You Can See Forever* (1970) and *The Little Prince* (1974), both of which flopped. Depressed by the whole experience of bad decision-making, miscasting, creative interference, money-wasting and general ineptitude, Eastwood vowed never to put himself in such a situation again. As it turned out, he would have to deal with a couple more troubled projects before finally ridding himself of other people's incompetence.

No doubt feeling the need to return to more familiar territory, Eastwood got together with Elizabeth Taylor with a view to putting the *Two Mules for Sister Sara* script into production. Hoping to recapture some of the spaghetti western style which *Hang 'Em High* had badly fumbled, he contacted Sergio Leone and composer Ennio Morricone to offer them the film (also, in the former's case, to repair a dwindling relationship). Fully confident in the star after *Coogan's Bluff*, Universal agreed on a Malpaso co-production, with a budget of $4 million, to be overseen by producer Martin Rackin. A former writer, Rackin had recently been responsible for a tedious remake of

Stagecoach (1966), starring sensational discovery Alex Cord, but his earlier western credits, notably John Ford's *The Horse Soldiers* (1959) and the John Wayne punch-em-up *North to Alaska* (1960), appeared to make him a suitable candidate for the job. As with the later *Joe Kidd*, the story behind the production of *Two Mules for Sister Sara* is a lot more interesting than the finished film. The project originated with seasoned western director Budd Boetticher, who in collaboration with star Randolph Scott and writer Burt Kennedy had produced a number of stylish 'B' westerns during the 1950s (*Seven Men from Now* 1956, *The Tall T* 1957, *Ride Lonesome, Comanche Station* 1960). After making a successful switch in genres with the gangster movie *The Rise and Fall of Legs Diamond* (1960), Boetticher abandoned Hollywood for Mexico in order to shoot a documentary on the celebrated bullfighter Carlos Azzura. Dogged by disasters which made the problems on *Paint Your Wagon* look trivial, filming dragged on over seven years, with Boetticher enduring bankruptcy, divorce, near fatal illness, imprisonment and the death of his subject (and most of his film crew) in a car crash. By the mid 1960s, Boetticher realized that he needed to revitalise his Hollywood career and penned the script for *Two Mules* while still based in Mexico City. The rugged cowboy-bogus nun love story (with the latter eventually revealed as a prostitute) had possibilities and Boetticher hoped to interest either John Wayne or Robert Mitchum (or maybe Steve McQueen) in the lead role, with actress Silvia Pinal (best known for her roles in the Luis Bunuel films *Viridiana* 1961, *The Exterminating Angel* 1962 and *Simon of the Desert* 1966) cast as Sara.

By the time the *Two Mules* deal had been worked out by Eastwood and Universal, Boetticher's involvement on the project had long ceased (he received a modest 'original story' credit on the finished film). Rackin decided not to use his script, hiring Albert Maltz to undertake an extensive rewrite. A prolific screenwriter during the 1940s (including scripts for *This Gun for Hire* 1942 and *The Naked City* 1948), Maltz's reputation had suffered during Senator Joseph McCarthy's communist 'witchhunt' towards the end of the decade, leaving his career all but dead. *Two Mules* proved an ill-chosen comeback as Maltz had difficulty reworking Boetticher's story into a vehicle for Eastwood's No Name persona, Taylor's aggressive glamour and the expensive spectacle (an exploding bridge, a pitched battle) that Rackin felt the film needed. Unimpressed by the result (which made the plot 'twist' obvious in the first few minutes), Leone rejected Eastwood's offer (never repeated), though Morricone agreed to supply the music, providing he could work from Rome with Italian musicians. Elizabeth Taylor remained content with the script, but didn't like Rackin's choice of Mexico as a location, insisting on the less authentic setting of Spain instead (where Richard Burton currently had a film in production). Rackin refused to budge and Taylor departed. With filming set to begin in early 1969, Eastwood and Rackin now needed to find a substitute director and a new star.

The choice of Don Siegel for the former can't have been too difficult. Rackin had worked with the director on *Hell is for Heroes* and, after *Coogan's Bluff*, Eastwood regarded Siegel as both a highly talented professional and a friend. As a Universal contract director he would have no problem being assigned to the film, though matters may have been complicated by Siegel's reluctant involvement on the troubled production of *Death of a Gunfighter* (1969). Originally envisaged by Jennings Lang as a vehicle for Eastwood (despite the fact that the leading character is supposed to be near retirement age), this film eventually starred Richard Widmark, with singer Lena Horne cast as his wife. Approached by executive producer Richard Lyons, Siegel turned down an offer to direct the film, suggesting television director Robert Totten as an alternative. Widmark quickly decided that he didn't like Totten, and asked Siegel to replace him. Siegel arranged a temporary peace between star and director, before Widmark, Lyons and head of Universal Lew Wasserman ganged up on him to take the job, completing the last ten days of shooting (*Death of a Gunfighter* was released with the pseudonym 'Alan Smithee' on the director credit, the first use of this *nom de film*). Reunited with Eastwood on *Two Mules,* Siegel's hopes of a smoother production were dashed, thanks mainly to the efforts of Rackin and new co-star Shirley MacLaine.

By no means a guaranteed box-office name (following hits such as *The Apartment* 1960 and *Irma La Douce* 1963 with several undignified flops), MacLaine got the role of Sara on the strength of her performance in Bob Fosse's as yet unreleased *Sweet Charity*, a Universal production overseen by Robert Arthur, Arthur Lubin's regular producer back in the days of Universal-International. Confident that the film would confirm MacLaine's star status (it failed), the studio executives agreed to her request for top billing on *Two Mules*, leaving Eastwood to take second place for the third film running (he got top billing on the advertising, which suggests some fierce preproduction negotiations). Blatant miscasting aside (Sara is supposed to be Mexican), MacLaine didn't appeal to either Eastwood or Siegel. A confirmed Democrat, she had little time for Eastwood's politics or his alleged macho posturing (MacLaine claimed at the time that he liked to play cowboy whether or not the cameras were rolling). Siegel found MacLaine difficult to work with, her temper not improved by the burning Mexican sun. Often late on location, MacLaine eventually fell ill, holding up production for a week. One unforeseen difficulty was her inability to ride a mule, necessitating a contrived scene where Sara swaps the animal for a donkey (rendering Boetticher's title a little pointless).

If MacLaine's behaviour exhibited star temperament at its least attractive, Martin Rackin tried hard to outdo Leonard Freeman and Alan Lerner in the interfering producer stakes. Often present on the Mexican location (based around the town of Cocoyoc), he insisted on hiring cheaper local labour (whether actors, technicians or horses) rather than import more experienced people from Hollywood (excepting stuntman Wayne Van Horn). This cost-cutting measure backfired, as Siegel found to his (and the film's) cost. Native horses, unused to film crews, panicked when confronted by camera cranes (one nearly bolted from underneath Eastwood during the first day of shooting). The construction crew built an elaborate garrison set, the production designer forgetting that army barracks usually have locks and bolts on the doors. Siegel didn't like any of the sets built for *Two Mules*, describing them in his autobiography as unimaginative and virtually unusable. Even when Rackin opted for quality over economy, he chose carelessly. For the film's director of photography, he hired top Mexican cameraman Gabriel Figueroa, who after training in Hollywood during the 1930s had worked with the likes of John Ford (*The Fugitive* 1947), Luis Bunuel (*Los Olvidados* 1950, *The Exterminating Angel*) and John Huston (*Night of the Iguana*). What Rackin failed to consider was that Figueroa had only shot one previous film in colour (*The Big Cube* 1969, an unlikely LSD melodrama), and still felt ill at ease away from black and white. Figueroa's inexperience with colour film stock led to a slowdown in production while Bruce Surtees advised him on how best to light for it. In fairness, *Two Mules* looks perfectly okay (glossy rather than atmospheric) and Eastwood felt sufficiently impressed with Figueroa to hire him for *Kelly's Heroes*.

As with *Paint Your Wagon*, the various production troubles on *Two Mules* are not really evident in the bland, mildly entertaining end product. The film opens with soldier turned mercenary Hogan (Eastwood) rescuing a woman from three would-be rapists (he shoots the men dead and then robs the corpses). Much to his surprise, he finds that he has saved a nun ('Jesus Christ'), a plot development that provides the opportunity for lines such as 'Maybe a nun ought not to be so good looking', 'Too bad nuns don't play poker, you'd be sharp at it' and the expected 'I sure wish you weren't a nun'. The audience realizes pretty quickly that Sara is not all she claims to be (puffing on cigars and swigging whisky when Hogan isn't looking), yet her new protector doesn't catch on until they end up at Sara's old brothel, where the madam greets her in less than reverent fashion. Hogan has been hired by the Juaristas to help them rob the French garrison at Chihuahua, and finds a useful ally in the pro-Juarista Sara (During the 1860s, Mexico was ruled for three years by the Austrian puppet emperor Maximilian, placed on the throne in 1864 by opponents of the displaced liberal leader Benito Juarez, with armed support from the French government. The latter had troops based in Mexico to reclaim money lent to the former President Miramon. Pressure from the American government forced the French to withdraw in 1866, leaving Juarez free to overthrow Maximilian the following year. Not that the film explains any of this.) Having first derailed a French army train by blowing up the bridge underneath it, Hogan and Sara meet up with the Juaristas, storm the garrison and live happily ever after, Hogan accepting his new role as Sara's second mule (or donkey).

Following the opening credits sequence, where Hogan goes on a nature tour of the Mexican countryside, riding past an owl, fish, rabbits, a mountain lion, a snake and a tarantula (squashed under his horse's hooves), Siegel directs *Two Mules* in an efficient, impersonal style far removed from his best work. He later claimed to be satisfied only with the first scene and the garrison battle, though the latter includes several gory inserts (a bayonet in the chest, a machete in the face, a lopped-off arm) which seem ill-judged. Despite not having final cut on the film, a privilege which went to Rackin, Siegel took more or less full responsibility for it, claiming that his 'cut in the camera' style did not leave the producer with much scope for re-editing. Morricone's score is intricate, with a Latin chorus for Sara (intoning 'Lead Us Not into Temptation') and a simulated mule bray for Hogan, yet the end result is curiously lacklustre. Eastwood claims to have worked on the music with Morricone, in which case he should keep quiet about it (the star later made credited contributions to the scores for *Tightrope*, *City Heat*, *Pale Rider* and *A Perfect World*, among others). Dressed up in a No Name influenced costume, with a leather hat, red-brown waistcoat, heavy stubble and plentiful cigars, Eastwood delivers a competent performance, falling down only in the badly scripted romantic interludes (he seems ill at ease displaying affection towards Shirley MacLaine). A drunk scene where Sara painstakingly removes an arrow from the intoxicated Hogan is drawn out to a wearying degree (though it does give Eastwood another chance to sing), and when Sara later loses her temper with the man ('Sober up you dirty bastard'), she has the audience's full sympathy.

Marketed with such slogans as 'A hard drinking gun with a cigar smoking nun', *Two Mules for Sister Sara* enjoyed solid box-office success when released in 1970, even picking up some favourable reviews, though most critics were not slow to point out the dud plot 'twist' and the utter lack of sexual chemistry between Eastwood and MacLaine (anyone who thinks film nuns can't be sensual should check out Deborah Kerr in *Black Narcissus* 1947 and *Heaven Knows Mr Allison* 1956). Eastwood later cited the film as a rare example of a western with a strong female character, yet in truth *Two Mules* did little for either of its leads. Its only real significance for Eastwood lay in the fact that he wouldn't take second billing to another star again until *A Perfect World* nearly 25 years later. During production on the film, Jennings Lang sent Eastwood a copy of Thomas Cullinan's novel *The Beguiled*, a weird gothic melodrama set during the American Civil War. Agreeing with Lang that the story could make a fascinating film, Eastwood passed the book on to Siegel, who also expressed strong interest. The story of an injured Union soldier finding refuge behind enemy lines in a decaying mansion full of sexually repressed women might not immediately appeal to the star's regular fanbase, but it offered a tempting (and challenging) change of pace. For the time being, Eastwood had a commitment to MGM to make *Kelly's Heroes* (starring as Kelly), another World War II action-adventure which made even *Where Eagles Dare* look like sober realism. As with the latter, there would be no Malpaso involvement, nor did Eastwood have control over the final cut.

An American-Yugoslavian co-production, *Kelly's Heroes* apparently began life as an anti-war black comedy, scripted by British writer Troy Kennedy Martin, before transforming into an overinflated big screen homage to the television favourites *The Phil Silvers Show* (Sergeant Bilko et al) and *Hogan's Heroes*. While Kennedy Martin's previous screen credit, the comedy caper *The Italian Job* (1969) could hardly be termed thoughtful (or anti-crime), he had a high reputation for his realist television dramas (including the police series *Z Cars*) and Eastwood felt the script offered more than the standard heroics and pyrotechnics (The star claims to have been opposed to the then ongoing Vietnam conflict, though in his usual, understated fashion.) The go-to-Europe-and-steal-some-gold storyline bore more than a passing resemblance to *The Italian Job*'s basic plot, yet this did not necessarily mean a similarity of approach or style. Aside from Gabriel Figueroa and associate producer Irving Leonard, the old hands recruited included *Eagles* veterans Brian G. Hutton and editor John Jympson, plus composer Lalo Schifrin. The major supporting roles went to Telly Savalas, then enjoying temporary big-screen bankability following parts in *The Dirty Dozen* and *On Her Majesty's Secret Service* (1969); fellow *Dozen* veteran Donald Sutherland, fresh from starring in Robert Altman's rather more successful military black comedy *M*A*S*H* (1970), and comedian Don Rickles, playing a blackmarket hustler called Crapgame (a good indicator of the film's wit/satire level). Shooting commenced on location in Yugoslavia in the latter half of 1969, taking a total of five months. Eastwood later remarked that the lengthy production seemed to have an adverse influence on the script, discarding the harder, blacker edge of Kennedy Martin's original for a straightforward heist plot. Stuck in post-D Day France with little to do but fight Germans, a group of morally dubious American soldiers capture an enemy general and accidentally discover the whereabouts of a fortune in Nazi gold (worth $16 million at the going market rate). Pausing for the occasional battle (courtesy of second unit director Andrew Marton), they locate the bank where the bullion is hidden (all 14,000 bars), resteal it and drive away.

Despite the utter lack of surprises in its storyline, *Kelly's Heroes* is watchable fare, competently directed by Hutton, with entertaining turns from Savalas, as the loudmouth platoon sergeant Big Joe, and Sutherland, playing a defiantly anachronistic bearded hippie named Oddball ('Why don't you knock it off with them negative waves ?'), a tank commander who drives into battle accompanied by country and western music (a decade before *Apocalypse Now*'s helicopter 'Ride of the Valkyries'). The comedy angle does become a little self-indulgent, especially in the sequence where Hutton and Schifrin pay homage to *The Good The Bad and The Ugly* as Kelly, Big Joe and Oddball stride down a street Leone-style to confront an obstinately dutiful German tank driver (they cut him in for a share of the gold). At this point the film seems to have given up on any pretence of satire or serious comment on the futility of war, opting instead for injokes and slapstick. Overlong, overloud and overacted (Eastwood excepted), *Kelly's Heroes* ultimately sinks under the weight of its own exuberance, throwing in more rain, more mud, more shouting and more explosions than the audience can bear. It does, however, boast a memorable theme song, *Burning Bridges*, written by Schifrin and lyricist Mike Curb.

Despite the prolonged and less than satisfactory production (with rumours of studio interference), Eastwood had enough confidence in the resulting footage to request a rescheduling of the film's release date while Hutton re-edited it to his (and Eastwood's) satisfaction. In more prosperous times, the MGM executives might have at least considered his wishes, but by 1970 the studio showed little inclination to put artistry before business. Financially precarious for a number of years, MGM had just undergone a takeover by Las Vegas businessman Kirk Kerkorian, who installed former CBS production chief James Aubrey as the new studio head. Aubrey instantly instigated a drastic economy drive, sacking MGM personnel and reducing production schedules. For all Eastwood's arguments about boosting the film's box-office chances, Aubrey saw no reason to distinguish *Kelly's Heroes* from the other pending MGM releases produced before his appointment and refused to postpone its launch date. Unable to improve on the initial, studio approved cut of *Kelly's Heroes*, Eastwood could only take bitter satisfaction in being proved right when the filmed opened in 1970 to dismissive reviews and mediocre business. Happy to hold grudges if the crime was great enough, he never worked for MGM again. The year didn't look like getting much better as he now felt uneasy about starring in *The Beguiled*, in preproduction with Universal during his stay in Yugoslavia. Despite his initial enthusiasm for the book, doubts about his suitability for the main role had surfaced. Jennings Lang, who'd suggested the project in the first place, worried about the film's commercial viability. While audiences would be happy to watch Eastwood beaten to a pulp and then resurrected for violent revenge, they might not prove so keen on paying good money to see their hero die.

6

American Gothic

My mother told me it just might stunt my growth.
Corporal John McBurney, *The Beguiled*

You ever find yourself being completely smothered by somebody ?
DJ Dave Garver, *Play Misty for Me*

I'm all broken up about that man's rights.
Inspector Harry Callahan, *Dirty Harry*

If the disappointment of *Kelly's Heroes* gave Eastwood a less than satisfactory start to the 1970s, the film did at least mark the end of a bumpy phase in the star's career. There would be no more inflated budgets, drawn-out production schedules, difficult co-stars or interfering producers. With only a couple of exceptions (*Bronco Billy*, *In the Line of Fire*), he would never again make a film without the full involvement of the Malpaso Company, with Eastwood ensuring that he retained control over his movies right through to the completion of post-production (he later cited the editing stage as his favourite part of the film-making process). Back with Universal Studios for *The Beguiled*, he enjoyed a reasonably harmonious relationship with production executive Jennings Lang, and would continue to use the company as his base of operations until the middle of the decade, when Eastwood decided that Malpaso's best interests lay with Warner.

1970 also saw the retirement of Irving Leonard from the Malpaso presidency. Perhaps worn down by the protracted wranglings on *Kelly's Heroes*, Leonard made way for Robert Daley, a longstanding friend (and former neighbour) of Eastwood's from his Universal-International days, when Daley worked as a studio accountant. In his joint capacity as company president and regular producer/executive producer (up to 1980), Daley lost no time implementing Eastwood's strict medium budget-medium schedule production policy, considering only 'tightly and accurately' budgeted screenplays with no expensive spectacle (big crowds, big explosions), no intricate (and therefore costly) special effects (until *Firefox*) and locations favoured over studios wherever possible. Malpaso also frowned on 'package' deals, whereby an enterprising producer would approach a studio offering a particular script, star(s) and director as an indivisible, often non-negotiable item (*Where Eagles Dare* is a good example). Eastwood would only ever make one exception to this rule, the action comedy *City Heat* (1984), with feeble results (see Chapter 11). With the business side of his career placed under stringent financial management, Eastwood felt he could afford a little more freedom when it came to the choice of subject matter, as *The Beguiled* soon made clear.

With the star still stuck in Yugoslavia back in late 1969, most of the preproduction work on the new project had been undertaken by Don Siegel, whose enthusiasm for *The Beguiled* countered the doubts expressed by Eastwood and Lang. Serving as both director and producer, Siegel commissioned a script from Albert Maltz, apparently happy to forgive/forget the latter's unsatisfactory work on *Two Mules for Sister Sara* (which, in fairness, resulted as much from Martin Rackin's meddling as Maltz's own difficulties).

Siegel's faith went unrewarded, however, as Maltz's screenplay completely lost the flavour of Cullinan's book (in the fevered, nightmarish style of Edgar Allan Poe and Ambrose Bierce), even substituting a happy ending for the violence of the original (the main character is mutilated, then poisoned by the women he has abused). Maltz departed to make way for Irene Kamp, who proved no more successful, transforming the dark, gothic fantasy into an innocuous period romance disliked by Siegel, Eastwood and Lang (Siegel later remarked that both Maltz and Kamp seemed uneasy with the casual cruelty and tortured sexuality of the book. The latter went on to daintify another grim literary original, turning Charles Dickens' *Old Curiosity Shop* into the innocuous movie musical *Mister Quilp* 1975). No doubt fearing another *Coogan's Bluff*-style fiasco, Siegel found a literary saviour in the form of Claude Traverse, the project's associate producer, who came up with a faithful adaptation in only three drafts (Rather unfairly, the final screen credit for the script went to the pseudonymous 'John B. Sherry' (Maltz) and 'Grimes Grice' (Kamp).)

Armed with the new, approved script, Siegel now needed a sinister, decaying Southern mansion to stand in for the ladies finishing school where most of the story takes place. Never one to hang around the studio backlot when ideal locations beckoned (a trait soon adopted by Eastwood), Siegel took his crew down South, finally selecting the Belle Helene Plantation in Baton Rouge, Louisiana. Universal agreed to a ten week schedule, with Eastwood taking a slightly reduced fee of $600,000 (to be topped up by his profit share). Aware that the script offered a number of strong, if not entirely sympathetic roles for women (still a rarity in American movies), Siegel asked Universal to approach French actress Jeanne Moreau for the co-starring part of Martha Farnsworth, the sexually messed-up school head. A major star in her native country, Moreau had a number of impressive English-speaking roles to her credit (*The Trial* 1962, *The Train* 1964, *Viva Maria* 1965, *Chimes at Midnight* 1966) and was currently working in the United States on the downbeat western *Monte Walsh* (1970), starring Lee Marvin and Jack Palance. Neither Moreau's status nor her availability cut much ice with Lang and Wasserman, who wanted an American actress for the role, obliging Siegel to settle for Geraldine Page (to do the Universal executives some credit, they weren't insisting on a box-office name). An acclaimed stage actress, Page's sporadic film career had seen her paired off with the likes of John Wayne (*Hondo* 1953), Paul Newman (*Sweet Bird of Youth* 1962) and Tommy Steele (*The Happiest Millionaire* 1967), making her an ideal co-star for the macho, yet sensitive Eastwood. The second major supporting role of repressed teacher Edwina Dabney went to Elizabeth Hartman, who'd appeared with Page in *You're a Big Boy Now* (1967), an early effort from director Francis Coppola.

The plot of *The Beguiled* is just about the strangest of any Eastwood film (though *High Plains Drifter* runs it a close second). As the Union troops slowly advance through the southern, Confederate states during the latter stages of the American Civil War, Amy (Pamelyn Ferdin), a twelve year old pupil at the Farnsworth school, discovers a badly injured Union soldier in the woods beyond the school gates. Martha reluctantly agrees to give Corporal John McBurney (Eastwood) shelter until he is well enough to be handed over to the Confederates as a prisoner of war. Realizing that he could be onto to a good thing, the amoral, manipulative McBurney plays the situation to his advantage, paying flattering attention to Martha, Edwina, their domestic slave Hallie (Mae Mercer) and even Amy, who decides she loves McBurney as much as her pet turtle Randolph. All

● *The Beguiled:* **Martha Farnsworth (Geraldine Page) tends to the injured Corporal McBurney.**

four soon give in to his charms, with Martha and Edwina finding that McBurney has awakened their long-stifled sexual urges. McBurney's schemings become a little unstuck when he is distracted by the advances of Carol (Jo Ann Harris), a seventeen year old pupil who makes her attic bedroom freely available. A jealous Edwina knocks McBurney down a flight of stairs, shattering his already injured right leg, which Martha then amputates, claiming that otherwise fatal gangrene will set in. McBurney awakes from his impromptu operation in a less than grateful mood ('You dirty bitch. Just because I didn't go to your bed'). Violently drunk, he gets hold of the school's only pistol, threatens Martha with violence and Hallie with rape, and kills Randolph when Amy tries to interrupt his disclosure of Martha's unsavoury past (she had an incestuous affair with her brother). Despite this episode, Edwina decides she still loves McBurney, who quickly sobers up, expressing apparently heartfelt apologies to one and all. As he and Edwina discuss plans to leave the school and get married, the other women plot his death. During a farewell dinner, he is fed poisonous mushrooms, dying in agony. Martha and her pupils bury him in the woods beyond the gates.

Opening with a series of sepia Civil War photographs (some the genuine article taken by Matthew Brady, others ingeniously faked to incorporate Eastwood), accompanied by the ominous drumbeat of Lalo Schifrin's score, *The Beguiled* is a striking fantasy of repression, passion, deceit and revenge (Eastwood calls it a film about 'the illness of war'). Retaining the black and white for a minute or so after the credits, Siegel has the camera crane down the forest trees while Amy passes underneath in her search for fresh mushrooms. As the film slowly switches to colour, McBurney staggers monster-like from behind a tree, burned, bloody and barely conscious. Despite his near-death condition, he retains enough of his survival instinct to distract Amy from approaching Confederate troops by kissing her on the lips (twelve years is 'old enough' for such attentions). This unsettling, dreamlike atmosphere is sustained throughout the film

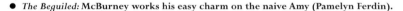

● *The Beguiled:* **McBurney works his easy charm on the naive Amy (Pamelyn Ferdin).**

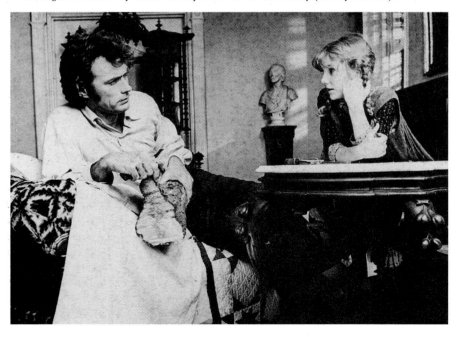

through the use of weird, disorienting camera angles and pans, fast edits, double exposures, triple exposures, split screen, flashbacks (revealing McBurney's lies, Martha's affair and her brother's attempted rape of Hallie), hushed voiceovers (expressing various characters' thoughts) and fantasy sequences (Martha imagines making love to both McBurney and Edwina). Siegel even throws in a little blasphemous religious allegory as Martha stares at a picture of the Virgin Mary holding the body of Christ after the crucifixion and then dreams of herself and McBurney taking their places. This striking direction is well complemented by Bruce Surtees' photography (mostly brownish hues) and Schifrin's score (making effective use of a harpsichord and church organ). There is a slight element of straining for effect (the device of characters articulating their thoughts is perhaps overused), yet overall the style is remarkably assured.

As the smooth-talking McBurney, Eastwood gets the chance to put an unsavoury slant on his established romantic image, casually flirting with the blatantly voracious Carol before making a move on an envious Edwina's more heartfelt (if understated) affection ('All that anger in those pretty green eyes'.) Having won Martha's trust by pretending to be a pacifist Quaker who abandoned farming to serve the Union as a medical officer (carrying bandages instead of a gun), McBurney rapidly progresses from confined prisoner to welcome houseguest to potential live-in lover. Of the five principal female characters, only Hallie remains sceptical of McBurney. Perhaps the most intriguing (and disturbing) of his relationships is with Amy, who develops a crush on McBurney after rescuing him from a lingering death in the forest (or a Confederate prison). Despite McBurney's numerous philanderings, Amy retains her trust in him, turning against the man only after he kills Randolph (an act for which McBurney is immediately sorry). Having saved McBurney while out picking mushrooms, Amy then brings about his death (implicitly encouraged by Martha) with another crop of mushrooms, this variety as poisonous as the atmosphere in the house (McBurney's fate is paralleled by that of an injured crow tended by Amy (perhaps a reference to Poe's raven), which dies exhausted by its attempts to escape her restraining tether.) As the shrouded corpse is taken out for burial, the film fades back to black and white (a symmetry described by Siegel as 'rounding'). Pamelyn Ferdin's performance as the awkward, well-meaning Amy equals those of Eastwood, Page, Hartman and Mercer, displaying none of the cuteness nor precocity all too common among child actors. 1971 seems to have been her peak year in movies, with another impressive appearance in the Kurt Vonnegut fantasy *Happy Birthday Wanda Jane*, though like many pre-teen performers, Ferdin's film career never gained much momentum post-adolescence, sputtering to a halt with such unlovely exploitation items as *The Toolbox Murders* (1978).

Both Eastwood and Siegel were pleased with *The Beguiled* (the latter regarding it as his best film), and looked to Universal for a gradual, initially low-key release that would allow it to pick up an audience through word of mouth rather than saturation promotion. Bearing in mind the film's decidedly offbeat quality, Siegel felt it merited serious consideration for the various film festivals (Berlin, Cannes, Venice), where *The Beguiled* would stand a good chance of winning a prize or two (chances boosted by Eastwood's reputation as a serious artist in Europe). Uninterested in the festival circuit, Universal decided to try the film out in Italy, opening *The Beguiled* in a Milan cinema specializing in no-nonsense action movies. Lured by promotional material suggesting a war film where Eastwood took on the Confederate army single-handed, audiences were not impressed. In Italy to receive an award for services to the national film industry, Eastwood agreed to attend the premiere, witnessing first hand the result of Universal's witless marketing. Things did not improve back home, where *The Beguiled* was released with ad-lines such as 'One man...seven women...in a strange house !' and 'All of them wanted his love...but one of them wanted his life'. A handful of good reviews were countered by accusations of rampant misogyny, typified by Judith Crist's terse 'A must for sadists and woman-haters'. According to Christopher Frayling, Universal did experiment with an 'arthouse'-style release in Britain, though without any more success. The only country to show much enthusiasm for *The Beguiled* was France, where an enterprising distributor retitled it *La Proie* ('the prey'), shifting the emphasis from the various women to Eastwood.

If the mishandling and subsequent commercial failure of *The Beguiled* left Eastwood unhappy with Universal, he didn't immediately let it show. Siegel claimed in his autobiography that the arguments over distribution marked the beginning of the end of the star's relationship with the studio, yet the five subsequent Malpaso-Universal collaborations suggest otherwise. Perhaps Eastwood accepted *The Beguiled* as a risky change of pace/image which simply hadn't worked out (the film did eventually find an appreciative audience on television and video). It probably helped that by the time *The Beguiled* did the cinema rounds, Eastwood had already made a deal with Lang and Wasserman to make *Play Misty for Me*, his official debut as a director-star (a potentially hazardous dual role previously attempted by the likes of Burt Lancaster, John Wayne, Marlon Brando and Albert Finney, none of whom felt inclined to repeat the experiment more than once).

An effective, if unremarkable thriller involving a womanizing disc jockey persecuted by a deranged fan (and one-night-stand lover), *Play Misty for Me* originated as a story outline by Jo Heims, first encountered by Eastwood as a legal secretary at Universal-International. Impressed by Heims' ambition to become a writer, Eastwood had bought the rights to the *Misty* idea back in the 1960s, only to let it go when Heims received a more generous offer from Universal. Some sources claim that at one point Steve McQueen obtained the project for Solar Productions, then decided that the female lead was too dominant. Several years on, Universal had done nothing with the story and Eastwood decided the time was right to put it into production, hiring fix-it specialist Dean Riesner to work with Heims on the script. The studio executives weren't so sure, unconvinced that audiences would go for the star as a disc jockey any more than they had liked him as a one-legged, womanising, turtle-killing soldier. Some hard bargaining followed, with Lew Wasserman eventually agreeing to the deal if Eastwood took no fee for directing (effectively netting Universal two creative talents for the price of one). As the only official qualification for becoming a director was to have a job, Eastwood promptly hired himself for *Misty*, Don Siegel co-signing his application to join the Screen Directors Guild. Siegel also agreed to play a small role in the film (as a bartender), finally getting a chance to use his RADA training forty years on (he had trouble remembering his lines). Supposedly on hand in case Eastwood became unstuck, Siegel later denied there'd been any serious concern about the star's ability to handle the film, though Eastwood admitted afterwards that he became so preoccupied with the directing side, he forgot about learning his lines until the night before shooting.

Not that Lang and Wasserman were really taking too much of a risk. Granted a brisk six week schedule and a modest $950,000 budget, Eastwood chose to shoot *Misty* on location in and around Carmel and Monterey, making the film something of a home movie. For the choice role of psycho-villain Evelyn Draper he selected Jessica Walter, a Broadway actress with some television experience (*The Defenders*, *Ben Casey*) and a handful of film roles (*Lilith* 1964, *The Group* 1966, *Grand Prix* 1967). Unsure about Walter, Universal agreed to her casting nevertheless, perhaps feeling that a post-*Beguiled* Eastwood might not be in the mood for argument. Finding the right actress for the undemanding part of Tobie, DJ Dave Garver's wholesome on-off true love, proved mysteriously difficult. Eastwood apparently tested 300 actresses before taking a hot tip from old friend Burt Reynolds and casting Donna Mills, a television soap opera star with no previous film experience. Starting filming with the Siegel scenes (shot in a disused sardine factory dressed up as a bar), Eastwood avoided shooting too much of his own performance for the first week (especially close-ups). For an objective view of his acting, he videotaped his scenes, giving him an instant playback of his performance. Rapidly gaining in confidence, Eastwood completed the film four days ahead of schedule and $50,000 under budget. Much to his (and Universal's) relief, *Misty* proved a critical and commercial success, enjoying several profitable rereleases after its initial run in 1971.

The plot of *Play Misty for Me* is as straightforward as could be wished. Dave Garver is a successful Carmel late night disc jockey with a line in poetical quotation ('Men have destroyed the roads of wonder and their cities squat like black toads') and a persistent fan, Evelyn, who repeatedly phones in requesting the Erroll Garner song 'Misty'. Encountering Evelyn at the Sardine Factory, Garver takes up her offer of a supposedly no-strings-attached one night affair, only to find his latest conquest becoming increasingly possessive. Refusing to listen to Garver's protests that there's nothing between them (especially now Tobie is back in town), Evelyn rapidly establishes her credentials as an all-out headcase. Starting off with unprovoked verbal abuse, she spies on Garver and Tobie, slashes her wrists, wrecks Garver's meeting with a television executive, grovels before Garver in public, trashes his house, attacks his maid with a butcher's knife (a scene trimmed for the film's original British release), sticks another knife in a pillow next to Garver's head as he sleeps and murders an investigating policeman (John Larch). Having assumed the name 'Annabel' (a reference to the Edgar Allan Poe poem 'Annabel Lee'), Evelyn moves in with Tobie, ties her up and then attacks Garver with yet another knife as he comes to the rescue. His patience sorely tested, Garver punches Evelyn, sending her through a window and over the balcony of Tobie's clifftop house.

Eastwood's direction of *Misty* is assured, if equally straightforward, with a brisk pace, a mobile camera and much use of aerial shots of the Carmel coastline and roads taken from a helicopter. The title sequence makes effective use of natural sounds, slowly fading in on the noise of waves and gulls as Garver takes a·stroll around the absent Tobie's house before leaping into his sports car to drive to work. Misjudged shots, such as a low angle look up Jessica Walter's skirt, are balanced by more effective touches, notably the lingering close-ups of Garver's haunted/hunted face as he finds his life stifled by Evelyn. Eastwood's only major blunders are two utterly gratuitous musical breaks that completely disrupt the tension of the storyline. The first of these involves a love scene (not in the original script) as Garver and Tobie walk on the beach and in the forest, pausing for a little sex under a modest waterfall. All this unreels to the strains of the pop song 'The First Time Ever I Saw Your Face', sung by Roberta Flack. Ending with a coastline stroll backlit by a setting sun, the sequence looks like an advert for the record, which it proved to be. Unnoticed on its original release, Flack's single became a hit on the strength of the *Misty* plug (Flack later repaid the debt, providing an end credits tune for *Sudden Impact*.) The second musical sequence is a short promotional film for the Monterey Jazz Festival, a clear case of Eastwood letting his hobby override his editing sense (Universal wisely shortened this scene for the foreign release prints.)

Other drawbacks include some weak dialogue ('I'm just trying to play it cool') and the eyeball-wincing yellow blouse, leather mini skirt, pink woollen hat, purple t-shirt and pink lounging pyjamas the costume department saw fit for Jessica Walter to wear (though the frightful wardrobe might be taken as an insight into the character's unbalanced mind). And whoever advised Eastwood that strolling around clad only in white Y-fronts made for greater suspense was not being kind. For all that, *Misty* holds up fairly well, especially in comparison with its unofficial remake/rip-off *Fatal Attraction* (1987), a prurient and vacuous melodrama with Michael Douglas and Glenn Close in the Eastwood and Walter roles. While Eastwood would have been justified in contemplating legal action over such a blatant piece of plagiarism, he dealt with the matter in casually, informing *Fatal Attraction* co-producer Sherry Lansing that she owed him a beer.

A curious footnote to *Play Misty for Me* is Eastwood's later revelation that the story contained an element of autobiography. As a teenager, he had been the unwilling object of an older woman's sexual obsession. It is difficult to know what to make of this, especially given the star's accompanying claim that the whole episode was really no big deal (no carving knives involved). A more strikingly autobiographical element of *Misty* is Garver's apparently pathological promiscuity. The scene where he attempts to explain his infidelity to Tobie, arguing that her possessiveness and jealousy drove him into the arms of other, less demanding women comes over as a case of celluloid imitating (or at least drawing on) life. For Garver, Evelyn represents the pick-up from Hell, a clinging, emotionally draining parasite posing as a casual fling. Those who accuse *The Beguiled* of misogyny would do better to focus their attentions on *Misty*. The women encountered by McBurney are the stuff of dark fairytale, with no more connection to the real world than the operatic brutalities of the Leone spaghetti westerns. Furthermore, their cruelty is not without reason, a response to the soldier's own emotional and physical abuse.

● *Play Misty for Me:* **Dave Garver finds his relationship with Evelyn Draper (Jessica Walter) at a low point.**

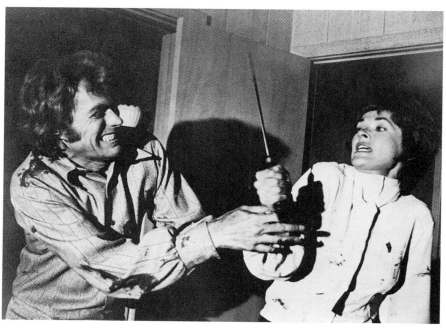

Existing in the contemporary, non-fantasy setting of 1970s California, Evelyn has no such motivation for her mania. There is no exploration of why she behaves as she does (this is a psychological thriller without much psychology). Though well enough acted by Walter, Evelyn is merely a monster to be slain by the heroic (if flawed) Garver before she can harm Tobie, his fair maid.

Eight films into his post-spaghetti career, Eastwood had good reason to feel pleased with his progress: undisputed star status (with a regular place in the top five of Hollywood leading men), generous paychecks (usually boosted to the magic $1 million mark by his percentage points), his own company, creative control over his films and only minimal press reportage of his private life. His two commercial failures could be safely written off as the results of general incompetence (*Paint Your Wagon*) and mismanaged distribution (*The Beguiled*); in both cases the blame lay with decisions made by other people beyond his control. Eastwood had yet to pick up much critical acclaim in his native land, not that this made him heartbroken. A more pressing matter for the star was his as yet unfulfilled desire to find a contemporary, urban action man role which would make as much impression on moviegoers as Joe the Stranger/No Name back in the mid 1960s. *Coogan's Bluff* had gone some way to providing such a character, yet the deliberate playing off of the Arizona lawman's cowboy style with the more uptight ways of the New York cops left audiences with little doubt that Coogan's real place lay back in the West, driving his jeep over dusty trails. Eastwood needed a character who retained Coogan's contempt for City Hall bureaucracy while at the same time being an undisputed (if maverick) member of it's law enforcement team. He finally found such a role in the shape of Inspector Harry Callahan (badge no.2211) of the San Francisco Police Department. As with *A Fistful of Dollars* seven years earlier, the circumstances that led Eastwood to *Dirty Harry* involved a little sound judgement and a lot of luck.

Written by the husband and wife team of Harry Julian Fink and Rita M. Fink, the original script for *Dirty Harry* (initially titled *Dead Right*) involved an ageing, disillusioned New York cop pursuing an exceptionally nasty serial killer. Frustrated by his superiors' desire to play the investigation strictly by the rulebook, the cop finds his quarry slipping through his fingers, hiding behind the legal technicalities that failed to protect the killer's victims. Rather than let the man walk free, he steps outside the law, turning vigilante, finally destroying both the murderer and his own career. An experienced Hollywood screenwriter, Harry Fink had worked on the likes of *Major Dundee* (1965), for which he also wrote the original story, *Ice Station Zebra* and *Big Jake*. On good terms with star John Wayne after the latter, Fink offered the *Dirty Harry* script to Wayne's producer son Michael, who felt it would be ideal for his father. Unhappy with the level of violence and swearing in the screenplay, Wayne senior declined the project (a decision he later regretted, attempting to cash in on the success of *Dirty Harry* with the routine police drama *McQ* 1974). Jennings Lang then showed an interest in acquiring the script for Universal and Eastwood (despite the latter's relative youth) but wouldn't pay the Finks' asking price. The latter finally got a break with Warner, who picked up the project as a vehicle for actor-singer Frank Sinatra. After a variable, intermittently impressive film career (highlights including *On the Town* 1949, *From Here to Eternity* 1953, *The Man with the Golden Arm* 1956 and *The Manchurian Candidate* 1962), Sinatra wanted to retire with a suitably striking final bow. He had recently scored a notable big screen success in the title role of the downbeat police drama *The Detective* (1968), another New York tale of crime and corruption, and *Dirty Harry* offered a more striking (and brutal) variation on reassuringly familiar material. With Sinatra signed up, Warner hired Irvin Kershner to direct, only to put the production on hold when their star injured his hand in an accident. When it became clear that Sinatra would not recover in time for the start of filming (in the summer of 1971), the studio looked around for a replacement (Sinatra, in the meanwhile, dropped out of films for a decade, eventually making a one-off star comeback in *The First Deadly Sin* 1980, a relentlessly depressing cop-ver-sus-ice-pick-wielding-psycho movie from the producer-director team of Elliott Kastner and Brian G. Hutton.) Happy to reduce the age of the main character, Warner approached Paul Newman, 1970's number one box-office attraction following the run-away success of *Butch Cassidy and the Sundance Kid* (1969). Unsure of the script's politi-cal sympathies, the fervently liberal Newman turned the film down (as did a *Bullitt*-fatigued Steve McQueen). Following the precedent established by Richard Harrison back in 1963, he tempered his flat-out rejection with the suggestion of an alternative leading man: Clint Eastwood. If a supposedly veteran cop could suddenly become a rel-atively youthful forty five, there was no reason why he couldn't be further rejuvenated to forty one. Eastwood accepted Warner's offer of *Dirty Harry*, despite a few reserva-tions about the studio-authorized rewrites of the script, turning it into a Malpaso co-production and one of the most important career moves of his life.

Assembling his usual team of collaborators (Robert Daley, Bruce Surtees, Lalo Schifrin, Wayne Van Horn), Eastwood again found himself without a director or a satis-factory script (post *Misty*, he had announced that he would in future alternate between acting and directing rather than combine the two). Don Siegel was the obvious choice for the former, but his exclusive Universal contract made hiring him problematic. Having failed to recruit Ted Post (tied up with television commitments), Eastwood asked Lew Wasserman to release Siegel from the studio as a one-off favour, enabling the latter to work on *Dirty Harry* as both director and producer (perhaps a tacit acknowl-edgement on Wasserman's part that the film should have been a Universal production). Discarding the various rewrites inflicted on the Fink script (including one by Terrence Malick), Siegel and Eastwood brought in Dean Riesner to make their desired changes (prominent among them Eastwood's wish to reduce the less savoury aspects of Callahan's character). Feeling that he'd exhausted the best New York locations with *Madigan* and *Coogan's Bluff*, Siegel suggested switching the locale to San Francisco, enabling the film to make use of such landmarks as the Golden Gate Bridge (an impas-sive backdrop to the killer's various atrocities), Mount Davidson Park (where the killer beats up Harry under the shadow of an enormous concrete cross) and Kezar Stadium (where Harry tortures his wounded adversary to discover the whereabouts of a kidnap victim). For once, Riesner's rewrite did not quite meet all requirements (Siegel claimed to have come close to quitting when Warner executive John Calley suggested a return to the Fink version). The script's original climax, an airport siege where the killer attempts to escape by plane holding schoolchildren as hostages, was felt to be both too expensive and a distracting piece of spectacle. Siegel supplied a new ending, a chase across a quarry (filmed at San Anselmo, Marin County), that provided a man-to-man showdown between cop and killer. Satisfied with this alteration, Warner still wanted a few more changes and John Milius appeared on the scene for a last minute rewrite.

Now best known for his distinctive, if questionable brand of pseudo mystical/myth-ical action movie (typified by *The Wind and the Lion* 1975, *Big Wednesday* 1978, *Apocalypse*

● *Dirty Harry:* Callahan and Scorpio (Andrew Robinson).

Now 1979 and the underrated *Conan the Barbarian* 1982), Milius' film credits back in 1971 amounted to little more than the likes of *The Devil's Eight* (1968), a poverty row *Dirty Dozen* rip-off. Accordingly, Warner paid him a modest $35,000 (supplemented by a Purdy shotgun Milius coveted), and he delivered an approved final draft in three and a half weeks. While Siegel's autobiography makes no mention of Milius' work on *Dirty Harry*, his contribution to the finished film proved vital (he claims that he lost out on a screen credit only because he neglected to file his rewrite with the Screenwriters Guild). Hired mainly to streamline and sharpen certain passages of dialogue, Milius's major addition to the script is the final version of the famous 'lucky' speech recited by Harry twice during the course of the action, first to an injured bankrobber (Albert Popwell) reaching for his shotgun, then once more (with feeling) to Scorpio the psycho killer (Andy Robinson in his never-bettered film debut), during the film's climax. Riesner's version runs as follows:

The thing is you're not really sure whether I fired five or six. And if five, whether or not I keep one under the hammer. Tell you the truth I lost count myself. Now what you got to do, considering this is a forty-four Magnum and will blow your head into litty bitty pieces...if it's loaded...What you've got to do is ask yourself: Are you feeling lucky, punk?

Milius's improved, punchier version has the ring of a true gun enthusiast and offers one of cinema's best-known catchphrases:

I know what you're thinking. Did he fire six shots or only five? Well to tell you the truth, in all this excitement I've kind of lost track myself. But being this is a .44 Magnum, the most powerful handgun in the world, and would blow your head clean off, you've got to ask yourself one question: do I feel lucky ? Well do you, punk ?

The bank robber opts for caution, though the gun is in fact empty, as Harry sadistically demonstrates by pointing the weapon at the prone man and pulling the trigger. Riesner's version of the script had Harry point the gun at his own head, a wildly out-of-character gesture. Scorpio decides he is feeling lucky, only to be blown straight to hell. Eastwood liked Milius' work enough to hire him for *Magnum Force*, the first (and best) *Harry* sequel (which opens with an abridged version of the 'Do you feel lucky ?' speech). It is not known if the blatant plug for the Smith and Wesson gun company got Eastwood any kind of sponsorship deal.

Though most memorable as a two-hander between Harry and Scorpio, *Dirty Harry* features a good array of supporting characters, far removed from the paper thin stereo-types too often deployed in the sequels. Harry's partner is the Mexican Chico Gonzales (Reni Santoni), a college graduate with a degree in sociology. Intially treated with wari-ness by Harry, Chico later saves his over-confident partner's life when a machine-gun toting Scorpio corners Harry in Mount Davidson Park. Curious as to how Callahan got his nickname, Chico sees enough of his partner's life on the beat to work out the answer for himself: Harry 'always gets the shit end of the stick'. Injured during the Park episode, Chico decides to quit the force and pursue a career as a teacher, a decision accepted (and respected) by Harry. This 'odd couple' relationship works well and Eastwood repeated the trick in the sequels, pairing Callahan off with an African American (*Magnum Force*), a liberated woman (*The Enforcer*) and a kung fu kicking Asian (*The Dead Pool*). If this sounds like the glib, unimaginative deployment of racial/sexual cliches as a token gesture against accusations of conservative white male supremacy, at least *Dirty Harry* establishes Chico as a credible character rather than a plot device. A former television writer, Santoni had found an early acting break in films as the star of *Enter Laughing* (1967), an autobiographical comedy by writer-director Carl Reiner. His rather aggressive performance didn't attract too much attention, and Santoni's subsequent appearances were in routine supporting roles in indifferent action films (*Anzio* 1968, *Guns of the Magnificent Seven*). *Dirty Harry* proved to be the highpoint of his film career and in 1987 writer-star Sylvester Stallone recruited both Santoni and Andrew Robinson for his own maverick cop movie *Cobra*, no doubt hoping for a little quality by association (it didn't work).

First seen striding around a murder scene, wearing his trademark sunglasses and brown suit (slimfit), Harry wastes no time displaying his anti-liberal, anti-appeasement credentials. Summoned to the mayor's office to discuss Scorpio's demand for $100,000 ('or it will be my pleasure to kill a Catholic priest or a nigger'), he gives the Mayor (John Vernon) short shrift ('For the past three quarters of an hour I've been sitting on my ass, waiting on you'), expressing disbelief that the latter intends to co-operate with a blackmailing killer ('You gonna play this creep's game ?') For all the black humour in the scene ('When a naked man is chasing a woman through an alley with a butcher knife and a hard-on I figure he isn't out collecting for the Red Cross'), the underlying tension between the Mayor's wait-and-see approach and Harry's wipe-the-scum-off-the-streets-now attitude leaves no doubt where the film is heading. Backed by the full force of the law, the Mayor proves impotent when faced with a psycho like Scorpio. A street-smart cop like Harry can instantly recognize that this is one case where justice must come before legal niceties and is willing to throw away his career (symbolized by his badge) rather than see the killer go unpunished. Existing primarily as a hard-eyed Magnum-wielding avenger (Milius describes Harry as 'God's lonely man'), there is little attempt to explore Callahan's character. Aside from his penchant for one-liners, all we know about him is his frugality, telling an intern not to cut open his trouser leg to get at shotgun wounds ('For $29.50 let it hurt'); his voyeurism, looking through a window at a naked woman or two when he is supposed to be tracking Scorpio, and his dead wife, killed in a car accident caused by a drunk. Harry is so busy being a lawman he doesn't even have time for a haircut.

Sharing Harry's preference for dull brown clothes and long hair, the twitching, grimacing, giggling Scorpio is otherwise a creature from another planet, tied to Harry only by their switching, interdependent roles as hunter and prey. (Riesner's script envisaged Scorpio as utterly nondescript, a Mr Nobody – a concept completely overturned by the casting of Andy Robinson). Sadistic, racist, anti-religious, cowardly and cunning, Scorpio could hardly be more deserving of Harry's brand of righteous wrath (he even kills children). Offering his pursuer a choice selection of insults that even Tuco Ramirez might regard as a little strong (ranging from 'Hubba, hubba, pig bastard' to 'You rotten wanker'), Scorpio taunts Harry over his choice of weapon ('My, that's a big one') and kicks him when he is down (repeatedly). While Siegel suggested that Scorpio might be a crazed Vietnam veteran (society is to blame ?), he functions best as an embodiment of pure evil, played with gleeful relish by Andy Robinson, especially when he smacks small children on the back of the head.

Filming on *Dirty Harry* went fairly smoothly, finishing ahead of schedule and under budget (an achievement common to all the Eastwood-Siegel collaborations). Eastwood got to do an impressive stunt, jumping from a railway bridge onto the roof of a hijacked schoolbus, achieving an ambition much frustrated in the past (Siegel had Wayne Van Horn try out the jump first, just in case). He also got to direct a short scene (where Harry deals with a would-be rooftop jumper) when Siegel fell ill. Shooting the scene in just one night, Eastwood did a creditable job. Director and star clashed on only one detail, Harry throwing his police badge into a quarry sump after he kills Scorpio. Eastwood didn't like the action's implication ('Quitting my job'), obliging a reluctant Siegel to suggest an alternative (included in Riesner's script) where Harry places the badge back in his jacket after hearing approaching police sirens (some sources claim that Eastwood delayed shooting the scene for a few days while he agonized over the badge issue). Eastwood finally relented on the day of filming, tossing Badge no.2211 into the water on the first take (a good thing, as the props man didn't have any spares). As Harry offers to quit on two occasions before the quarry climax, Eastwood may have felt uneasy about the visual impact of the act, rather than the idea behind it. Perhaps he recalled John Wayne's public disgust at Gary Cooper dropping his star in the dust in *High Noon*.

Following a sombre (perhaps misjudged) dedication to officers of the San Francisco Police Department killed in the line of duty, *Dirty Harry* unreels in a stark, hard edged style, with a measured pace and an aggressive score (vocals, electric guitar and drums). Siegel makes effective use of low angles (introducing Scorpio behind the looming barrel of his rifle silencer) and fast cuts, depicting a brutal world where violent death appears out of nowhere for no apparent reason. Among the film's most potent images are a murdered girl floating in a rooftop swimming pool (Scorpio's first victim), Scorpio's screaming face (partly hidden behind a ski mask) as Harry sticks a switchblade into his leg, an extreme long shot of Harry torturing Scorpio to find out where he's hidden a kidnapped schoolgirl, and the girl's naked body being removed from a drain at dawn, the Golden Gate bridge looming in the background. The final glimpse of Scorpio, floating in the quarry sump as his blood mingles with the water, mirrors the opening killing, bringing his murder spree full circle. Whatever one's reservations about the film's alleged politics/morality/ideology, *Dirty Harry* succeeds in making its hero's course of action seem the only possible response to the horrors he confronts. Never a great fan of the 'scope format (which he likened to the shape of a Band-Aid), Siegel provides an unforgettable Panavision image of Harry taking up a firing stance, his Magnum looming in the right foreground of the frame. This is Justice, supercop-style, comic-book mythology played with a compelling straight face (and it makes a great poster, too).

Premiered in San Francisco in December 1971, *Dirty Harry* proved a highly respectable box-office success, earning nearly $18 million in the United States and close on $50 million worldwide. More liberal reviewers attacked the film as irresponsible, ultra-right wing propaganda, giving *Dirty Harry* the kind of free publicity only dreamed of by most marketing executives. Warner's advertising division appears to have deliberately played on the lone wolf vigilante angle, selling *Dirty Harry* with lines such as 'You don't assign him to murder cases – you just turn him loose !' Among the critics swallowing the bait was star reviewer Pauline Kael, who labelled the film 'fascist medievalism', displaying a talent for a clever turn of phrase if nothing else (Kael subsequently became a dedicated Eastwood hater for the rest of her reviewing career.) Twenty five years on, this controversy seems more than a little absurd, reflecting a desire by left-wing pundits to reaffirm their right-on credentials rather than any dangerous message sent out by *Dirty Harry*. The film is a wish-fulfillment fantasy, enabling audiences to vent their feelings of helplessness in the face of violent crime as lawman turned vigilante

● *Dirty Harry*: **Callahan gets ready for the climactic shootout with Scorpio.**

Harry Callahan blows away the embodiment of all that is foul with modern society. Siegel rejected any political interpretation of *Dirty Harry*, arguing that the extreme actions of one frustrated cop were never intended to be read as a general endorsement of police brutality (especially as he loses his job). Confirmed Republican Eastwood may have felt a little differently, though the most worrying element in his four increasingly cartoonish sequels is their dwindling quality (*Sudden Impact* is one of his very worst films). The only obvious consequence of *Dirty Harry* was an increasingly dull succession of 'vigilante' movies, featuring either a rogue cop or concerned citizen, such as *Walking Tall* (1972), *Death Wish* (1974) and the blatant rip-off *Blazing Magnum* (1976).

Dirty Harry proved to be the last Eastwood-Siegel collaboration for eight years. The teacher-pupil (or even father-son) part of their relationship probably made this split inevitable, with Eastwood rapidly gaining in confidence as a director in his own right. Of the ten films made between *Harry* and *Escape from Alcatraz*, five were directed by the star. As with Sergio Leone a few years before, Eastwood's still rising star status (boosted no end by *Dirty Harry*) dictated a change in the balance of power between actor and director. The mutual respect might still be there, but Eastwood would now have the last word in all matters of film-making. It is significant that only one of the four directors employed by Eastwood between 1972 and 1978 had not been nurtured by Malpaso (and only two thereafter). By 1979, Eastwood felt little need for directors who brought their own creative input and his reunion with Siegel for *Alcatraz*, a downbeat (and not very commercial) prison drama, proved a one-off.

A further factor in the Eastwood-Siegel split was the former's more or less exclusive relationship with Warner Bros from the mid 1970s onwards. While both men said goodbye to Universal in 1975 (Siegel unhappy over the studio's mishandling of his films *Charley Varrick* 1973 and *The Black Windmill* 1974), Siegel felt no inclination to follow Eastwood's lead. Unhappy with the drawn-out arguments with Warner over the *Dirty Harry* scripts, his resentment grew during shooting when the studio refused to okay a short scene Siegel felt to be important. In the bank robbery/shootout sequence early on in the film (where Harry is injured in the leg by shotgun pellets), all the robbers are black. Worried that Callahan might be taken for a bigot (despite his Mexican partner), Siegel devised a follow-up scene where Harry's injuries are looked after by a black intern, whose dialogue makes it clear that he and Callahan are old friends. Claiming that this addition was unnecessary, Warner wouldn't agree to either scheduling or funding it, obliging Siegel to shoot the scene in a hurry with second assistant director Charles Washburn cast as the doctor. Adding insult to injury, Warner further irritated Siegel by declining to push *Dirty Harry* for Academy Award nominations, even though it made several 'ten best' lists in late 1971. From now on Eastwood (and Malpaso) would be on his own, with no mentors to guide or advise him (would Eastwood have made *The Beguiled* without Siegel's encouragement ?), a position that suited the star just fine. His new superstar status received unexpected confirmation from the Hollywood Foreign Press Association, which presented Eastwood with a Golden Globe as the world's most popular film star of 1971. *Time* magazine ran a cover story on the award, treating it as something of a joke ('no kidding !'). While Eastwood would have to wait a little while for any 'authentic' home-grown awards, it took him only a few years to prove the HFPA right with some of the best work of his career.

7

Magnums and Thunderbolts

They say the dead don't rest without a marker of some kind.
Sarah Belding, *High Plains Drifter*

There's nothing wrong with shooting, as long as the right people get shot.
Inspector Harry Callahan, *Magnum Force*

Following the success (and controversy) of *Dirty Harry*, Eastwood could have taken on virtually any film project he wanted, regardless of box-office considerations. Even the most abject commercial failure could be easily cancelled out by another shoot-em-up (especially a *Harry* sequel). To Eastwood's credit, he decided to leave Inspector Callahan alone for a couple of years, confident that there would still be an open door at Warner when he felt the time was right. To his discredit, he picked just about the dullest follow-up imaginable, a pedestrian 'honest farmers versus corrupt land baron' western called *Sinola*, soon retitled *Joe Kidd*.

In fairness, *Joe Kidd* appears to have been a rushed substitute for the project Eastwood really wanted to film, a remake of the Italian-French spaghetti western *The Big Silence* (1968), directed and co-written by Sergio Corbucci. The story of a mute gunfighter who takes on a sadistic bounty killer, falling in love with the widow of one of his victims, *The Big Silence* is a gripping, genuinely powerful film, with a truly horrible ending (the bounty hunters win). Corbucci's use of composition, camera movement and pacing is outstanding, complemented by Silvano Ippoliti's photography (making exquisite use of the winter setting) and Ennio Morricone's haunting score (far removed from the style of the *Dollars* films). Working with a first rate script, the cast includes French star Jean-Louis Trintignant as Silence, Klaus Kinski as the witty, intelligent killer Loco, and black American actress Vonetta McGee (in her film debut) as Pauline, Silence's employer and lover. More restrained and realistic than *Django* (Silence relies on an automatic pistol rather than superhuman gunfighting skills), *The Big Silence* dispenses with the surreal, blackly humorous world of the earlier film, making the climactic murders of Silence and Pauline all the more disturbing. Despite the presence of Leone regulars Mario Brega and Luigi Pistilli, Corbucci's film has little in common with the work of Eastwood's mentor.

Impressed by both the film and its commercial success in Europe, Eastwood is rumoured to have approached Corbucci with a view to buying the rights (one reason why *The Big Silence* never received a release in either the United States or Britain). Whatever Corbucci's response to the star's interest, nothing came of it. The resounding box-office failure of *The Beguiled* may have deterred Eastwood from any script where the main character dies (he wouldn't do it again until *Honkytonk Man*, another flop). That said, Corbucci had bowed to pressure from his distributors, and shot a different, happy ending for *The Big Silence*'s release in Eastern territories, giving Eastwood a ready-made alternative. A further problem was the non-speaking central role. While audiences were used to Eastwood as a man of few words, they would be disconcerted by Eastwood as a man of no words at all. His reasons for abandoning the proposed remake may have been as much artistic as financial. Box-office and image considerations aside, Eastwood knew he stood little chance of equalling Corbucci's original. The only vestige of *The Big Silence* to be found in *Joe Kidd* is the machine pistol used by Eastwood in the latter half of the film (the kind where the wooden holster doubles as a rifle stock).

Another Malpaso-Universal coproduction, *Joe Kidd* employed the usual Malpaso crew, with newcomer James Fargo taking his place as assistant director. The son of bit-part actor George Fargo, an old friend of Eastwood (he appears in *Kelly's Heroes*), Fargo Jr. would serve in this capacity for four further films (*High Plains Drifter*, *Breezy*, *The Eiger Sanction*, *The Outlaw Josey Wales*) before graduating to director with *The Enforcer*. As Malpaso did not provide full-time work for all its regular employees, Fargo also served on several non-Eastwood Universal productions, notably Steven Spielberg's *Jaws* (1975), whose underwater cameraman, Rexford Metz, later photographed *The Gauntlet* and the Fargo-directed *Every Which Way But Loose*. Another addition to the Malpaso team was editor Ferris Webster, whose career dated back to the 1940s with films such as *The Picture of Dorian Gray* (1945), *Father of the Bride* (1950), *Forbidden Planet* and *Cat on a Hot Tin Roof* (1958). During the 1960s, he had enjoyed successful collaborations with the directors John Frankenheimer (*The Manchurian Candidate*, *Seven Days in May* 1964, *Seconds* 1966) and John Sturges (*The Magnificent Seven*, *The Great Escape*). Always ready to learn from top talent, Eastwood retained Webster's services on every Malpaso production up to (and including) *Honkytonk Man*. Respected novelist Elmore Leonard provided the script for *Joe Kidd* (proving conclusively that his talents didn't extend to the big screen), which Eastwood placed in the supposedly safe hands of aforementioned western veteran Sturges. Aside from his important (if indirect) role in launching Eastwood's career along the *Seven Samurai-The Magnificent Seven-Yojimbo-A Fistful of Dollars* route, Sturges could boast a list of impressive movies (*Bad Day at Black Rock*, *Gunfight at the OK Corral*, *The Great Escape*, *Hour of the Gun*). Satisfied with these credentials, the normally on-the-ball Eastwood neglected to pay much attention to Sturges' more recent work, the dull *Ice Station Zebra* and the duller *Marooned* (1969). Location filming commenced in 1972 in High Sierra, California and Tucson, Arizona.

Running a mere 87 minutes (20-30 minutes shorter than the average Eastwood vehicle), *Joe Kidd* is a flimsy piece of work. Set against the picturesque backdrop of mountainous New Mexico, the plot features bounty hunter turned rancher Joe Kidd getting caught up in the conflict between a group of honest, if aggressive Mexicans attempting to reclaim their land and a corrupt, racist capitalist determined to hold on to it. Initially uninterested, Joe is none too pleased when the Mexicans' leader, Luis Chama (John Saxon), steals his horses during a flight to the hills (having first pulled a gun on the local judge and set fire to property deeds). Joe signs on with land baron Frank Harlan (Robert Duvall on autopilot), leading the latter's posse of hired guns in their hunt for Chama. Deciding that Harlan is not a nice man at all (he threatens to gun down unarmed villagers if Chama doesn't surrender), Joe switches sides, killing most of his ex-employer's men on the ride back to Sinola, where he shoots Harlan in the courthouse. Impressed by Joe's moral example, Chama gives himself up to American justice. Aside from a well staged shootout with high-powered telescopic rifles (making good use of delayed sound), *Joe Kidd* is routine, competent entertainment, indifferently handled all round. Eastwood makes a half-hearted attempt at varying his standard cowboy act, beginning the film with a hungover Joe languishing in a prison cell on a drunk and disorderly charge. Clad in a 'civilian' outfit (suit, collar, tie, bowler hat), Eastwood's impersonation of a habitual drunk is no more convincing than his supposedly alcoholic cop in *The Gauntlet*, and his performance doesn't even begin to spark until the cowboy clothes are on. The script lacks any real tension and the 'grand finale' involving a train being driven through the town saloon seems included mainly to wake the audience up. Worse is the fumbled, uncertain depiction of Chama, despite the best efforts of John Saxon (Richard Widmark's opponent in *Death of a Gunfighter*). Offscreen for much of the film, the supposedly idealistic Chama is revealed as selfish, egocentric and misogynist, happy to let others die for his cause (without consulting them first) and informing his tough, independently-minded girlfriend that women exist only to give men pleasure. Chama's decision to follow Joe's advice and surrender to the law seems just as bogus, if only because the earlier courtroom scene makes it clear that the Mexicans have no hope of justice from American courts. Eastwood found working with Sturges a disappointing experience, with no sense of rapport between the two men. Then in his early sixties, Sturges no longer had any great interest in film-making except as a means of funding his retirement. After three more routine efforts, *Valdez Horses* (1973, aka *Valdez the Halfbreed* aka *Chino*), *McQ* and *The Eagle Has Landed* (1976), Sturges counted his money and packed his bags. The most interesting aspect of *Joe Kidd* is the presence of character actor Gregory Walcott in the role of Sinola's ineffective sheriff. Best known for surviving a starring role in Edward D. Wood's infamous poverty row sci-fi epic *Plan 9 from Outer Space* (1956), not to mention a co-starring part opposite John Agar in *Jet Attack* (1958), Walcott signed on for three further Malpaso productions (*Thunderbolt and Lightfoot*, *The Eiger Sanction*, *Every Which Way But Loose*), enjoying the kind of modest career revival later handed out to Mara Corday.

With little to show for *Joe Kidd* apart from a modest profit, Eastwood had to look elsewhere for the big events of 1972. Inspired by the British pubs he visited with Richard Burton during the shooting of *Where Eagles Dare* (and perhaps also by the 'English' pub in the 1960 *Rawhide* episode *Incident of the Garden of Eden*), he opened his own bar-restaurant in Carmel, naming it 'The Hog's Breath' (apparently Eastwood's idea of an authentic Olde Englishe pub name). Aside from an embarrassing run-in with the town's health inspectors during the 1980s (resulting in a brief shutdown of the restaurant), the Hog's Breath has been a thriving concern ever since. On the Hollywood front, Eastwood found himself (and Maggie) in demand for various social events. Not a great lover of the party circuit, he nevertheless felt obliged to pay his movie-star dues, and the Eastwoods agreed to host the Celebrity Tennis Tournament. If this wasn't honour enough, Eastwood received an invitation/order to present the Best Picture Oscar at the 1972 Academy Award ceremony (it went to *The Godfather*). On the night, an already reluctant Eastwood found himself coerced into delivering the opening speech as well, original choice Charlton Heston being stuck on a freeway with a flat tyre. Stuck in front of an autocue reeling off bad jokes about Moses and *The Ten Commandments* (1956), Eastwood vowed never to go near the ceremony again. On a happier note, Maggie announced that she was pregnant again, eventually delivering up Alison Eastwood, the star's second daughter.

For his next film project, Eastwood chose to remain in Western territory with the bizarre morality tale *High Plains Drifter*. This involved a certain amount of risk, as by 1972 the western genre was generally felt to be on the verge of terminal decline. The mediocre receipts from *Joe Kidd* indicated that paying audiences now preferred Eastwood as a cop rather than a cowboy (a disappointment to a star whose creative imagination and love of the great outdoors made the latter role ideal). Sticking to his artistic guns, Eastwood went ahead with an idea that might alienate die-hard western fans as much as *Harry* enthusiasts. Inspired by the recent real-life case of Kitty Genovese, a New York resident stabbed to death outside her apartment building while her neighbours looked on from their windows, he wanted to make a statement about public apathy and group responsibility. Eastwood liked the idea of a whole western town punished for the murder of its sheriff and commissioned a script from Ernest Tidyman. An experienced writer of action movies, notably *The French Connection* (1971) and the blaxploitation hits *Shaft* (1971) and *Shaft's Big Score* (1972), Tidyman resurrected Eastwood's No Name persona as the late sheriff's avenger, initially identifying him as the dead man's brother. Eastwood didn't want such a clear cut (not to say predictable) motivation/explanation and the main character became simply The Stranger. Jennings Lang agreed to make the film a Universal co-production, with filming on location at Winnemucca Dry Lake, Nevada. Art director Henry Bumstead designed an entire town, built in three weeks on the shore of Lake Mono, North California, with both exteriors and interiors. Abandoning his earlier decision not to act as both star and director on the same project, Eastwood gave himself six weeks to direct his first western (also his first film in Panavision), completing the filming two days ahead of schedule. Keen to extend the sense of group effort as far as possible, he instructed editor Ferris Webster to set up shop near the town set, cutting the amount of studio-based post-production down to the bare minimum.

Described by Eastwood as a 'medieval' morality play, *High Plains Drifter* is also an effective ghost story, achieved an uncanny atmosphere all too rare in films dealing with the supernatural. Set shortly after the Civil War, the story centres on the recently established mining town of Lago, thriving on the proceeds from its natural source of wealth. This new found affluence is threatened when the dutiful town sheriff, Dave Bliss (Wayne Van Horn), discovers that the mine is on government property, invalidating Lago's claim to its riches. The mine owners send three 'troubleshooters' to deal with Bliss, who is bullwhipped to death in the town's main street while the inhabitants look on. A year passes by, and a stranger rides into town (passing by the graveyard). By the time he rides out, over a dozen men are dead and Lago is a burned-out ruin.

The most immediately striking aspect of *High Plains Drifter* is the sheer confidence of the whole enterprise. Opening with a long shot of The Stranger emerging from a distant horizon blurred by heat-haze, Eastwood and cameraman Bruce Surtees make good use of the landscape, contrasting the light brown timbers of the town with the deep blue of the lake and the white chill of the surrounding mountain range. Obviously at ease with the 'scope format, Eastwood's direction employs impressive tracking shots and camera angles, not to mention a plethora of flashbacks as The Stranger relives the death of Bliss (their faces are intercut, establishing an unexplained bond between them). Eastwood also exhibits a good eye for offbeat detail, such as open coffins resting against a cart, soon filled by the three men gunned down in the opening sequence. Installed by the townspeople as their official protector, The Stranger takes full advantage of them, looting the various shops and giving goods away to passing Indians (an anti-capitalist theme ?).

While most of the townspeople are simple, vicious caricatures (with a shared taste in greed, cowardice, hypocrisy and corruption), this approach works well with the overall allegorical style. Eastwood claims that the people of Lago represent the Seven Deadly Sins (they certainly cover most of them), with The Stranger either a vengeful ghost or an avenging angel. The only townspeople to escape his wrath are Mordecai (Billy Curtis), a put-upon dwarf who shares The Stranger's memories of the murdered sheriff, and Sarah Belding (Verna Bloom), the one person who tried to intervene when Bliss was killed. Having painted the town blood red and renamed it 'Hell', there is little left for The Stranger to do other than take on Bliss's three killers (returning to Lago after their former employers put them in jail), setting fire to Lago in the process (which makes for great backlighting). One is whipped to death, another hanged and the last shot. Mordecai gets to be a real hero, gunning down the surviving mine owner when the latter points a rifle at The Stranger's back (presumably a homage to Silvanito's last minute gunplay in *A Fistful of Dollars*). His work done, The Stranger rides back into the heat haze, pausing only to bid farewell to Mordecai as the latter carves an inscription on a previously blank grave marker: 'Marshal Jim Duncan rest in peace'.

Considering its ambitions, *High Plains Drifter* hits remarkably few false notes. Dee Barton's mournful score lingers in the mind, the dialogue ranges from the satisfyingly predictable ('Couldn't be worse if the devil himself had ridden right into Lago') to the poetically offbeat ('Someone left the door open and the wrong dogs came home') and the distinctive bit players (Geoffrey Lewis, John Quade, Dan Vadis, John Mitchum) earn their paychecks. The only problematic element is the second female lead role of Callie Travers (Mariana Hill), an immoral bitch on permanent heat. Alternating between lusting after The Stranger and throwing insults at him ('That squinty-eyed sonofabitch'), Callie is presented as a woman 'asking for it' (she gets it).

Released in 1973, *High Plains Drifter* didn't quite catch on with either the public or the critics. For all the violent set-pieces (such as a shootout in a barber's shop), the film proved too off-kilter for regular action fans, grossing a modest $7.5 million at the American box-office. Reviewers found the supernatural-allegorical elements self-conscious and heavyhanded, a strained near-parody of the *Dollars*-No Name style. Neither spaghetti western nor traditional western, *Drifter* managed to alienate major players in both camps. Sergio Leone disliked the film, perhaps feeling that Eastwood had bastardised the original Joe/No Name character. John Wayne felt moved to write Eastwood a letter, arguing that: 'This is not what the West was all about.' Having acknowledged Eastwood as his natural heir in the cowboy hero pantheon, Wayne expressed major reservations about the star's choice of scripts. When *A Fistful of Dollars* opened in the United States back in 1967, Eastwood had announced 'I do all the stuff John Wayne would never do', and his subsequent films bore this out. For all Wayne's dislike of the 'excessive' violence and swearing in Eastwood's vehicles, there appears to have been a mutual respect between the old-style star and his young(ish) successor (Eastwood hoped, in vain, that he and Wayne might one day co-star in a film).

Despite *High Plains Drifter*'s unspectacular box-office performance, the film comfortably recovered its costs (plus a reasonable profit) and Eastwood felt no pressing urge to go for an all-out hit (i.e. *Dirty Harry II*). More interested in honing his directing skills on a completely different style of film, he chose the generation gap romance *Breezy* (1973). If writer Jo Heims had got her way, this pleasant, utterly predictable love story would have been the first onscreen collaboration between Eastwood and actress Sondra Locke. Having followed *Play Misty for Me* with another Universal-backed thriller, the routine *You'll Like My Mother* (1972), Heims felt that both she and Eastwood needed a change of pace and wrote *Breezy* with the latter in mind. Pleased with the script (allegedly based on one of his ongoing relationships), Eastwood decided he would not be comfortable as a romantic lead (with no-one to shoot) and chose to make the film his first project as a director only. Jennings Lang had no problem with the idea, so long as Eastwood could shoot *Breezy* in under five weeks for less than $300,000. Confident of his experienced, tight-knit crew, the star saw no difficulty in this. The only significant change in personnel was cameraman Frank Stanley, who would shoot four Malpaso films in a row while Bruce Surtees took a little time out to work on non-Eastwood productions such as *Conquest of the Planet of the Apes* (1972), *The Outfit* (1973) and Bob Fosse's black and white biopic *Lenny* (1974). For the male lead, a divorced, world-weary estate agent, Eastwood selected William Holden. A star since his film debut in *Golden Boy* (1939), Holden peaked in the 1950s with *Sunset Boulevard* (1950), *Stalag 17* (1953), and *The Bridge on the River Kwai*. Apart from a starring role in *The Wild Bunch* (1969), Sam Peckinpah's epic hymn to slow motion bloodspurting (a style disliked by Eastwood), his recent career had shown unmistakable signs of decline and Holden happily accepted *Breezy*. Immediately impressed with Eastwood, Holden even agreed to waive his fee, settling for a share in any profits.

Casting for the part of Breezy, an easygoing, life loving young hippie, Eastwood got his first glimpse of Sondra Locke. Academy Award nominated for her film debut *The Heart is a Lonely Hunter* (1968), where the 21 year old Locke played the 14 year old friend of deaf-mute Alan Arkin, she had found little subsequent success, apart from a supporting role as rat-lover Bruce Davidson's girlfriend in the horror-thriller *Willard* (1971). Whatever his personal response to Locke at this time, Eastwood the director felt the actress looked both too old and too worldly for the role. Despite Heims's lobbying for Locke, he chose 20 year old television actress Kay Lenz, recommended for the part by editor Ferris Webster. Even if Eastwood did feel an immediate attraction to Locke, his love life already offered quite enough complications. During location shooting in Encino, a suburban district of Los Angeles, Maggie paid an unexpected visit to her husband, only to find Roxanne Tunis already there. Their meeting proved cordial, if hardly friendly, much to the relief of an unusually agitated Eastwood.

Though well enough made and acted, *Breezy* is little more than a shallow, bittersweet romance (William Wellman liked it). Frank Harmon (Holden) picks up a hitchhiking Breezy, they fall in love, but he is too uncomfortable with the age difference (35 years, so one sees his point) and their wildly different lifestyles for the relationship to last. Not the easiest film to market, *Breezy*'s box-office chances were further undermined by the Motion Picture Association of America's insistence on an 'R' rating (because of some brief nudity), which barred it from audiences under 17 (unless they took an adult with them to the cinema). Whether or not *Breezy* would have appealed to teenagers is open to question. It certainly didn't appeal to Eastwood's adult followers (as a non-violent Eastwood film which didn't even have Eastwood in it) and flopped. Aside from any wounds to the director's pride, the failure of *Breezy* later created an awkward situation between Malpaso and the Screen Actors Guild. As there were no profits to be shared, William Holden's earnings from the film amounted to exactly nil. This contravened Guild regulations, and Eastwood was obliged to pay his star the union minimum of $4000. Deciding that he'd done enough artistic experimentation for the time being, Eastwood made a return trip to Warner for *Magnum Force*, to be filmed in the summer of 1973.

As brutal and straightforward as its title (an unsubtle reference to both the first *Harry* and its own basic plot), *Magnum Force* is a good example of a well-crafted by-the-numbers sequel which gives the audience exactly what they want (and expect). Having been last in line with the *Dirty Harry* script, writer John Milius got the first shot at the new story. Taking his inspiration from reports of Brazilian 'death squads' operating from within the police force, Milius' storyline pitted Callahan against a group of renegade motorcycle cops gunning down criminal scum beyond the law's grasp. This way, the vigilante theme of *Dirty Harry* stayed intact but Harry himself now worked strictly to the rulebook (apart from harassing a gangster or two). Feeling that Harry was still too much of a rootless loner, Eastwood recruited new writer on the block Michael Cimino to add a little more personality and background. Cimino only had one filmed screenplay to his credit, the eco-friendly science fiction melodrama *Silent Running* (1972), which made him both inexpensive and eager to please. He added a subplot featuring glimpses of Harry's home life (a spartan apartment) and a tentative relationship with his young Japanese-American neighbour Sunny (Adele Yoshioka). Combined with the good-natured interplay between Harry and his black partner, Early Smith (Felton Perry), this would neatly counter any lingering suspicions of racism.

More than a little schematic, the plot of *Magnum Force* alternates between the rogue cops' cold blooded executions (unacceptable neo-fascism) and Harry's own violent hijinks (simply the result of a good cop doing his job). Four mobsters are gunned down at point blank range in their car. Harry foils an attempted airplane hijack (economically reusing the original climax to *Dirty Harry*). A swimming pool full of crooks and their girlfriends is bombed and machine-gunned. Harry takes on a gang of armed robbers attempting to hold up a hardware store. A whore-killing pimp (Albert Popwell) is shot up in his 'pimpmobile'. Harry trails a gangster suspected by his superior, Lieutenant Briggs (Hal Holbrook), of being behind the killings. A bisexual crime boss is blown away along with his drugged-up lovers in their penthouse apartment. Harry is sent to arrest the gangster, only to end up in a gun battle (the gangster has been mysteriously tipped off that rival mobsters dressed as cops are about to hit him). As the storylines converge, it is revealed to no great surprise that the head of the murder squad is Harry's own boss, the supposedly wishy-washy liberal Briggs. Harry takes on the rogue cops (including a pre *Starsky and Hutch* David Soul), chucks a bomb into Briggs' car (a bomb previously planted in Harry's mailbox) and walks home a sadder, wiser man.

Apart from its disappointing finale (a drawn out chase around a disused aircraft carrier), *Magnum Force* works fairly well in a crude fashion, transforming the familiar figure of the motorcycle cop (black leather jacket, breeches, leather boots, white helmet and sunglasses) into a faceless angel of death. Even with Harry in toned down mode, Eastwood still gets to strut his macho stuff, riding on the bonnet of a fleeing villain's car and taking part in another motorbike chase with the surviving killer-cop. Reunited with Eastwood after five years, Ted Post directs energetically, going a little overboard with the restless camera and wild angles. Lalo Schifrin's standard mix of electric guitar, vocals and drums is also overdone, lacking the quieter interludes that made his score for *Dirty Harry* so effective. The film stumbles a little in the logic department (why does David Soul take his weapon of execution, a .357 Magnum, to a police department shooting contest?) and the emphasis on naked women being shot full of holes is dubious to say the least (one also takes a plunge from a highrise apartment window). Audiences weren't bothered by such petty details and *Magnum Force* grossed over $40 million at the box-office.

The only downside to the first *Harry* sequel was Eastwood's rapidly deteriorating relationship with Ted Post. Post later claimed that Eastwood had changed for the worse since *Hang 'Em High*, letting his business instincts override his artistic judgments to a harmful extent (hardly the case with a film such as *High Plains Drifter*). Success had gone to the star's head, inflating his ego to a Leonard Freeman-Alan J. Lerner-Martin Rackin level. Eastwood allegedly interfered with Post's direction during the shooting of

Magnum Force, vetoing several camera set-ups the latter wanted to use, and then proceeded to re-edit the footage behind Post's back. The latter felt the resulting film suffered from a sluggish pace and a number of noticeable gaps in the editing (such as a proper establishing shot for the final sequence). While Post might have been willing to accept Eastwood's creative 'suggestions' on *Hang 'Em High*, where the director had every reason to be grateful for the star's patronage (reviving Post's film career after a decade of television), things had changed a little in the intervening five years. By 1973 Post had worked on three more features, the relatively lavish *Beneath the Planet of the Apes* (1970), *The Baby* (1972) and *The Harrad Experiment* (1973), and could no longer be content as a mere Eastwood lackey. Star and director also clashed over the characterization of Lieutenant Briggs, a thinly written role disliked by actor Hal Holbrook. Post advised underplaying, only to be contradicted by Eastwood, who wanted unsubtle aggression. The latter won out, resulting in a strident, rather crass performance by Holbrook (who later accused Post of failing to exert his authority as a director). Post remained on civil enough terms with Eastwood to deliver a glowing tribute in the 1992 television documentary/hagiography *The Man from Malpaso*, but they never worked together again.

On a happier note, Eastwood's productive working relationship with writer Michael Cimino resulted in one of the star's best films, *Thunderbolt and Lightfoot*. Trained as an actor, Cimino had worked in documentaries and television commercials before trying his luck in Hollywood with a number of script ideas. On the strength of the *Magnum Force* rewrite, Cimino approached Eastwood with his screenplay for *Thunderbolt*, a quirky combination of road movie, heist movie and 'buddy' movie (with accompanying gay subtext). Not one to undersell himself, Cimino also wanted to direct the film and wouldn't make any deal without this proviso. Three days after receiving the script, Eastwood bought the project, novice director and all. United Artists agreed to distribute the film, perhaps concerned that they were missing out on the Eastwood boom the company had helped to create back in 1967. With a $4 million budget and a seven week schedule, *Thunderbolt and Lightfoot* went into production in the autumn of 1973. Fully aware of Eastwood's brisk shooting pace (which the star claims is as much to do with sustaining momentum as saving money), Cimino planned the filming down to the last detail. For the pivotal co-starring role of Lightfoot, a hippie drifter with a penchant for stolen cars and leather trousers, Eastwood and Cimino selected Jeff Bridges. Academy Award nominated for his performance in Peter Bogdanovich's *The Last Picture Show* (1971), Bridges had continued to impress in offbeat films such as *Bad Company* (1972) and John Huston's *Fat City* (1972).

Set against the tranquil backdrop of Montana, complete with blue skies, golden wheatfields, rolling hills and wooden churches, *Thunderbolt and Lightfoot* begins in engagingly offbeat vein, turning darker and violently downbeat in the second half. Driving a stolen car through a field, Lightfoot encounters decorated Korea veteran turned bank robber turned phony preacher John 'Thunderbolt' Doherty (Eastwood), on the run (literally) from a former associate. A few years back, Thunderbolt took part in an elaborate scheme to rob the Montana Armored Depository of $500,000, blasting the doors open with a 20mm cannon (hence his nickname). The loot was hidden behind the blackboard of a small town schoolhouse, which has now been replaced by a more modern building. Pursued by two more ex-colleagues, Red Leary (George Kennedy) and Goody (Geoffrey Lewis), Thunderbolt eventually reaches an uneasy truce with the men, despite Leary's intense dislike of his new buddy Lightfoot. At the latter's suggestion, the partly reformed gang agree to rob the depository a second time. Despite elaborate

● *Magnum Force*: Sidney the Pimp (Albert Popwell) questions his 'bitch' (Margaret Avery) regarding misappropriation of funds.

planning (dwelled on in almost clinical detail), the heist is a failure, with both Goody and Leary ending up dead (Leary having first kicked Lightfoot unconscious). Fleeing with Lightfoot across the countryside, Thunderbolt comes across the original school-house, relocated and rebuilt as a historic monument. The loot from the first robbery is still there.

Demonstrating a striking flair for both writing and directing (especially in his use of the moving camera and 'scope format), Michael Cimino supplements his well achieved heist plot with a mass of quirky detail and characterization. Hitch-hiking on the free-way, Thunderbolt and Lightfoot are given a lift by a mad driver (Bill McKinney) who keeps a caged raccoon on his passenger seat and pipes his car's exhaust fumes back into the vehicle (Best remembered as the rapacious hillbilly in John Boorman's *Deliverance* 1972, McKinney played supporting roles in six further Malpaso films, most notably as Eastwood's arch enemy in *The Outlaw Josey Wales*.) Having skidded his car across the road and then rolled the vehicle over through 360 degrees, the driver gets out and opens his boot to reveal a multitude of white rabbits, which he unsuccessfully attempts to blast with a shotgun. Unsettled by all this, Thunderbolt knocks the man out and steals his car, obliging Lightfoot to sit in raccoon shit of varying vintage. This sense of off-kilter absur-dity recurs throughout the film, albeit in less manic style. A lady motorcyclist responds to Lightfoot's playful advances by hitting his (borrowed) van with a hammer. The four gang members are obliged to obtain honest jobs in order to finance their robbery scheme (Thunderbolt finds employment in a steelworks, a rare touch of autobiography from Eastwood.) As part of the heist plan, a self-admiring Lightfoot dons drag ('You sexy bitch'). The thuggish, leeringly sadistic Leary suffers from both asthma and hay fever. Cimino's one error of judgment is to present the only substantial female charac-ters (one played by a pre *Dukes of Hazzard* Catherine Bach) as empty-headed purveyors of casual sex, a common failing of 'buddy' movies.

The relationship between Thunderbolt and Lightfoot is one of the most memorable and believable in the Eastwood filmography. Thunderbolt takes an instant liking to the cocky, amoral drifter, despite having his shoulder dislocated by Lightfoot's driving antics on their first meeting (the arm is pulled back into place with a belt and a convenient tree branch). At first reluctant to respond to Lightfoot's offer of a more longterm friendship ('You're ten years too late, kid'), he soon comes round to the idea of their 'partnership', though it is the sight of Leary toting a barely hidden shotgun that initially sends Thunderbolt back to Lightfoot's car. The latter seems to regard their friendship as preordained by fate ('Thunderbolt and Lightfoot. That sounds like something doesn't it'), perhaps the means by which he will achieve his dream of buying (not stealing) a white Cadillac convertible, paid for in cash. A far more expressive (not to say versatile) actor than Eastwood, Bridges' style makes an effective contrast to his co-star's tightlipped cool and understated humour, providing a WASP variation on the Joe-Silvanito/Blondie-Tuco relationships of *A Fistful of Dollars* and *The Good The Bad and The Ugly*. The final sequence of the film is genuinely touching. Showing definite signs of severe internal injuries inflicted by Leary, Lightfoot nevertheless helps Thunderbolt recover the money hidden in the schoolhouse. Thunderbolt buys the Cadillac for his rapidly ailing friend, who tells him it's time to move on: 'Lets see what's over the next mountain.' Lightfoot dies in the car. Pausing briefly to check on Lightfoot, Thunderbolt drives on. While the film keeps any suggestion of a gay element in the friendship fairly subliminal (though at one point Thunderbolt and a dragged-up Lightfoot pretend to be a dating couple at a drive-in movie), Eastwood's performance conveys a sense of tenderness towards Bridges absent in many of his safely heterosexual onscreen relationships.

Perhaps disconcerted by some of *Thunderbolt and Lightfoot*'s more offbeat ingredients, United Artists decided to play it safe with their marketing campaign for the film, released in the summer of 1974. Disregarding Eastwood's objections, the studio promoted *Thunderbolt* as a straightforward heist/action movie ('He has exactly seven minutes to get rich quick !') The trailer used a misleading *Dirty Harry*-style score in the place of the much gentler Dee Barton soundtrack employed for the film. While *Thunderbolt and Lightfoot* eventually grossed a respectable $25 million, Eastwood felt that UA's mishandling of the film had thrown away the chance of a full blown hit and swore never to work with the company again (he didn't). At least he could take some consolation from the favourable reviews and Jeff Bridges' Academy Award nomination for Best Supporting Actor (making *Thunderbolt and Lightfoot* the first Malpaso production to attract 'serious' industry acclaim). Michael Cimino's subsequent career as a writer-director proved notoriously disappointing. Having produced an outstanding film on a modest budget and tight schedule (even completing the last 56 set-ups in twenty four hours instead of the scheduled three days so Eastwood could go home early), he later seemed to react against this enforced economy in a disastrous fashion. While his Vietnam epic *The Deer Hunter* (1978) scored a controversial (and questionable) success with audiences and critics alike, *Heaven's Gate* (1980), *The Year of the Dragon* (1985), *The Sicilian* (1987) and *The Desperate Hours* (1990) all display painful evidence of a talent overwhelmed by ego, pomposity, self-importance and a general lack of sound judgment. Perhaps Eastwood should have stuck to the original schedule.

Having nurtured a new film-making talent, Eastwood now looked for a chance to work with one of the cinema's most respected veterans, director-producer Howard Hawks. Aside from the seminal *Red River* (see Chapter 2), Hawks' work included 'classics' from virtually every popular genre: comedy (*Twentieth Century* 1934, *Bringing Up*

Baby 1938, *His Girl Friday* 1940), *film noir* (*The Big Sleep* 1946), gangster movies (*Scarface* 1932), war films (*Sergeant York* 1941), westerns (*Rio Bravo* 1959) and action-adventure (*To Have and Have Not*). Semi-retired since the modest John Wayne western *Rio Lobo* (1970), the seventy seven year old Hawks had a new project in development, a comedy about the oil business called *When It's Hot Play It Cool*. An admirer of Eastwood's films (particularly the *Dollars* trilogy), the director wanted to work with him, despite thinking the star a little effeminate compared to John Wayne, as well as lacking much aptitude for comedy (what about the humour in *The Good The Bad and The Ugly* ?) Eastwood was willing to dispense with his standard fee (which Hawks considered excessive), settling for a share in any profits, as he wanted to study Hawks' working methods (and renew a very slight acquaintance dating back to the late 1940s). Despite the interest from both Eastwood and Steve McQueen (whose career had started to slow down a little), *When It's Hot...* never got beyond the discussion stage and *Rio Lobo* remained the last entry in Hawks' filmography (he died in 1977). Eastwood later expressed regret that he'd never worked with any of the top film-makers from Hollywood's 'golden' age, citing Hawks, John Ford, Alfred Hitchcock and Henry Hathaway as his particular idols. In truth, he achieved American stardom too late for this wish to ever come true. Ford retired (not entirely by choice) after *Seven Women* (1966), and the other three were talents in noticeable decline by the late 1960s. Hitchcock never made another outstanding film after *Marnie* (1964), though the clumsy, unpleasant *Frenzy* (1972) has its admirers. Another fan of Eastwood, the elderly director did approach the star in the late 1970s with a project idea; flattered by Hitchcock's invitation, Eastwood quickly realized that the director's ill health made the proposed film no more than a pipe-dream. Hathaway produced only one good movie, the John Wayne Oscar winner *True Grit* (1969), among a lot of dross (*The Last Safari* 1967, *Five Card Stud* 1968, *Raid on Rommel* 1971, *Shootout* 1971). Even Hawks had faltered after the mid 1960s, recycling his past efforts with only modest results (*Red Line 7000* 1965, *El Dorado* 1966). Eastwood's experiences with John Sturges on *Joe Kidd* had taught him only too well that an impressive back catalogue could count for little if the director no longer had the ability or inclination to make the necessary effort. Bearing this in mind, it is surprising that Eastwood never got together with John Huston (even more surprising when one considers *White Hunter Black Heart*). Two decades on from the likes of *The Maltese Falcon* (1941) and *The Treasure of the Sierra Madre* (1948), one of Eastwood's all-time favourites, Huston's career took a nosedive with the failures of *Casino Royale* (1967), *Reflections in a Golden Eye* (1967), *Sinful Davey* (1968) and *A Walk with Love and Death* (1969). Unlike Hitchcock, Hathaway and Hawks, Huston recovered from this slump to make at least four more outstanding films: *Fat City*, *The Man Who Would Be King* (1975), *Wise Blood* (1979) and *The Dead* (1987). An erratic talent throughout his career, Huston's hits were still well balanced by his duds and misfires (*The Kremlin Letter* 1970, *The Mackintosh Man* 1973, *Phobia* 1980, *Victory* 1981, *Annie* 1982), yet Eastwood could have taken a chance.

Opting to take a chance of a rather different kind, Eastwood decided to make his next project an espionage thriller, based on a bestselling novel. *The Eiger Sanction* tells the familiar tale of the disillusioned former secret agent brought out of retirement for one last mission, an assassination in this instance (the 'sanction' of the title). For various uninteresting reasons, the killing must take place halfway up Mount Eiger in Switzerland. Back with Universal Studios after a two film break, Eastwood wanted to make his production as authentic as possible. Not only would he use the genuine Eiger as his location, he would do all his own mountaineering, despite a total lack of climbing

● *Thunderbolt and Lightfoot*: **just good friends.**

experience. To the latter end, Eastwood took a three day climbing course at Yosemite National Park, California. Perhaps overconfident of his new abilities, he narrowly avoided serious (if not fatal) injury on a practice climb. Unperturbed by this experience, Eastwood soon found that his enthusiasm for the project was not universally shared. Don Siegel turned down his offer to direct, partly because of the dull script, mostly because the sixty two year old Siegel didn't fancy spending prolonged periods stuck halfway up a Swiss mountain. Other directors expressed similar sentiments, leaving Eastwood with little choice other than to abandon the production or direct himself. Choosing the latter proved to be the worst mistake of his career. Arriving in Switzerland in August 1974, Eastwood based his production team in the town of Wengen, at the foot of the Eiger. On the second day of filming, Eastwood and his team of professional climbers (doubling for less adventurous actors) were caught in a rock fall. Eastwood's personal trainer, Mike Hoover, suffered a fractured pelvis. David Knowles, a British mountaineer and stuntman, was struck on the head and killed. Understandably traumatized by this tragedy, Eastwood's first inclination was to abandon the film. Swayed by his responsibilities to Universal, Malpaso and the paying public, he continued shooting. Later reports suggested that the Eiger should never have been used for filming, as the mountain's crumbling rock and poor weather made regular avalanches and rockslides inevitable. Eastwood at least took the lessons of the production to heart, never again placing either himself or any Malpaso employee in a dangerously unpredictable situation (though some claim that the shooting of the escape sequence in *Alcatraz* exposed Eastwood and his costars to unnecessary risk). The desire to do his own stunts remained, but tempered by a first hand awareness of the possible cost, both to himself and others.

Overshadowed by the death of David Knowles, *The Eiger Sanction* itself is almost insultingly routine, a standard mixture of intrigue, killings and doublecross. If some of the plot devices (Eastwood's former government assassin is now a lecturer in art history) and character names (Jonathan Hemlock, Dragon, Miss Cerberus, Pope) suggest an element of self-parody, this is not borne out by Eastwood's plodding direction and a fairly dismal screenplay. What the star failed to appreciate is that drawn out sequences showing men trying to climb up big rocks in bad weather do not necessarily make for enthralling viewing. The one element of interest is the presence of Vonetta McGee as Eastwood's contact agent and lover. After *The Big Silence*, McGee had taken roles in the less than choice efforts *The Kremlin Letter*, *Blacula* (1972) and *Shaft in Africa* (1973) and *The Eiger Sanction* didn't make for a great improvement. Her interracial romance with Eastwood suffered a severe toning down when the film was released outside the United States. Citing reasons of overlength (the American print runs 128 minutes), not helped by the indifferent box-office back home, Universal chopped around ten minutes from *The Eiger Sanction*, losing a sex scene between McGee and Eastwood and much of the background to the sanction itself. It didn't help.

The Eiger Sanction proved to be the last (and least) Malpaso-Universal co-production. Questioned at the time, Eastwood explained that the crowds drawn by the studio's popular on site tours distracted him and his staff in the Malpaso office. This smacks more than a little of an agreed 'official version' and the actual reasons are no doubt many and various: the unhappy circumstances behind *The Eiger Sanction*, the studio's re-edits on the film, lingering resentments over *The Beguiled*, tempting overtures from Warner, perhaps even memories of the bad old days of Universal-International. For all the various problems, Universal had played its part in developing Eastwood's career, financing the pivotal *Coogan's Bluff*, the noncommercial *Beguiled* and the star's first four films as a director (two of which could hardly be termed wildly lucrative). 1975 also marked the end of another longstanding relationship. Eastwood had kept in regular contact with Roxanne and Kimber Tunis, paying his non-official family overnight visits at least four times a year. Ever since Kimber's birth eleven years earlier, Roxanne had accepted this less than satisfying arrangement in the increasingly vain hope that Eastwood would one day leave Maggie and make their own union permanent. She eventually came to accept that the only relationship she could ever have with the star would be the one he'd arranged back in the *Rawhide* days, especially now that Maggie outgunned her in the child department. Roxanne Tunis left the United States to restart her life in France, still tied to Eastwood by their mutually agreed financial arrangement. Whatever regrets Eastwood had about this development, there were other matters that required his attention. Unconcerned with the prevailing industry opinion, he wanted to make his next film another western. With shooting scheduled for the autumn of 1975, he didn't yet have a distribution deal with any studio but he did have complete confidence in the script. *The Outlaw Josey Wales* would prove to be the crowning achievement of Eastwood's career as a director. It would also reacquaint him with Sondra Locke.

8

The Outlaw Josey Wales

Get ready little lady, hell is coming to breakfast.
Lone Watie

In 1973 an unassuming tale called *Gone to Texas* appeared in book form, with a print run of less than a hundred copies. The publishers described its author, one Forrest Carter, as a poet and story-teller of Cherokee descent, persuaded to commit one of his stories to paper. Set against the aftermath of the American Civil War, *Gone to Texas* is the tale of Josey Wales, a peace-loving farmer turned Confederate guerrilla by the murder of his wife and son. Still looking for revenge when the war ends, Wales refuses to surrender, pursuing his vendetta as an outlaw. Chased by Union soldiers and bounty hunters, he unwillingly attracts a growing band of followers: an elderly Cherokee Indian, a Navajo Indian girl, an old lady, her granddaughter and a dog. Growing to appreciate this new 'family' group, Wales is torn between his as yet unattained vengeance and a growing desire to put away his guns and return to the land. The soldiers are still on his trail, led by the two men who turned Wales into an outlaw.

By some fortunate quirk of fate, a copy of *Gone to Texas* found its way to Robert Daley, who immediately appreciated its potential as an Eastwood vehicle. Eastwood agreed and hired Philip Kaufman to both write and direct the film version, unsubtly renamed *The Outlaw Josey Wales*. Active in low budget, independent cinema during the 1960s (with films such as *Goldstein* 1964, and *Fearless Frank* 1969), Kaufman had attracted Eastwood's attention with *The Great Northfield Minnesota Raid* (1972), a western in the low key 'realist' style. Backed by Universal (Jennings Lang served as executive producer), the film made no great box-office impact, but Eastwood liked Kaufman's sense of period, with authentic background detail, enhanced by Bruce Surtees' photography. Reuniting Kaufman and Surtees for *Josey Wales*, Eastwood also recruited production designer Tambi Larsen, who'd worked on *Thunderbolt and Lightfoot*. This way, the film would be guaranteed to look good, if nothing else.

With Malpaso regulars Robert Daley, Ferris Webster and James Fargo in place (Fargo also got to serve as an associate producer), Eastwood decided to recruit a few new personnel, notably old schoolfriend Fritz Manes (as a humble production assistant) and Joel Cox, assisting Webster in the editing department. The Webster-Cox team would work together on *The Enforcer*, *The Gauntlet*, *Every Which Way But Loose*, *Escape from Alcatraz*, *Bronco Billy* and *Honkytonk Man*, after which Cox graduated to senior editor following Webster's retirement. Having collaborated with a number of composers after Lalo Schifrin's brief-but-fruitful tenure as Malpaso's virtual musician-in-residence (Dee Barton on *Misty*, *Drifter* and *Thunderbolt*; Michael Legrand on *Breezy*; John Williams on *The Eiger Sanction*), Eastwood selected Jerry Fielding to provide the score for *Josey Wales*. Previously associated with the directors Sam Peckinpah (*The Wild Bunch*, *Straw Dogs* 1971, *Junior Bonner* 1972, *Bring Me the Head of Alfredo Garcia* 1974) and (going down-market) Michael Winner (*Lawman* 1970, *The Nightcomers* 1971, *Chato's Land* 1972, *The Mechanic* 1972, *Scorpio* 1972), Fielding proved the ideal choice. Drawing largely on traditional Civil War tunes, his unobtrusive, oddly memorable score blends well with the overall style of *Josey Wales*. Eastwood used Fielding again on *The Enforcer*, *The Gauntlet* and *Escape from Alcatraz*, with only moderate results.

Casting for the supporting roles, Eastwood (and Kaufman) again exhibited either great judgment or great luck. The part of aged but unbowed Indian chief Lone Watie went to Chief Dan George, a seventy six year old Canadian Indian who'd scored a big success (and an Academy Award nomination) in the jokey epic western *Little Big Man* (1970), effortlessly upstaging star Dustin Hoffman. Unknown Geraldine Keams was cast as the squaw Little Moonlight, offering a dignified, sympathetic portrayal of an abused yet tough-minded woman finding a place in the Wales 'community'. For the more conventional role of fierce but honourable Comanche chief Ten Bears, Eastwood and Kaufman chose the imposing Will Sampson (Jack Nicholson's apparently mute friend in *One Flew Over the Cuckoo's Nest* 1975). Discussing the *Josey Wales* script some years later Eastwood drew attention to the way it presented Indians as people with a sense of humour, especially Lone Watie's deadpan wit ('They call us civilized because we're easy to sneak up on'.) The Indians certainly emerge from the film a lot better than most of the non-native Americans (without *Josey Wales* becoming a selfconsciously right-on pro-Indian diatribe). As the cast and crew were regularly transported to the locations in Kanab, Utah in planes piloted by Navajo Indians, this was perhaps just as well.

For his non-Indian characters, Eastwood rounded up many of his usual Malpaso players, finding roles for John Mitchum (a lecherous trader), John Quade (a comanchero leader), William O'Connell (a ferryman adept at switching between the Confederate and Union anthems without pausing for breath) and Bill McKinney (as Captain Terrill, the Kansas redleg turned army officer who wipes out Wales' home and family, then pursues him from Missouri to Texas). The star also called on John Vernon, cast as Fletcher, a former ally of Wales who betrayed their band of guerrillas for cash, and Paula Trueman (who appeared in *Paint Your Wagon*), cast as the diminutive, plain-speaking Grandma Sarah. Having exhausted his filmography, Eastwood then drew on his television days, finding a small part for *Rawhide* co-star Sheb Wooley, and his own family, casting a seven year old Kyle Eastwood as Josey's ill-fated son. This only left the part of Laura Lee, Sarah's shy, wide-eyed granddaughter, who falls in love with Josey.

Since her brief encounter with Eastwood (and his casting director) back in 1972, Sondra Locke's career had gone nowhere in particular. A co-starring role opposite the troubled husband and wife team of Robert Shaw and Mary Ure in the thriller *Reflection of Fear* (1972) sank without trace when the film did likewise. Never overly concerned with an actor's public profile (unless it raised their fee too high), Eastwood offered Locke the role of Laura. To what extent this decision rested on his interest in the woman rather than the actress is impossible to determine (especially now Locke is legally constrained from discussing her relationship with Eastwood). Locke is certainly well cast as Laura, her best film role by a long way. Unlike her later Malpaso appearances, Laura earns audience sympathy, especially during her touchingly awkward courtship of Josey (which doesn't get going until the last twenty five minutes of the film), complete with tastefully staged lovemaking. An uncharitable observer might argue that Locke succeeds here where she failed later simply because Laura has very few lines. *Josey Wales* also initiated the dubious tradition of Locke being violently assaulted in Eastwood's films. Stripped by rapacious comancheros (outlaws specializing in selling stolen guns, liquor and women to the Comanches), Laura is only saved from rape when their leader decides she is worth more as a virgin (maybe as much as twenty horses), though a watching Josey is standing by with a gun in his hand. Locke also undergoes sexual assault in *The Gauntlet*, attempted rape in *Bronco Billy* and rape followed by brutal assault in *Sudden Impact*. As co-star Eastwood also directed all three of these efforts, one wonders how he felt subjecting the then love of his life to these simulated ordeals.

Appreciating that *Josey Wales* had no guarantee of a large audience, Eastwood decided to budget the film at a modest $3.7 million. Still without a distributor, the production got underway in the late autumn of 1975 (Eastwood would also shoot *Pale Rider* and *Unforgiven* at this time of year, arguing that the season of fruition and decay offers the ideal backdrop for his style of western.) Two weeks into filming, what appeared to be a project made in heaven took a sharp downward turn when Eastwood fired Kaufman. There had already been some difference of opinion regarding the screenplay, which Eastwood handed over to Malpaso script reader Sonia Chernus (see Chapter 1) for a little rewriting. While neither Eastwood nor Kaufman have been forthcoming over the exact reasons for the latter's dismissal, this may well have been one case where the oft cited 'creative differences' rang true. Kaufman had his own very definite vision of the film which simply didn't coincide with Eastwood's (as later efforts such as *The Right Stuff* (1983) clearly demonstrate, Kaufman is not just another director-for-hire). Interviewed by Christopher Frayling fifteen years later, Kaufman claimed to have made most of the artistic decisions during preproduction on *Josey Wales*, selecting the cast and supervising the sets and costumes. While the last two factors are open to question, the number of Eastwood veterans in supporting roles suggests that it was the star, not Kaufman, who had the last word in this respect.

Rather than look for another director, Eastwood decided to take on the job himself (perhaps the most important creative choice of his career). Whatever his problems with Kaufman, this potentially disastrous behind-the-scenes rift is nowhere evident in the finished film. Eastwood's controlled, unshowy direction is a model of expert storytelling which hits no false notes at all. Though relatively long at 135 minutes, *Josey Wales* is beautifully paced, with no dull spots or drawn out scenes. Bruce Surtees' photography makes effective use of subdued, sombre colours, with the emphasis on brown/green hues, disrupted by regular splashes of red. If any of Kaufman's footage did survive in the final version of the film, it doesn't show in any variation in style. Bearing in mind the assured even-handedness of the direction, plus the fact that *Josey Wales* went a few days and $200,000 over budget (officially attributed to bad weather), it seems plausible that Eastwood scrapped most of the first two weeks' work and made a fresh start. Warner certainly had enough confidence in Eastwood to buy up the distribution rights for *Josey Wales* weeks before shooting was completed, not even waiting for a look at the rough cut.

A long way from the phantasmagorical landscape of *The Good The Bad and The Ugly*, the Civil War backdrop of *Josey Wales* is depicted as a brutal disruption of a man's life, destroying the work of years in a matter of minutes. The precredits sequence shows a cleanshaven Josey at his plough, sunlight filtering through the trees above. Little Josey walks ahead, removing stones from his father's path as Mrs Wales calls the boy in for dinner. Black smoke in the distance and hooves on the soundtrack herald the arrival of the redlegs, Kansas-based mercenaries under Union pay. The farm is burned to the ground and Josey's family murdered (there is some implication that Mrs Wales is gang-raped first). Josey's hopeless intervention is cut short when Terrill knocks him unconscious with a swipe from his cavalry sabre, leaving a scar that the redleg will have cause to remember. Burying his family in improvised shrouds (a hand falls out of the sacking), Josey attempts to pray, only to tearfully reject religious consolation (Eastwood is utterly convincing in this scene). Returning to the burnt-out farmstead, he pulls a gun from

● Farmer Josey Wales abandons his plough and picks up a gun.

the ashes (symbolising Josey's rebirth as a lethal avenger) and embarks on a little shoot-ing practice (Eastwood intercuts shots of Josey firing and reminders of what he has just lost). Confederate guerrillas appear out of the woods, led by 'Bloody' Bill Anderson (John Russell, an actor with a passing resemblance to Lee Van Cleef). Josey joins up and the credits roll over a montage of the guerrillas at work. Anderson is eventually killed and a bearded Josey takes his place as leader.

With the last credit comes the end of the war, and Fletcher persuades his fellow rebels to surrender, unaware that his Union contact (an evil senator) will massacre them. Now a fugitive outlaw, Josey can save only one of the men, Jamie (Sam Bottoms), who tells him of Fletcher's deceit. Jamie soon succumbs to wounds inflicted by Terrill, leaving Josey on his own. The latter rapidly acquires a reputation as a notorious killer, though his only serious crime is spitting tobacco (during the course of the film, Eastwood spits on carpetbagger Woodrow Parfrey, a dead bounty killer, a scorpion, a dead horse trader, a beetle and his dog (3 times)). As Grandma Sarah later says, 'nasty habit, young man'.

Jamie's death ends the first act of *Josey Wales*. The second begins with the arrival of Lone Watie, clad in his 'civilised' outfit of top hat and frock coat (he later burns them when he decides to follow Wales). Years before, Watie lost his family when the United States government put the Cherokee nation on a forced march to reservation land (the point being that the Civil War gave white Americans such as Josey a taste of the tragic injustices endured by the Indians throughout their history). While Josey falls asleep lis-tening to Watie's story, he is sympathetic, recognizing a kindred spirit (the battle with the comancheros implies some kind of mental link between them, with the distant fig-ure of Josey following the instructions mouthed by the captive Watie). Moving through Indian territory towards Texas, the two men (and their dog) are joined by Little

Moonlight, the ill-treated servant of a sniveling storekeeper (when two traders molest her, Josey arrives on the scene, an ominous silhouette framed in the store's doorway). For all Josey's objections ('I don't want nobody belonging to me'), Little Moonlight is soon part of the family.

Leaving behind a trail of dead soldiers and comancheros (expertly staged shootouts), Josey and friends make their way through Texas, now joined by Sarah and Laura. This group finally arrives at a ranch belonging to Sarah's dead son (also Laura's father), a redleg killed by Missouri raiders, near the ghost town of Santa Rio. When the few remaining townspeople join them to get the ranch working again, Josey is within sight of the life he lost back in Missouri. A blood pact with Ten Bears ensures peace with the local Indians ('Governments don't live together. People live together') yet Josey can't forget the soldiers on his trail (signified by brief flashbacks to the precredits carnage). Riding out from the ranch in order to ensure peace for his 'family', Wales is confronted by Terrill. Second time round, Josey is not an unarmed farmer on his own and the redlegs are wiped out (even Laura Lee proves a decent shot). Having emptied his guns, Josey throws his weapons away (no longer the outlaw ?) and impales Terrill on his own sabre, a neat reversal of their first meeting. With the story of Josey Wales already entering the realms of myth, Fletcher makes his own peace with the man ('The war is over'), deciding not to recognize Josey when he strolls into the town saloon. Josey Wales rides into the sunset, free to head for home.

Whether looked at as a tale of redemption, a spiritual odyssey, a Vietnam allegory or simply a rousing Western yarn, *The Outlaw Josey Wales* remains by far Eastwood's finest post-Leone/Siegel film. None of the star's later efforts as a director come close to touching it, with even the more lauded *Unforgiven* claiming only second place as an

● *The Outlaw Josey Wales:* **Lone Watie (Chief Dan George) demonstrates his 'sneaking up' skills on Josey.**

honourable also-ran. Unlike Eastwood's other westerns, *Josey Wales* offers a very traditional hero, a character with whom audiences can readily identify. While Joe/No Name
exhibits traces of humanity, he remains a mysterious, largely amoral figure. The
'Stranger' characters in *High Plains Drifter* and *Pale Rider* are supernatural dispensers of
justice, not even pretending to be human. Jed Cooper, Hogan and Joe Kidd are clumsy
attempts to meld Italian and American cowboy styles. Even *Unforgiven's* William Munny
is too eaten up by his past as a bounty killer to forget his guns and make a new start.
Josey Wales began as a farmer and can return to being one once his enemies are dealt
with (though Eastwood deliberately makes the ending a little ambiguous). As *Time*
reviewer Richard Schickel pointed out at the time, *Josey Wales* has a strong nostalgia
appeal, offering a world where an honest man can be content with a wife, a ranch, a
thriving community and the trust of others, white man and Indian. Naive and sentimental, perhaps, but it works.

As Eastwood no doubt expected, *The Outlaw Josey Wales* enjoyed respectable rather
than spectacular box-office success, grossing $13.5 million in the United States. There
were some positive reviews (even Pauline Kael thought it was okay) and an unexpected
tribute from veteran director-genius-rebel-exile Orson Welles, who called the film one
of the best directed of all time. Welles also suggested that Eastwood's involvement with
the film (and the accompanying critical snobbery) prevented *Josey Wales* from receiving
the recognition it deserved. While Jerry Fielding netted an Academy Award nomination
for his score, Eastwood would have to wait another ten years or so before earning his
place as a 'serious' film-maker. For now, he could content himself with retaining complete control over the release of his Malpaso productions, Warner leaving the decisions
regarding publicity and distribution (even the release dates) in his hands. The studio didn't
want to make the same mistakes as Universal and United Artists.

A rather bizarre epilogue to the *Josey Wales* story arrived in the form of an article in
the *New York Times* shortly after the film's
release. According to this piece, *Gone to Texas*
author 'Forrest' Carter was not an Indian
storyteller at all, but a whiter-than-white
political speechwriter called Asa Carter.
Ultra right wing, Asa Carter worked for such
racist politicians as George Wallace (State
Governor of Alabama from 1962-1966) and
openly supported the Ku Klux Klan. An
interesting 'revelation' (never proved),
though not one that makes much difference
to the film. Phil Kaufman told Frayling that
while he believed the Forrest/Asa Carter
story, his script had dispensed with the more
dodgy politics/ideology of the book. The
pro-South, anti-North element is still present, but this has been a staple of American
historical melodramas throughout film history (*Gone With The Wind*, 1939, for example).
Presumably impressed by the success of the
film, Carter brought out a literary sequel the
same year, *The Vengeance Trail of Josey Wales*.

● *The Outlaw Josey Wales:* **Laura Lee
(Sondra Locke).**

Eastwood thought this new story fair enough, but didn't feel that *Josey Wales* needed a follow-up (very wise). A few years later, actor-director Michael Parks produced a low budget sequel/rip-off unimaginatively entitled *The Return of Josey Wales*, which deservedly languished in video oblivion before surfacing briefly in 1986 on the back of *Pale Rider*'s commercial success.

A rather more publicized offshoot from *The Outlaw Josey Wales* was Eastwood's rapidly developing friendship with Sondra Locke. While both were married (Locke to childhood friend Gordon Anderson in 1967), neither felt any need to conceal the mutual attraction. Within two years (so Locke says) they were living together as man and wife. Having put up with Roxanne Tunis for over fifteen years, Maggie Eastwood now found her husband in a new relationship he didn't need to hide from the media (times having changed a little). Furthermore, Eastwood's contact with Locke would amount to a lot more than a few overnight visits a year, being an ideal combination of business and pleasure (or so he thought at the time). Less than four years after *Josey Wales*, Maggie would request a formal separation.

● *The Outlaw Josey Wales.*

9

Men with a Mission

You got a lot of class Harry.
Detective Frank DeGeorgio, *The Enforcer*

Somebody's betting I can't do my job. Well they're full of shit.
Detective Ben Shockley, *The Gauntlet*

When it comes to sharing my feelings with a woman, my stomach just turns to royal gelatin.
Philo Beddoe, *Every Which Way But Loose*

I guess anything you want bad enough is worth a chance.
Frank Morris, *Escape from Alcatraz*

Orson Welles was not the only maverick film-maker to be struck by the quality of *The Outlaw Josey Wales*. In 1976, Eastwood received an invitation from writer-director-producer Francis Coppola to take a starring role in *Apocalypse Now*, Coppola's attempt to top the success of his acclaimed gangster epic *The Godfather Part II* (1974). An uncredited adaptation of Joseph Conrad's 1902 story *Heart of Darkness* (two years out of copyright), the Coppola-John Milius screenplay relocated the action to the all too recent setting of the Vietnam War, not one of Hollywood's favourite places at the time. The initial approach to Eastwood appears to have been made by Steve McQueen, cast as the 'hero' Willard, a US Army Captain sent on a mission to eliminate his dangerously berserk colleague Colonel Kurtz. Having decided that he would rather play the latter, McQueen asked Eastwood to take his place as Willard. Coppola seconded his request, no doubt hoping for a potent (and unique) star combination. Eastwood expressed more than a passing interest, despite some reservations about the rather esoteric script (which he claimed not to understand). Christopher Frayling suggests that the star also felt unsure about how the 'no-win' scenario (inevitable with the Vietnam conflict) would go down with his fans, though in the final version of the script, this factor becomes fairly irrelevant by the end. When Eastwood finally declined Coppola's offer, he cited the more down to earth reason of time, arguing that the scheduled sixteen weeks' filming (largely on location in the Philippines) was too long a period for him to spend on the one project. He had no wish to repeat the experiences of *Paint Your Wagon* and *Kelly's Heroes* (even the production of *Where Eagles Dare* had left him bored and impatient). Eastwood later claimed that he would have been happy to star in *Apocalypse Now* on an eight week schedule (much closer to the usual Malpaso production period), though it soon became clear that his and Coppola's film-making styles were universes apart. McQueen rapidly departed from the project, marking the second and last time that Eastwood came close to co-starring with his former role model/rival (McQueen dropped out of films for three years, making a desultory comeback in 1979 with the unremarkable *Tom Horn* and *The Hunter*, only to die of lung cancer in 1980.) Coppola replaced him with Harvey Keitel, who was quickly fired in favour of Martin Sheen, who suffered a heart attack during shooting (and a career slump thereafter). The original schedule soon became a joke, with filming and post-production dragging on over nearly three years. While the finished film has its admirers, Eastwood's decision not to become involved seems (on balance) the right one.

Firmly established with Warner after *Josey Wales*, Eastwood decided to follow his western with a more straightforward action movie. The previous film had witnessed a marked mellowing of his macho-man persona (with even a touch of family/domesticity thrown in); now the time had come to go back to scum-killing basics. The box-office returns from *Magnum Force* made a second *Harry* sequel an attractive proposition and by the summer of 1976 *The Enforcer* was in production. Clearly not intending to exert himself overmuch with this film, Eastwood put James Fargo in the director's chair, confident that his regular crew would help the former assistant director out of any difficulties. For the script, he called on the services of Dean Riesner once more, this time working with Stirling Silliphant. Like Riesner, Silliphant had Don Siegel's seal of approval (Silliphant wrote the screenplay for *The Line-up*), which still counted for something with Eastwood. An experienced television writer (*The Naked City*, *Route 66*, *Rawhide*), Silliphant's film career included work on *Village of the Damned* (1960), an impressive British science fiction thriller, *In the Heat of the Night* (1967), for which he won an Academy Award, and *Marlowe* (1969), an updated version of Raymond Chandler's novel *The Little Sister*, starring James Garner. By the mid 1970s, Silliphant's talent appeared to have suffered from a surfeit of disaster movies (*The Poseidon Adventure* 1972, *The Towering Inferno* 1974) and blaxploitation (*Shaft in Africa*). The script for *The Enforcer* is strictly writing-by-numbers, adding a few contemporary concerns (urban terrorism, feminism, black militancy) to the standard rogue cop versus psycho villain storyline. After *Coogan*, *Misty* and *Harry*, Riesner could have written an Eastwood vehicle in his sleep and on this occasion would appear to have done so. Directed by Fargo with little more than technical competence, *The Enforcer* comes across as a large scale television movie, distinguishable from its small screen equivalent only by the Panavision format; the extra gore, swearing and nudity and Eastwood himself (still looking cool as Inspector Callahan).

Still clashing with his prissy superiors, Harry continues to endure abuse from the 'punks' of San Francisco (a liquor store robber spits on Callahan, then kicks his ass) before blowing them away in the name of justice. Having dealt with Scorpio and the motorcycle vigilantes, Harry now finds himself up against the People's Revolutionary Strike Force, an apparently fanatical gang of terrorists who kidnap the dim-witted mayor and demand a $5 million ransom. Revolutionary or not, a punk is a punk and Harry discovers via Black activist Big Ed Mustapha (Albert Popwell) that most of the PRSF are only in it for the money (a plot device used to better effect in the Bruce Willis thriller *Die Hard* 1988). The leaders are Bobby Maxwell (DeVeren Bookwalter), an ex-pimp who gets a sexual thrill out of killing, and Wanda (Samantha Doane), an ex-whore who likes to dress as a nun (the gang receives help from a misguided liberal priest). And they wear ridiculous headbands. When Maxwell kills Harry's partner, Frank DeGeorgio (John Mitchum), a character briefly glimpsed in the previous films, it becomes personal and the PRSF's days are numbered.

Just as superficial (not to say crass) as the terrorism angle, the feminist slant of *The Enforcer* is a lot more successful thanks to the casting of Tyne Daly as Inspector Kate Moore, an inexperienced policewoman promoted to the homicide division as part of the mayor's politically motivated positive discrimination programme. Chosen by Eastwood on the grounds that she looked like a police officer, Daly ensures that Moore comes across as likeable, strongwilled and intelligent. Parts of the film undermine her credibility (she becomes ill during an autopsy, nearly gets blasted by rocket backfire on an army firing range and has trouble with the city's steep streets during a chase sequence), yet the scenes between Callahan and Moore save *The Enforcer* from utter mediocrity. Initially unimpressed ('She wants to play lumberjack, she's going to have to learn to handle her end of the log'), Callahan grows to accept and like Moore both as a dedicated cop and a person, handing out his greatest compliment: 'Whoever draws you as a partner could do a hell of a lot worse.' Moore cheerfully mocks Harry's ultra-macho style ('Cold bold Callahan with his great big .44') and saves his life on two occasions. When Maxwell guns her down during the finale on Alcatraz island, Harry gets really mad. Having lost two partners during the space of one film (definitely misfortune rather than carelessness), Harry makes it clear what he thinks of this evil hippy-nazi ('You fucking fruit'), before blasting him to pieces with a disposable rocket launcher.

Released in late 1976, *The Enforcer* went down extremely well with audiences, grossing nearly $24 million in the United States and Canada alone. With each *Harry* film more profitable than the last, Eastwood could shrug off the largely hostile reviews (appropriately enough, *Harry* no.3 proved to be Malpaso's third biggest hit of the 1970s). Somewhat rashly, the star announced that Inspector Callahan would now be put into retirement, ending the series on something less than a high point (that said, *The Enforcer* is infinitely preferable to the sluggish, sleazy *Sudden Impact*). It would take a seven year gap and two box-office disappointments in a row to change his mind. For Tyne Daly, *The Enforcer* turned out to be a mixed blessing. Never a great fan of America's gun culture, she accepted the role of Kate Moore in order to work with Eastwood and boost her less than thriving film career (appearances in *John and Mary* 1969, *Angel Unchained* 1970, *Play*

● *The Enforcer:* **Inspector Kate Moore (Tyne Daly).**

It As It Lays 1972 and *The Adulteress* 1973 made little impression). Having completed the film, Daly found herself out of work for a year before landing a poorly conceived supporting role in the Charles Bronson Cold War thriller *Telefon* (1977), directed by Don Siegel from a script co-written by Stirling Silliphant (which Siegel hated). *The Enforcer* remains her best known film and (if nothing else) provided useful experience for Daly's role in the hit television police series *Cagney and Lacey* (1982-88), co-starring Loretta Swit (in the 1981 pilot episode, directed by Ted Post), Meg Foster and Sharon Gless (one at a time).

Eastwood might have brought Harry Callahan's career to a temporary halt but he had no intention of abandoning cop movies altogether, following *The Enforcer* with a curious police drama-love on the run hybrid. Written by Michael Butler and Dennis Shryack, *The Gauntlet* was originally intended as a vehicle for singer-actress Barbra Streisand. Ten years on from her Academy Award winning debut in *Funny Girl* (1968), Streisand's career continued in good health, though some felt that her most recent effort, a remake of *A Star is Born* (1976), represented a clear case of ego winning out over talent (not that her fans cared). The film's distributor, Warner, certainly had no complaints. Sensing an opportunity to unite two of their biggest stars in one film (Streisand had already vetoed Steve McQueen), the studio approached Eastwood with *The Gauntlet* screenplay, which chronicles the hate-love relationship of a burned-out cop and a foul-mouthed (though intelligent) prostitute as they go on the run from the law and the Mafia. Enthusiastic about the script, Eastwood didn't want to co-star with Streisand (whether for reasons of star status, creative control, billing, temperament, politics or memories of Shirley MacLaine) and bought the project for Malpaso. To no-one's great surprise he selected Sondra Locke as his leading lady, granting her co-star status with her name above the title. Opting to direct himself, Eastwood put the $5.5 million film into production on location in Arizona and Nevada.

As schematic as *The Enforcer*, *The Gauntlet* works a little better thanks to a fast moving script and Eastwood's well paced direction. The story opens with disillusioned, hard-drinking Phoenix cop Ben Shockley (Eastwood) being assigned an apparently routine escort job by his boss, Blakelock (William Prince). Shockley is to travel to Las Vegas to pick up a trial witness, one Gus Malley (Locke), who will provide testimony for a minor case back home (shades of *Coogan's Bluff*). Mildly surprised to discover that Malley is a woman, he is unimpressed by her hysterical claims that people are out to kill her. Needless to say, Malley is quite right. Picked up by a Mafia henchman to service one of their corrupt police contacts, Malley found herself face to face with Shockley's superior. Blakelock plans to have both Malley and Shockley killed on the trip back to Phoenix, using police and mob firepower.

Once the basic premise is established, *The Gauntlet* becomes essentially one long chase, as Shockley and Malley employ a number of vehicles to fight their way through a series of attacks. Starting off in an ambulance (Shockley's cunning way of smuggling Malley out of her Las Vegas prison cell), they progress to a hire car (blown up before they can get in), a hijacked police car (driven by Bill McKinney), a stolen motorbike (leaving behind an angry biker or three), a train (where they are reunited with the aforementioned bikers) and a hijacked bus (bulletproofed with some handy steel plating). Their travels are rudely interrupted by four action set-pieces (costing $250,000 each to stage). Malley's house is shot to pieces by a battalion of policemen (who think there are dangerous criminals inside). The stolen police car gets as far as the Arizona State line before being shot to hell by Mafia hitmen. The motorbike is pursued by a helicopter over the western-style landscape (in an overextended sequence), a chase brought to an abrupt halt when the helicopter hits some power lines. In the grand(ish) finale, the armour-plated bus drives through Phoenix towards City Hall, as hundreds of policemen empty their guns into it from all sides. As no-one thinks to shoot at the tyres, Shockley and Malley make it to the steps of the building to confront Blakelock (nobody bothers to arrest the supposedly criminal couple). The latter's weakwilled assistant (a bent district attorney) spills the beans, Blakelock goes berserk with a gun, Shockley is wounded and Malley kills Blakelock. Cop and ex-hooker live happily ever after.

Offering a surprisingly unflattering view of the police (faceless automata who turn on one of their own without question when ordered), *The Gauntlet* stumbles badly in its closing stages, where the script seems in a hurry to tie up all the loose ends before anyone notices the gaping holes in the story. The action scenes tend towards the repetitive (Eastwood claimed they were deliberately over-the-top, but neglected to explain why) and the film relies on the Shockley-Malley relationship for most of its interest. Running the familiar gamut of antagonism-wary trust-respect-friendship-love, this partnership is nevertheless quite well done, presumably helped by the stars' offscreen romance. Locke gets to swear at Eastwood ('Big .45 calibre fruit'). Eastwood gets to slap Locke (twice). Locke kicks Eastwood in the groin. A college graduate, with a level of social and political awareness undreamed of by the rather dim Shockley, Malley is spirited, if not terribly likeable. In her most effective scene, Malley describes being sexually assaulted by a gun-toting Blakelock, Eastwood framing Locke in lingering close-up. Here, if nowhere else, Locke earns her co-star billing. Eastwood argues that Malley is the dominant character in the film and Shockley certainly seems a little dull by comparison. Apart from the opening scene where a hungover Shockley drops a whisky bottle from his car (hardly the kind of product placement Jack Daniels would be looking for), the drunk cop subplot never amounts to anything. As Edward Gallafent notes, this Eastwood cop doesn't even get to shoot anyone, often relying on Malley to help him out of trouble. In the odd train sequence, Malley saves Shockley from a serious beating at the hands of three bikers (Samantha Doane, Dan Vadis and Roy Jenson) by exposing her breasts and taunting the gang into sexually assaulting her. A recovered Shockley finally gets around to knocking the bikers off the train, accompanied by jarring comedy music (as this film and *Sudden Impact* demonstrate, it's okay for Eastwood to hit women if they are violent, foulmouthed lesbians). *The Gauntlet*'s most telling moment appears to have been quite unintentional. Questioned by Shockley about her clients, Malley replies that they are mostly 'married men cheating on their wives'. If either Eastwood or Locke saw any irony in this line, they didn't let it show.

Unconcerned by any flaws in *The Gauntlet*'s script, Eastwood remained on good terms with the Butler-Shryack writing team (the film's $17.7 million gross at the American box-office probably helped). The latter soon had another screenplay in development, a supernatural western called *Pale Rider*. Though fully aware of the genre's precarious (near terminal) state, Eastwood bought the finished script a year or so later, putting it to one side while he waited for a more western-friendly climate to hit Hollywood (Butler and Shryack also wrote another lone-cop script with Eastwood in mind. The star turned it down and in 1985 *Code of Silence* became a minor hit for second division action man Chuck Norris.) For the time being, he had a rather different style of film in mind, a knockabout comedy with a country-and-western score. Against the advice of both Warner and his Malpaso staff, Eastwood intended to make *Every Which Way But Loose*, playing opposite Sondra Locke and an Orang Utan.

● *The Gauntlet:* **Gus Malley (Sondra Locke) prepares to avenge both herself and the wounded Ben Shockley.**

Eastwood's reasons for this sudden change in direction appear to have been largely business oriented. He wanted to tap into the highly lucrative family market, going for a 'PG' (Parental Guidance) rated piece of entertainment rather than the usual 'R' fare. With Kyle Eastwood approaching ten years of age, Eastwood may also have been aware that few of his films were suitable viewing for his own, increasingly cine-literate children. The most blatant factor in the production of *Every Which Way* was the phenomenal success of the Burt Reynolds comedy *Smokey and the Bandit* (1977), which had grossed $60 million at the box-office, placing Reynolds above Eastwood in the movie star stakes. Produced for Universal, the film featured Reynolds as a grinning, beer-swilling, bar-room brawling trucker; Sally Field as his love interest and Jackie Gleason as the fat sheriff who chases them both. Looking for a near carbon copy, Eastwood found what he wanted in a script by Jeremy Joe Kronsberg, an country and western composer whose low key film work included the title music for *The Outfit*, a well-crafted revenge drama. Warner argued that the image-change wouldn't go down well with Eastwood's fans (the studio also had its own Reynolds movie, *Hooper*, scheduled for release in 1978). Various members of the Malpaso Company told their employer that Kronsberg's screenplay was awful. No doubt grateful for this candour, Eastwood made the film anyway, ending up with the biggest hit of his career so far.

Loud, crude (and a little overlong), *Every Which Way But Loose* follows the adventures of hard-drinking macho man Philo Beddoe, a trucker with a profitable sideline in bare-knuckle fighting. When not on the road, Beddoe lives with his diminutive, foul-mouthed mother, Ma (actress-writer Ruth Gordon, sixty three years on from her film debut in *Camille* 1915), and his friend Orville (Geoffrey Lewis), a dim-witted mechanic who organises Philo's fights. A more recent addition to this 'family' is Clyde the

Orang Utan (Manis, an eleven year old Las Vegas entertainer), who accompanies Philo just about everywhere, acting as his companion and confidant. When Beddoe falls in love with the elusive, rather mysterious country and western singer Lynn Halsey-Taylor (Sondra Locke), Orville and Clyde join him in his search for her. On the way, they repeatedly tangle with two off-duty policemen and a gang of overage, overweight bikers, The Black Widows (led by John Quade in a ridiculously camp outfit), who can't fight and keep losing their motorbikes. There are regular pauses for punch-ups and songs (several sung by Locke with creditable results), and the final showdown with the bikers is turned into a homage to *The Good The Bad and The Ugly*. Having failed to win Lynn's affections, Beddoe goes up against champion fighter 'Tank' Murdoch (Walter Barnes), deliberately losing the contest when he realizes that the spectators only care about the money to be made from him.

Adequately directed by James Fargo (his last collaboration with Eastwood), *Every Which Way* is amusing at times and Manis is not without a certain charm. Beddoe is at pains to provide a little background for his friend (won in a punch-up with four men), informing Lynn (and the audience) that Orang Utans come from Sumatra and have twelve ribs. The numerous fights, though competently staged, are mainly played for laughs, with the usual strange sound effects (often stripped to the waist, Eastwood demonstrates that a man can still look good at forty eight). The most memorable scene in the film is a bare-knuckle bout in a meat packing plant (the rows of hanging carcasses provide a telling, possibly unintentional comment on the proceedings). Dispensing with the humour of the earlier fights, this contest rapidly becomes more violent, with spilled blood and a cheating opponent. When Philo wins, the bookie refuses to pay up and it takes a little pistol work from Echo (Beverly D'Angelo), Orville's newly acquired girlfriend, to disperse the hostile crowd (a far more believable picture of the illegal fight world). The oddest aspect of the film is the character of Lynn. Manipulative, neurotic and unkind, she is blatantly unworthy of Philo's love. Aside from this failed romance, *Every Which Way* is expertly tailored to the requirements of its target audience. The irate reviewers who dismissed it as moronic drivel missed the point. *Every Which Way But Loose* is a shrewd film playing dumb.

Warner proved equally shrewd in their marketing of Eastwood's good-ole-boy epic. The studio wanted to launch the film as part of their Christmas line-up for 1978, along with the megabudget fantasy *Superman* (1978). Not wishing to place the films in direct competition, Warner opened *Every Which Way* in rural, small town territories (where most of its audience lived), while *Superman* premiered in the major cities. Both films cleaned up at the box-office. On a $5 million investment, *Every Which Way* grossed between $50 and $60 million in the United States, Warner's third most profitable film after *Superman* and *The Exorcist* (1973). Eastwood's commercial instinct had been rewarded beyond anyone's expectations, prompting him to return to the country and western milieu on three more occasions (*Bronco Billy*, *Any Which Way You Can*, *Honkytonk Man*). With over 40 per cent of the box-office gross going to Malpaso, he could take just about any chance he wanted for his next project. Three films on from *Josey Wales*, Eastwood's apparent preference for easy-on-the-brain entertainment did not appear to deter producers with more upmarket projects in development. In 1978, he was approached by Lorimar Pictures, a big-time television production company looking to break into films (having reached the pinnacle of small screen entertainment with *The Waltons*). Lorimar planned to make a film version of Richard Brautigan's novel *The Hawkline Monster* (a bizarre gothic western fantasy), combining the talents of Eastwood

● *Every Which Way But Loose:* **Clyde and Philo.**

and Jack Nicholson (in need of a post-*Cuckoo's Nest* hit after the disappointments of *The Missouri Breaks* (1976), *The Last Tycoon* (1976) and *Goin' South* (1978)). Despite the promising material (not a million miles removed from *The Beguiled* and *High Plains Drifter*) Eastwood showed no great interest, possibly because Lorimar had made a distribution deal with the out-of-favour United Artists (he may also have had reservations about co-starring with the exuberant, scene-stealing Nicholson). Probably a wise decision, as *The Hawkline Monster* never made it into production, though Lorimar did get around to producing a few interesting films (*The Ninth Configuration* 1980, *The Big Red One* 1980). Besides, agent Lennie Hirshan had already been in contact with news of Don Siegel's latest project, *Escape from Alcatraz*. Agreeing to play the lead in a sombre, low key prison drama whose author had never written a screenplay before, Eastwood no doubt felt that one 'quality' movie was quite enough for the time being.

Since *Dirty Harry*, Siegel had directed only four more films: *Charley Varrick* (1973), an engaging 'caper' movie which reunited him with Andrew Robinson, John Vernon and Lalo Schifrin; *The Black Windmill* (1974), a plodding thriller filmed in England with an uninterested Michael Caine; *The Shootist* (1976), an affecting western melodrama starring a cancer-ridden John Wayne as a cancer-ridden ex-gunfighter, and the dire *Telefon*. Dismissing the last of these as a prime example of film-making by committee (with predictably flat results), Siegel found working in Hollywood an increasingly joyless experience. His departure from Universal in 1975 over the studio's poor handling of his films left Siegel just another director-for-hire. Deciding to take a little more control over his career, he bought the screenplay for *Alcatraz* with his own money before looking for any studio backing.

Based on a 1964 book by J. Campbell Bruce, *Escape from Alcatraz* was the work of Richard Tuggle, a former editor for a San Francisco health magazine who'd decided to try his luck in films. An admirer of *Riot in Cell Block II*, Tuggle sent his script to Siegel, who took an instant interest, not least because Campbell Bruce had sent him a copy of the based-on-fact book for comment when it first appeared. An account of a 1962 breakout by three inmates (which may or may not have been successful), the script offered a dominant character in the form of recent arrival Frank Morris, a man whose desire to escape from the island prison (in San Francisco Bay) cannot be broken by the brutalities of its regime. Discussing the script with Hirshan (also Siegel's agent by this time), the director suggested Eastwood as the obvious choice for Morris.

Whatever the tensions between Eastwood and Siegel after *Dirty Harry*, they had not entirely lost contact. Hirshan aside, Siegel's production assistant, Carol Rydall, had worked in the Malpaso office for a number of years (her credits include *Thunderbolt and Lightfoot*). Both had experience of the now disused prison, Siegel while scouting locations for *Riot*, Eastwood during shooting on *The Enforcer* (since closing in 1963, Alcatraz had survived as a rather grim tourist attraction). Returning to the island in 1978, Siegel found it in a fairly dilapidated state, yet still felt that most of the filming could be done in the authentic locations. Once Eastwood and Malpaso were on board, the relationship between star and director-producer appears to have been largely harmonious, though Eastwood made clear his disappointment that Siegel had made a production deal with Paramount (which financed *The Shootist*) instead of Warner (the director still resented the studio's failure to push *Harry* for Academy Award consideration).

After a few rewrites on Tuggle's script (courtesy of Siegel, Rydall and Eastwood), *Escape from Alcatraz* went into production in January 1979. As locations go, the island prison was not the most inviting. Aside from the general decay, the building no longer had any form of heating and the regular daytime tourist visits obliged Siegel to rework his shooting schedule a little (several interior scenes were filmed at Paramount studios). Squatting Indians had left behind a large amount of graffiti which the Department of Parks and Recreation Commission now regarded as a historical document. Forbidden to clean the anachronistic graffiti off the building, the production team were obliged to paint over it and then remove the redecoration once shooting was completed. The most bizarre stipulation handed out by the DPRC involved the use of simulated rainfall during the filming of the opening sequence. The obvious method for effects man Chuck Gaspar was to draw water from the bay for redistribution via hose pipes. The DPRC vetoed this idea on the grounds that the salt content of the sea water would further erode the prison buildings, forcing Siegel to import a supply of fresh water from the mainland. While the director dealt with these logistical problems, his star found himself faced with difficulties of a more domestic kind. During the filming, Eastwood received the news that Maggie wanted a formal separation. Despite his well established (and well known) relationship with Locke, this request apparently came as a surprise to Eastwood, leaving one to wonder just how much he'd ever considered his wife's feelings regarding his various liaisons. It has been suggested that the numerous tabloid articles on the Eastwood-Locke affair played as big a role in Maggie's decision as the affair itself. Private grief was one thing, public humiliation quite another. Added to this was the fact that Eastwood and Locke looked like becoming a permanent couple, a development which never seemed likely in the Roxanne Tunis affair. While the Eastwoods would not divorce until 1984, their twenty five year old marriage seemed effectively over. All things considered, Eastwood was probably more than happy to be stuck on Alcatraz for the time being.

Filmed by Siegel in a detached, dispassionate style (enhanced by Bruce Surtees' cold photography), *Escape from Alcatraz* is a near documentary recreation of the historical events, with little in the way of drama or character development. Beginning with Morris' transfer to Alcatraz from Atlanta State Prison (on-screen text informs us that this is 'January 18 1960 San Francisco'), the story moves at a leisurely pace, observing the prison regime in great detail. The one concession to melodrama in this opening sequence is a guard's sardonic greeting of 'Welcome to Alcatraz', followed by a thunderclap. The first half of the film sees Morris adjusting to the new surroundings (though one prison must look much like another). His enemies include the coldly vindictive Warden (Patrick McGoohan, no longer *The Prisoner*), who boasts a fine collection of nail clippers, and the rapacious inmate Wolf (Bruce M. Fischer), whose thwarted lust for Morris quickly turns to hatred. Prominent among the 'good' convicts are Litmus (Frank Ronzio), with his pasta-eating pet mouse; Doc (Roberts Blossom), a gifted painter, and English (Paul Benjamin), elder statesman of the segregated black convicts (who include Danny Glover and *Cagney and Lacey* co-star Carl Lumbly). In one of the film's many indictments of prejudiced 1960s America, English reveals that he is serving two life sentences for killing two white men who attacked him with knives in an Alabama bar. Little is revealed about Morris, other than a brief allusion to his broken family background, his intelligence and his convictions for burglary, armed robbery and grand larceny. Most of the time he merely observes other people's miseries. Saddest of these is the fate of Doc, whose painting privileges are withdrawn after the Warden discovers an unflattering portrait of himself. Doc responds to this injustice by hacking off the fingers of his right hand (the film's one moment of graphic violence). Morris keeps a self-portrait of Doc in his cell to remind him of the inner sense of freedom the man stood for (and its cost).

The escape plot doesn't really get into gear until the arrival of two convict brothers encountered by Morris during his stay at Atlanta, Clarence Anglin (Jack Thibeau) and John Anglin (Fred Ward). With a fourth inmate, Charley Butts (Larry Hankin), they

● *Escape from Alcatraz:* **Frank Morris converses with senior convict English (Paul Benjamin).**

devise an elaborate escape plan involving the prison's ventilation system. Siegel dwells on the various elements of the scheme at length, eschewing suspense in favour of simple observation (though several scenes are in semi-darkness). Three of them get away in a raft made from old raincoats (working without doubles, Eastwood and his co-stars had problems with the currents around the island), but are later presumed to have drowned (no bodies were ever found after the historical escape).

Well made and acted (some may dislike McGoohan's mannered style), *Escape from Alcatraz* is more worthy than entertaining, a consistently interesting film that doesn't appear to seek audience involvement. As with the actual escape, there is no satisfying ending to the story, merely a brief written epilogue informing us that Alcatraz closed a year later. Bearing this in mind, Eastwood and Siegel must have been reasonably content with the box-office returns (around $10 million), which gave them a small profit. There doesn't seem to have been any doubt that their reunion would be anything more than a one-off, a low key coda to a highly successful relationship. After two more films, the ill-planned *Rough Cut* (1980) and the ill-fated *Jinxed* (1983), Siegel retired from the business. Waving goodbye to perhaps his greatest mentor, Eastwood also had to deal with the effective end of his relationship with Maggie. Unwilling to wait for the divorce, Eastwood decided to establish a subsidiary of the Malpaso Company, Robert Daley Productions, thereby denying his ex-wife-to-be any share in the profits of films made after the separation (a shrewd move as it turned out). The first of these productions would be *Bronco Billy*, a good natured comedy-drama promoting the virtues of friendship and love over mere money.

10

Never meanin' no harm

You should never kill a man unless it's absolutely necessary.
'Bronco' Billy McCoy, *Bronco Billy*

There's one too many women in your life.
Lynn Halsey-Taylor, *Any Which Way You Can*

A likeable, if wildly uneven tale of a man obsessively pursuing his dream of the Old West in a hostile modern world, *Bronco Billy* came close to passing Eastwood by. Dennis Hackin's script arrived unsolicited at the Malpaso office, which operated a policy of returning non-commissioned material unread. Obviously feeling a little indulgent, Eastwood decided to give it a look and found himself drawn to the theme of an old-fashioned idealist winning out over various corrupt, unfeeling and materialist opponents (Eastwood compares the film to the work of director Frank Capra, a near neighbour and acquaintance during shooting on *High Plains Drifter*, whose sentimental man-of-the-people-beats-the-system movies include *Mr Deeds Goes to Town* 1936 and *Mr Smith Goes to Washington* 1939.) *Bronco Billy* also offered a good opportunity for another country and western score (courtesy of the *Every Which Way* team of Snuff Garrett and Steve Dorff) and a co-starring role for Sondra Locke. Acquiring the screenplay, Eastwood agreed to Hackin's condition that the film be made under the banner of the latter's own company, Second Street Films, with Hackin and partner Neal Dobrofsky serving as *Bronco Billy*'s producers. Back in the director's chair after a two film gap, Eastwood took his cast and crew on location to Boise, Idaho, where *Bronco Billy* was filmed in six weeks for just over $4 million (well within the original $5 million budget).

Opening with a rather cloying theme song ('Everybody loves cowboys and clowns'), *Bronco Billy* follows the misadventures of William McCoy (Eastwood), a shoe salesman turned cowboy star. 'Bronco' Billy runs a tatty, sparsely attended Wild West show, which offers such traditional 'delights' as the Indian snake dance ('which no white man has ever seen'), trick roping, knife throwing, fancy horse riding and trick shooting (mostly of plates). Specializing in riding, shooting and knifing, Billy's fellow artistes include 'Doc' Lynch (Scatman Crothers), Lefty LeBow (Bill McKinney) and Chief Big Eagle (Dan Vadis), all of whom he met in jail while serving a seven year sentence for the attempted murder of his wife (she slept with his best friend). A more recent addition to the troupe is Leonard James (Sam Bottoms), revealed as a Vietnam deserter after being arrested during a bar-room brawl. Having apparently turned his back on James (a man should never run away from his duties), Billy covertly attempts to bribe the local sheriff (standard smartass-fatboy model), allowing the latter to humiliate him in order to secure his friend's release. As with *The Outlaw Josey Wales*, the theme of community/surrogate family is dominant throughout *Bronco Billy*, the misfit members of the Wild West show staying loyal both to the business and eachother (even conspiring to rob an obstinately unintimidated express train when the cash runs out). Kind to both orphans and lunatics (who get free shows), Billy finds friends among society's other rejects. When the show's tent burns down, he pays a visit to the asylum, where the inmates stitch him a new one made entirely from American flags (there may or may not be a 'state of the nation' message here).

This main storyline is fleshed out with a secondary plot involving Antoinette Lily (Locke), a cold, arrogant heiress who amply demonstrates that money doesn't make up for an unhappy, loveless childhood. Antoinette must marry before reaching the age of thirty in order to retain her inheritance, and settles for John Arlington (Geoffrey Lewis), whom she doesn't even like. Unhappy with his frigid bride, Arlington runs off, leaving Antoinette without money or transport. Reluctantly joining up with Billy and friends, she eventually comes to love this 'family' (there is a tedious, largely unresolved subplot involving the attempts of Antoinette's stepmother to have the missing heiress declared legally dead, thereby gaining the inheritance for herself). Stuck with an under-written role (Antoinette's change of heart over the initially despised Billy is too abrupt), Locke delivers a mediocre performance, overplaying her lines in a manner that suggests little aptitude for comedy. It doesn't help that this particular comedy features an ill-judged scene where two rednecks attempt to rape Antoinette (Billy sorts them out). When she and Billy finally get together, it soon becomes clear that all this woman needed was a good seeing to, a rather simplistic solution to thirty years of emotional deprivation and neglect. Berating Antoinette for her lack of passion, Billy delivers per-haps the least fortunate line of Eastwood's career: 'There must be thirteen year olds who're more woman than you are.' Aside from the overstated theme of being what you want to be ('You only live once. Gotta give it your best shot'), *Bronco Billy* can also be read as an unintended commentary on Eastwood's vision of his relationship with Locke: a strong, independent woman who nevertheless bends unconditionally to his will, becoming warmer and more feminine in the process (in fact, the offscreen Locke did not always put up with Eastwood's sexual wanderings, resulting in a brief separation between the couple in 1980).

Directed by Eastwood in a fairly straightforward style (the camera gets a little rest-less at times), *Bronco Billy* also suffers from a surprisingly slipshod production. Burdened by muddy colours, dim lighting and harsh sound recording, the film looks and sounds cheap, which cannot have been the star's intention. Always careful with his budgets, Eastwood's contention that 'the only reasonable price is the lowest possible cost consistent with telling your story well' may be laudable in theory, yet here the speedy filming and underspent budget are all too evident. While a good deal more substantial than Eastwood's other comedies, *Bronco Billy* has a very uncertain feel to it, throwing in elements of screwball comedy (forty years too late), black comedy (Billy's account of shooting his wife), drama, satire, social comment, good ole boy punch-up and straight action man heroics (pistol toting Billy foils a bank robbery in full cowboy gear). The end of the film, where the Wild West show becomes a big crowd puller, is pure wish-fulfillment, expressing an optimism hardly warranted by earlier events in the film. While Eastwood may have seen elements of himself in the stubborn, unfailingly self-confident Billy, his handling of the film lacks the sureness and lightness of touch required by the script. That said, the New York Museum of Modern Art thought highly enough of *Bronco Billy* to include it as the closing film in their 1980 Clint Eastwood retrospective, another tentative sign that the star might yet achieve recognition as a serious film-maker in his native country (following on from the Academy Award nominations for *Thunderbolt* and *Josey Wales*). Sadly, the next few years would bring precious few Eastwood movies worth including in any future tributes.

As with *Escape from Alcatraz*, *Bronco Billy* enjoyed solid rather than runaway box-office success, pleasing critics more than filmgoers. If Eastwood wanted bigger returns, he would have to resurrect either Harry Callahan or Philo Beddoe. Still feeling that the former had reached the end of his natural lifespan, he brought back the bare-knuckle fighter for *Any Which Way You Can*, a film which made its predecessor look a model of sophistication and satirical wit. Evidently confident that the project could virtually make itself, Eastwood appointed Wayne Van Horn as its director. Apart from his numerous tours of duty as Malpaso's stunt arranger, Van Horn had served as second unit director on *Magnum Force*, which was all the experience he really needed for this kind of film. He directs in an unsubtle, cartoonish style, which plods along between the numerous punch-up set-pieces. Recruiting most of the *Every Which Way* cast, Eastwood found himself in need of a replacement for Manis, now apparently too old and fat to recreate the role of Clyde. His unbilled successor does an adequate job, despite the undignified antics called for in the script. (Years later, rumours surfaced that both orang utans used for *Every/Any* had been ill-treated by their trainers in order to make them perform, something of an embarrassment for professed animal lover Eastwood.)

Lacking the bright moments of *Every Which Way*, the sequel rehashes bits of the original with negligible results. Philo is still punching away, though he now wants to retire. The Black Widows are still after him ('Whose hide you gonna nail to the gates of hell ?'), as incompetent as ever. Lynn Halsey-Taylor is now in love with Philo, who soon forgives her ill-treatment of him in *Every*. The major running joke is Clyde's tendency to defecate in police squad cars. Debut writer Stanford Sherman's one innovation is a Mafia subplot, with Philo obliged to take on their champion after Lynn is kidnapped. Luckily, the mob's king puncher, Jack Wilson (William Smith, better remembered as Arnold

● *Bronco Billy:* **Billy McCoy puts Antoinette Lily (Sondra Locke) in her place.**

Schwarzenegger's dad in *Conan the Barbarian*), is an honourable man who helps Philo rescue Lynn. The two men decide to fight anyway, Philo winning after an epic slugfest despite a broken right arm. If this isn't enough for his fans, Eastwood also duets with Ray Charles for the title song, 'Beers to You', his surprisingly flat rendition making one yearn for *Paint Your Wagon*. Opening during the 1980 Christmas season, *Any Which Way You Can* made nearly $50 million in American cinemas. Having achieved an exceptionally good return from this particular formula (one man and his orang utan), Eastwood wisely chose not to continue with the series (which inspired the short-lived rip-off television show *B.J. and the Bear*, 'Bear' being a chimpanzee). *Every Which Way* writer Jeremy Joe Kronsberg attempted to cash in the sequel's success, directing the abysmal comedy *Going Ape !* (1981), co-starring Jessica Walter and not one but three orang utans.

With *Any Which Way* lingering in the cinemas into early 1981, Eastwood evidently felt no pressing need to deliver another Malpaso production for release that year. When he did get around to selecting a new project, his choice resulted in just about the very worst film of Eastwood's career (*Sudden Impact* takes the dishonours for dumbest and most offensive), though for reasons which can't have been entirely evident prior to shooting. *Firefox* is based on a run-of-the-mill spy thriller by British writer Craig Thomas. Eastwood stars as ex-Airforce Major Mitchell Gant, a traumatised Vietnam veteran (complete with flashbacks) reluctantly brought out of retirement to steal the latest Soviet weapon, Firefox. A new design of supersonic fighter, the plane can't be detected by radar, has a speed in excess of mach 6 and works by thought control. As Gant is of American-Russian parentage, this last factor presents no problems. Briefed by NATO supremo Kenneth Aubrey (an overacting Freddie Jones, one of several British actors recruited for thankless roles), Gant heads off to the Evil Empire (as then was) to liaise with a group of largely Jewish political dissidents. Aided by the latter, several of whom have been forced to work on the Firefox project, Gant successfully steals the plane and heads for home.

Viewed a decade on, the most plausible explanation for *Firefox* lies with the final half hour, where Gant pilots the fighter out of hostile Soviet territory to Alaska and safety. Post *Star Wars* (1977), Eastwood could not help but be aware of the popularity of large-scale special effects driven fantasies. This last sequence offered plenty of scope for spectacular effects work, combining eighties high tech with the sixties-style Cold War espionage of the rest of the film. It might be argued that this unorthodox hybrid had no guaranteed audience appeal, yet Eastwood felt confident enough to throw Malpaso's usual budgetary caution to the wind, investing $18 million in the project. *Firefox* would be his first international production since *The Eiger Sanction*, with shooting in Finland, Greenland and Austria. When it came to staging the all-important flying sequences (including a dogfight with a second Firefox), Eastwood spared no expense, hiring *Star Wars* veteran John Dykstra to work his special effects magic. The unconvincing, not to say boring results are often cited as the film's biggest failure, though in fact they are merely the muddy icing on a supremely unappetising cake.

Tedious, humourless and depressing to look at, *Firefox* is a dreary failure from the word go, with no tension (always a plus for a thriller), no excitement and a style of violence that manages to be both excessive and unconvincing. The depiction of Soviet life must have been dated even at the time and the dialogue ranges from the dull to the risible ('Let's see what this baby can do'.) The subplot involving Jewish political prisoners fails to add any weight to the proceedings, appearing superficial (not to say offensive) right down to the moment Gant's new friends sacrifice their lives to aid his escape.

When Gant comes out with: 'What is it with you Jews? Don't you ever get tired of fighting City Hall?', it becomes all too clear how far Eastwood is out of his depth with the material.

The received wisdom regarding the failed special effects bonanza is that John Dykstra's models simply didn't work when superimposed against blue-white backdrops (snow, sky, sea) instead of the usual blackness of space. There is some truth to this, though *The Empire Strikes Back* (1980) features a convincingly staged part-aerial battle in near identical surroundings. A bigger problem for *Firefox* lay with the design of the models and the type of film they were appearing in. *Star Wars* and its sequels/rip-offs are science-fiction fantasies set on alien worlds. While *Firefox* might be regarded as a fringe fantasy (especially the thought control device), it takes place in recognizably earthbound surroundings, supposedly during the present day. This creates a different set of expectations on the part of the audience, prominent among them far less inclination to suspend disbelief. The Firefox fighters might not exist in reality, but their design is based on genuine aircraft. Thus any flaws in scenes with these models will be all the more glaring (the effects work in *Star Wars* is not perfect by any means). The crass echoes of *Star Wars* do not help. Several moments during Gant's flight through the icy wastes bear more than a passing resemblance to Luke Skywalker's triumphant attack on the Death Star (such as a chase through an icy canyon). Just as Jedi knight Obi Wan Kenobi's disembodied voice guided Luke in his moment of glory, so Gant's mentor, Aubrey, is heard on the soundtrack reminding the Major how to fly the plane. Exactly what Eastwood thought this crass homage would achieve is open to speculation. In a better film, it might raise half a smile. Two hours into *Firefox*, most audiences will be too bored to even notice (the film has the same running time as *The Outlaw Josey Wales*, yet feels about a week longer).

With director-star Eastwood also assuming the role of official producer for the first time (hardly the most promising start), the production of *Firefox* appears to have been largely harmonious. Eastwood got on well with his mostly British cast, earning the praise of Freddie Jones and Nigel Hawthorne (playing one of the Jewish scientists working on the Firefox project). Interviewed shortly after a television screening of the film, Hawthorne placed the blame for its failure squarely on the editors and the special effects team, absolving Eastwood of any responsibility. A charitable gesture towards his former employer, if a little unfair on a veteran member of the Malpaso production crew. While Ferris Webster might have been in the editor's chair, the last word on the shape of the film lay with Eastwood and no-one else. Webster could certainly not be blamed for the dull footage he had to work with. As a Malpaso production entirely under the control of the company's star asset and major stockholder, the embarrassment of *Firefox* belongs to Clint Eastwood alone.

Premiered in June 1982, *Firefox* received a much deserved trashing from the critics, most of whom were too numbed by its extraordinary dullness to bother overmuch with the unpleasant violence and crude right-wing politics. With Eastwood favourite Ronald Reagan in the White House, the film should have been a natural to cash in on God-fearing America's less than tolerant attitude towards the Soviet Union. It is a measure of *Firefox*'s poor quality that it proved a box-office disappointment in the US, generating only a negligible profit (though the French liked it). This unexpected setback must have produced a little unease in the Malpaso office, especially as Eastwood planned to make his next film a commercially doubtful adaptation of Clancy Carlile's Depression-era novel *Honkytonk Man*. Apparently unconcerned, Eastwood proceeded to put the latter into pre-production, commissioning Carlile to adapt his book into a screenplay. While

Warner were happy enough for Eastwood to cast himself as tubercular singer-songwriter Red Stovall, the studio worried about the downbeat ending (Stovall succumbs to the disease just as his new record is released) and suggested a more cheerful alternative. Showing the utmost respect for his source material, Eastwood refused. Serving as star-director-producer once again, he filmed *Honkytonk Man* on location in California, Nevada, and Nashville, Tennessee (country-and-western capital of the world), completing production in five weeks. Among the key Malpaso personnel working on the film was art director Edward Carfagno, an industry veteran with forty years worth of impressive credits (*Quo Vadis*, *The Bad and the Beautiful*, *Ben Hur*, *The Cincinnati Kid*) plus three Academy Awards. Following his Malpaso debut on *Honkytonk*, Carfagno would work on eight Eastwood films in a row, becoming the star's longest serving production designer.

Eastwood's attraction to Carlile's original book appears to have been threefold. His childhood years had given him firsthand experience of the Depression and the importance of both music and dreams in the lives of impoverished rural communities (the film seems more nostalgic than bitter). He could also identify with Stovall's restless, on-the-move lifestyle, viewed largely through the eyes of the singer's young nephew, Whit. Furthermore, the latter role required an actor in his early teens. Having enjoyed a taste of the film world with *The Outlaw Josey Wales* and *Bronco Billy* (where he and Alison Eastwood appear as orphans), Kyle Eastwood had been asking his father for a more substantial part in a Malpaso production. Kyle had no real acting experience or training and casting his son would lay Eastwood open to charges of blatant nepotism. His decision to give Kyle the role of Whit enabled Eastwood to placate two of his nearest and dearest at once. There was no suitable role in the film for Sondra Locke (the brief part of Whit's mother went to Verna Bloom), who instead served as Kyle's acting coach.

In the time-honoured tradition of the road movie, *Honkytonk Man* follows the episodic adventures of Red and Whit as they travel across the country to Nashville, where Red hopes to perform his new, as yet unfinished song at the Grand Ole Opry. When Red appears dead drunk at his sister's farm during a dust storm, her impressionable son is immediately entranced by his uncle's car, cowboy hat and guitar. Whit is permitted to accompany Red on the Nashville trip on the grounds that his uncle needs to be kept out of trouble. Inevitably, the film develops into a rites of passage tale for Whit, who gets to drive the car (Red isn't safe on the road), drink whisky (during Prohibition), arrange a jailbreak for his uncle, fight a bull matador style, write some lyrics for Red's song and have sex (for $2). An incompetent thief, Red makes some effort at paying his way singing in various bars (Eastwood's light but tuneful voice is well used in this film). Arriving in Nashville, Red suffers a violent coughing fit during his audition, losing the chance to perform during a live radio broadcast (for reasons of health rather than talent). Offered a meagre recording deal ($20 flat fee per record), he manages to get his song, 'Honkytonk Man', on disc before expiring amid much bloody coughing and shivering (a very drawn-out deathbed scene). Wearing his uncle's hat, Whit plays the guitar at Red's graveside. The dream lives on.

Obviously an important personal project for Eastwood, *Honkytonk Man* is both funny and touching at times, with a convincing sense of period. On the downside, the film is slow, overlong, self-indulgent and sentimental (not to say depressing). Despite dying his hair red, Eastwood has a few problems with his supposedly alcoholic, tuberculosis-ridden character, appearing neither drunk nor ill for much of the film. Several of Red's misadventures verge on out-and-out slapstick (such as unwittingly bathing in a bull's drinking trough) and his treatment of Whit's tentative love interest, the tone deaf

● *Honkytonk Man:* **Red Stovall and Whit (Kyle Eastwood) strike a confident pose at the Grand Ole Opry. Stovall's subsequent performance is slightly less assured.**

would-be singer Marlene (Alexa Kenin), seems unnecessarily callous. Concentrating mainly on the central father-son relationship, Carlile's script betrays signs of uncertainty over the character of Whit's Grandfather (John MacIntire), who accompanies Red and Whit on the trip to Tennessee (he wants to die in his birthplace) without being given anything to do. In his co-starring debut (sharing top billing with his father) Kyle Eastwood is perfectly adequate but lacks any real trace of Eastwood senior's charisma. That said, his dad gets all the best lines, notably the unusual boast: 'I got money ten miles up a bull's ass.'

With *Honkytonk Man* scheduled for release in late 1982, Eastwood realized that he needed a surefire commercial property for his next film. Even if *Honkytonk* scored with the critics, it stood little chance of pulling in much of an audience. The lure of Inspector Harry Callahan had finally become too strong and Eastwood hired writer Joseph C. Stinson to incorporate the character into an existing script, a sleazy rape-revenge tale. By the time *Honkytonk Man* appeared to decidedly mixed reviews and unprofitable box-office, *Sudden Impact* was well into preproduction, rendering the previous film's commercial failure largely unimportant (Eastwood still regards *Honkytonk Man* as one of his finest achievements.) Kyle Eastwood's big movie break didn't make much impression outside his family circle. He hoped to consolidate his budding film career with the lead role in *The Karate Kid* (1984), a highly lucrative Columbia production which spawned two sequels. Keen to help his boy along, Eastwood offered to take a leave of absence from Warner and serve as the film's director. Furthermore, he would also star in a second Columbia film, leaving the choice of project entirely up to the studio executives. Following Eastwood's huge success with *Sudden Impact*, it says something about Columbia's opinion of Eastwood Jr that they felt able to turn his old man down. The studio cast Ralph Macchio as their junior league martial artist, with *Rocky* veteran John G. Avildsen directing. Just as Clint Eastwood's career was receiving a welcome shot in the arm, Kyle Eastwood found himself prematurely retired, obliged to remain a one-off footnote in his father's filmography.

11

Spill your Guts

Listen punk. To me you're nothing but dogshit.
Inspector Harry Callahan, *Sudden Impact*

Early on in *Sudden Impact*, a female judge reprimands Inspector Callahan for yet another violation of a suspect's rights. As the bad guy gets off the hook on a legal technicality (an illegal search), she remarks: 'This is an old story', a comment applicable to the whole wretched film. 'Dirty' Harry is back on the streets of San Francisco, leaner and meaner than ever. His superiors might cringe and mock ('You're a dinosaur, Callahan'), but the audience knows better. Armed with a new weapon, a .44 Magnum Automag, and a new catchphrase ('Go ahead. Make my day') Callahan is the only man who knows how to combat the violent criminal scum lurking on every street corner. Making no distinction between rich and poor scum, he takes on supposedly untouchable Mafia bosses (taunting one into cardiac arrest) and run-of-the-mill street hoods. In the film's one good scene, a diner waitress (Mara Corday) alerts Callahan to the presence of armed robbers by pouring the entire contents of a sugar dispenser into the savoury-toothed policeman's coffee (he realizes that the lady's mind is not on her work). The ensuing shootout may be a little dumb (why do the bad guys always wait for Harry to pull out his weapon and make his speech ?), but things get a lot dumber later on when Callahan pursues another robber in a retirement home bus filled with applauding senior citizens (a homage to the school bus sequence in *Dirty Harry* ?) After a brush with mob hitmen, he is put on temporary assignment to the nearby coastal resort of San Paulo, where the local police are baffled by a series of killings where the victim is shot first in the groin and then in the head. Someone evidently means business.

The finger on this particular trigger belongs to sensitive artist Jennifer Spencer (Sondra Locke), seen in lethal action at the beginning of the film (plenty of murder here but not much mystery). Ten years earlier, Jennifer and her sister were brutally gang-raped at the local funfair by a group of extraordinarily nasty scum, including a foulmouthed lesbian. Her sister reduced to a persistent vegetative state, Jennifer struggled on with her life until recently, when she spotted one of the rapists in the street, triggering her long suppressed rage with murderous results. The shooting spree continues, while Callahan pursues a rather cack-handed investigation. Inevitably, he becomes involved with Jennifer, not finding anything in the least strange about her pronouncements on the breakdown of law and order: 'This is the age of lapsed responsibilities and defeated justice' (perhaps not typical artist talk). Recognizing a kindred spirit, Callahan neglects to inform the local police when he finally links his lover to the killings, deciding to sort things out his own way. In the ludicrous funfair finale, Harry receives a severe beating at the hands of the surviving rapists, leaving Jennifer at their mercy. After she has been kicked around a bit (a prolonged sequence tinged with leering sadism), Eastwood/Callahan does his usual resurrection act, reappearing as a backlit avenger. The psycho leader of the gang gets shot four times, falls off a bridge, and plunges through a glass roof, ending up impaled on the horn of a carousel unicorn (Eastwood's homage to *Strangers on a Train* ?) With the San Paulo police convinced that the now deceased ringleader carried out all the killings (gullible or what), Callahan and Jennifer are free to stroll off together, while the credits roll to the strains of Roberta Flack's forgettable ballad 'This Side of Forever'.

Sudden Impact deserves all the flack aimed (a little unfairly) at *Dirty Harry*, and then a lot more besides. A crude, reactionary fantasy with none of the original film's style or sense of ambivalence, this third sequel marks the nadir of Eastwood's career. All the way through he takes the easiest options, lazily pandering to viewer expectations. We are given simple-minded lectures on justice; uptight, humourless liberals; designer violence; tame nudity; subhuman villains; lavatorial comedy (a pissing, farting bulldog); gory retribution and a token attempt at appeasing ethnic audiences (Harry's best friend is a black policeman). Aside from some reasonable suspense and a few effective close-ups of Locke's staring eyes, Eastwood's direction is competent at best, with a plodding pace and a dull, murky visual style (all too common in the star's later work). Joseph Stinson's script is truly abysmal: cliched, repetitive, contrived, sluggish and crass, with characters who don't even register as stereotypes. The evil lesbian stands as one of the worst pieces of writing, acting and directing in film history. In what should have been a gift of a role, Locke is no more than adequate, though she is hardly outplayed by a sleepwalking Eastwood. A lengthy flashback to the rape (an uncomfortably voyeuristic scene) gives Jennifer all the motivation/justification she needs for her actions. Unlike *Magnum Force*, there is never any serious doubt as to whether or not Callahan will side with this bold vigilante, who is after all merely claiming the justice denied her by the law. Without the respectability provided by Eastwood, *Sudden Impact* would barely qualify as straight-to-video fodder. As it is, the film comes uncomfortably close to being straight sado-exploitation, trash unworthy of its creator. For Locke, *Sudden Impact* would prove the end of her onscreen relationship with Eastwood. While they would stay together as a real-life couple until 1989, Eastwood appeared to be winding down his professional contact with the actress from here on. He may have become a little uncomfortable with the dual nature of their relationship, or simply run out of scripts that offered suitable parts for Locke. Whatever the case, after co-starring in six films together, the Eastwood-Locke team dissolved.

Released during the 1983 Christmas season, *Sudden Impact* proved an astonishing hit with American audiences, evidently not sold on the idea of goodwill to all men. Despite hostile reviews (many of which dubbed Locke's character 'Dirty Harriet'), the film grossed around $150 million at the box-office, with domestic revenue accounting for at least half the total. Harry Callahan's no-nonsense brand of policework struck a chord with many of Eastwood's fellow-countrymen, who a few years later would find another taciturn hero in the form of Sylvester Stallone's John Rambo, a traumatized Vietnam veteran turned American Avenger (in *Rambo: First Blood Part II* 1985). The simplistic world-views offered by these films and their imitators (with equally simplistic solutions) were perhaps not a million miles away from the public utterances of minor film star turned superpower president Ronald Reagan, no stranger to doing what a man has to do in westerns such as *Santa Fe Trail* (1940) and *Cattle Queen of Montana* (1954). While Eastwood shared many of Reagan's political beliefs, he at least managed to make a clear distinction between movies and the real world.

Back on top as America's number one film star (a position held up to 1982 by Burt Reynolds), Eastwood felt able to take a bit of a risk with his next production. *Tightrope* reunited him with *Alcatraz* writer Richard Tuggle, who had made little subsequent progress in the film business, apart from a brief stint working on the script of Don

● *Tightrope:* **Wes Block enjoys an off-duty moment with daughter Amanda (Alison Eastwood).**

Siegel's unsuccessful comedy-caper movie *Rough Cut* (his rewrite wasn't used). The intriguing tale of a detective tracking a serial killer who apparently shares his tastes in unusual sexual practices (chiefly light bondage), the screenplay definitely offered a change from Inspector Harry Callahan. A divorced father of two (a situation similar to Eastwood's), worn-out cop Wes Block finds his personal and professional worlds increasingly difficult to reconcile. Warm and caring towards his daughters (the oldest to be played by Alison Eastwood), he confines his lovelife to sordid, joyless encounters with prostitutes. As with Michael Cimino a decade earlier, Tuggle would not sell his project unless he also got to direct the film, a condition Eastwood found acceptable despite Tuggle's lack of experience. Originally set in San Francisco, *Tightrope* was rapidly relocated to New Orleans, partly to avoid confusion with the *Dirty Harry* series, partly because the city's reputation for decadence matched the atmosphere of the film. For the co-starring role of Beryl Thibodeaux, a rape counsellor who helps Block to overcome his resentment and fear of women (he likes to use handcuffs during sex), Eastwood chose French-Canadian actress Genevieve Bujold. Like most of the star's leading ladies, Bujold had no real box-office name, despite tentative bids for stardom in the late 1960s and 1970s (*Anne of the Thousand Days* 1969, *Earthquake* 1974, *Coma* 1978). Eastwood claims to operate a policy of hiring gifted actresses he feels are neglected by other mainstream film-makers. This is fair enough, though it might be added that employing non-stars also reduces the budget and prevents any major ego clashes.

Up until its disappointing finale, *Tightrope* is an above average thriller which carefully balances its central find-the-killer storyline with well drawn domestic asides. Unable to get over the trauma of his divorce, Wes Block seeks solace with paid women who mean nothing to him, the bondage element symbolizing his supposed control over them (for a few hours at least). When these same women are tortured, raped and murdered by a masked assailant (often only a short time after their liaisons with Block), he is forced to confront his own sexual needs and the unsavoury thought that the killer might be merely a more extreme version of himself. (In a rather predictable dream sequence, Block becomes a hooded killer attacking new girlfriend Beryl.) Coping alone with the hazards of growing children ('What's a hard on, daddy ?'), Block does a praiseworthy job, anxious to shield his daughters from the darker, corrupting sides of life he must confront every day. When the killer strikes at Block's house, leaving an unharmed Amanda Block (Alison Eastwood) gagged and handcuffed on her father's bed (incestuous undertones ?), Block can no longer keep his two worlds apart, accepting that his problems with one will always affect the other. As Beryl teaches him how to love again (without fear of being hurt or abandoned), Block gets into supercop mode, more than a little mad at the killer: 'I'm gonna break your motherfuckin' ass.'

Inventively written and directed by Tuggle, who makes good use of his shadowy, sleazy New Orleans locations (with much red lighting, eerie sound and a spooky Ronald Reagan carnival mask), *Tightrope* works as a properly developed narrative, rather than a series of flashy set-pieces (unlike most of the *Harry* sequels). The opening scene at a prostitute's birthday party establishes a sense of community and friendship among the New Orleans branch of the oldest profession, which is then assailed by the stalking killer (very different from the 'pimp murders bitch' sequence of *Magnum Force*). Where the film falls down is in its halfhearted suggestion that cop and killer are two sides of the same personality. A psychiatrist talks to Block about the 'tightrope' we all tread over our dark side, the gulf between control and expression, and Tuggle often puts Eastwood's face in half shadow, suggesting a split identity, yet the idea amounts to nothing. Even if Eastwood's star image didn't prevent the viewer from taking the notion too seriously, the film eventually cops out of it (so to speak) very explicitly. The killer is revealed as an ex-policeman arrested by Block for rape ten years earlier. Thus the darker undercurrents explored in the previous hour and a half are dropped in favour of a straight revenge motive. In the climactic chase sequence (set at night during a thunderstorm), Block chases the man through a graveyard and onto a railway track. As the men struggle, a train approaches. Getting off the track just in time, Block is left clutching the splattered killer's severed arm, a throwaway sick joke more at home in a schlock horror film. Doubtless cured of his hangups, Block strolls away arm in arm with Beryl.

Premiered in September 1984, *Tightrope* earned some surprisingly positive reviews, with several critics acclaiming the film as a turning point in Eastwood's career. There was even vague talk of Academy Award nominations, rumours which the star sensibly played down. This level of elation is a little puzzling, though *Tightrope* certainly boasts good performances (Alison Eastwood included) and the 'daring' semi-admission from Block that he may or may not have dabbled in gay sex. Perhaps inevitably, the film did more for Eastwood than Tuggle, whose largely impressive work on *Tightrope* failed to launch him into a high profile career (later films such as *Out of Bounds* 1986 sank without trace). Doubtless worn out by his exploration of a tortured man's sick soul (which the film seems to blame on Block's ex-wife: 'she didn't want tenderness'), Eastwood felt ready for something a little more easygoing. Offered a $5 million paycheck and the chance to work with friend/rival Burt Reynolds, he signed on for a co-starring role in *City Heat*, a lightweight comedy-thriller which paid homage to the gangster films of the 1930s.

Six years younger than Eastwood, Reynolds had first come to public notice in various television series (*Riverboat* 1959-60, *Gunsmoke* 1965-67, *Hawk* 1967), which he supplemented with appearances in a number of low budget films, such as the interesting *Angel Baby* (1961), the routine *Armored Command* (1961) and the dull *Operation CIA* (1965), which gave him his first starring role. Taking his cue from the *Rawhide* veteran, Reynolds made a brief trip to Italy in the mid 1960s for the title role in the spaghetti western *Navajo Joe* (1965), a middling pre *Django* effort from Sergio Corbucci. Back in the United States, Reynolds enjoyed regular starring and co-starring film roles from the late sixties onwards, his career taking off after appearances in *Fuzz* (1972), a police comedy-drama, and the eco-parable *Deliverance*. Rather more easy going than Eastwood in both his onscreen persona ('good ole boy') and choice of scripts (usually undemanding action-comedy-adventure), Reynolds enjoyed a fair balance of hits and flops during the seventies and early eighties, scoring a particular success in stunt vehicles such as *Smokey and the Bandit*, *Hooper* (which Reynolds also produced), *Smokey and the Bandit II* (1980) and *The Cannonball Run* (1981), all directed by former stuntman Hal Needham. Unlike

Eastwood, he didn't attempt to secure a tighter measure of control over his career by forming his own production company, nor did he cultivate a strong relationship with any one studio, working for all the major companies. Exhibiting at least a touch of creative ambition, Reynolds had made three tentative stabs at directing from 1976 onwards, scoring two outright misses (*Gator* 1976, *The End* 1978) and one hit, the brutal cop movie *Sharkey's Machine* (1981). By 1984, Reynolds' films were largely pure dross (*Paternity* 1981, *The Best Little Whorehouse in Texas* 1982, *Stroker Ace* 1983), yet his fans kept the faith. Eastwood's recent smash hit with *Sudden Impact* had demoted him to number two top box-office attraction and Reynolds had to make do with a mere $4 million as his fee for *City Heat*. Confident that this unbeatable star combination couldn't miss with audiences, Warner agreed to a $25 million budget (the period setting necessitated a number of large scale studio sets) and waited for the money to roll in.

Created by veteran comedy writer-director Blake Edwards, *City Heat* (originally called *Kansas City Blues*) ran into deep trouble before filming even started. Having just worked with Reynolds on the romantic comedy *The Man Who Loved Women* (1983), Edwards looked forward to renewing their successful (if non-lucrative) relationship. He found Eastwood rather less amenable, arguing with the star from day one. While the 'package' nature of the *City Heat* deal didn't allow Eastwood to enjoy his usual level of control, the film was still an official Malpaso co-production, employing several Eastwood regulars (Fritz Manes, Edward Carfagno, Lennie Niehaus, Wayne Van Horn). Edwards found his authority rapidly undermined, finally quitting (or being fired) when his choice of leading lady, a newcomer named Clio Goldsmith (briefly in vogue after appearing in the French-Italian sex comedy *The Gift* 1982), was declared unsatisfactory by Eastwood, who wanted her replaced with the better known Madeline Kahn (Reynolds claims that Goldsmith stayed on with the production following Edwards' departure, only to be fired a few days into filming for 'unprofessional' behaviour). Still not satisfied, Eastwood and Warner hired *Sudden Impact* writer Joseph Stinson to rework Edwards' script. The new version did not go down well with fellow cast member Marsha Mason, who resigned from the film on the grounds that her character had been altered beyond recognition (Mason didn't hold a grudge against Eastwood, accepting his offer of a co-starring role in *Heartbreak Ridge* two years later).

With new director Richard Benjamin replacing Edwards and new co-star Jane Alexander replacing Mason, *City Heat* could finally go into production, though both Eastwood and Reynolds would have done better to run away very fast. If Edwards' original concept for the film contained any element of flair or invention it didn't make it into the finished version. More at home with romantic comedy (*My Favorite Year* 1982, *The Money Pit* 1985), Benjamin proved ill at ease with the film's violence, despite (or because of) the jokey tone (Eastwood is rumoured to have kept Benjamin firmly under his control throughout the production.) The thirties setting failed to convince, with neither Eastwood (cast as a stone-faced detective) nor Reynolds (cast as a laidback private eye) proving a natural successor to the likes of James Cagney, Humphrey Bogart, George Raft and Edward G. Robinson. Unimpressed by the offer of two megastars for the admission price of one, audiences weren't interested and *City Heat* flopped. For Reynolds, the film proved more than just another career blip, marking the effective end of his reign as a movie star. His subsequent film, the Universal production *Stick* (1985), was another disaster, with director-star Reynolds obliged to sit back and watch as the studio re-edited his footage, adding new material shot months later. A long term infection caused by an injury during shooting on *City Heat* added to his problems, with industry rumours of some deadly AIDS related illness reducing Reynolds' bankability to a negligible level. Dropped by most of the major studios, he struggled on for the remainder of the decade before returning to television (*BL Stryker*, *Evening Shade*). A one-off bigscreen comeback in the puerile comedy *Cop and a Half* (1993) didn't alter Reynolds' has-been status.

Eastwood, by contrast, could write *City Heat* off as another rare miscalculation, though having watched Warner throw away $25 million on a dud idea, he now found himself obliged to pay out at least that much on his divorce settlement. Five years on from their separation, Maggie wanted to make her split from Eastwood final (she would marry again, though not very wisely). Predictably, the sum involved is a well kept secret, with estimates varying from $25 to $50 million (the majority of commentators agree on $30 million as the most likely figure). The divorce appears to have been reasonably amicable, with the ex-couple occasionally meeting up for discussions on matters relating to their children. For all Eastwood's personal difficulties with Maggie (who had more than a few causes for complaint), he could be grateful for her help with his career, supporting him financially in the early days and encouraging him to take a chance when *The Magnificent Stranger* came his way (whatever the exact figure, Eastwood concedes that Maggie earned every dollar of her settlement). Twenty years after first riding into town as the Man with No Name, Eastwood now planned to appear as another mysterious gunfighter, the decidedly non-pacifist 'Preacher' of *Pale Rider*.

12

Old Friends, Creaking Bones

Spirit ain't worth spit without a little exercise.
Preacher, *Pale Rider*

If they kill me, it won't be because I helped them.
Dizzy Gillespie, *Bird*

There's nothing more dangerous than a screw-up with a .44.
Tommy Nowack, *Pink Cadillac*

If the western had been a moribund genre back in 1975, nine years on it was dead and buried, the commercial and artistic disaster of *Heaven's Gate* serving as its overly-ornate tombstone. His box-office standing barely rocked by the *City Heat* fiasco, Eastwood decided he could afford to take a chance with *Pale Rider*. The failure of the previous film may even have spurred him on. Designed by committee as a surefire crowd-pleaser, *City Heat* had nevertheless been rejected out of hand by audiences. By following his own instincts and making *Pale Rider*, Eastwood could perhaps reintroduce film-goers to the timeless pleasures of wide-open spaces, big hats and plentiful gunfighting (as he'd bought yet another western screenplay the previous year, a downbeat tale called *The William Munny Killings*, he must certainly have hoped so). As with *High Plains Drifter*, he wanted to use the western format as a vehicle for a statement or two, this time attacking the destruction of the natural environment for commercial gain. Basically a supernatural-allegorical retelling of George Stevens' *Shane* (1953), where mysterious gunfighter Alan Ladd helps out beleaguered homesteaders Jean Arthur and Van Heflin, *Pale Rider* pits small time gold prospectors against the ruthless LaHood (and Son) Company, whose large-scale hydraulic mining methods are ruining the landscape. The script also throws in a few bits from *High Plains Drifter*, with Eastwood's apparently deceased 'Preacher' on a personal mission of vengeance against the leader of LaHood's hired guns.

Shot on location in Sun Valley, Idaho in the autumn of 1984, the $6.9 million production proved to be the last collaboration between Eastwood and cameraman Bruce Surtees (camera operator Jack Green, a Malpaso regular since the early 1970s, took over as resident director of photography in 1986). Exhibiting his usual flair, Surtees's work on *Pale Rider* is undeniably striking, recalling both *Josey Wales* (sombre green/brown forest and wooden buildings) and *Drifter* (blue/white mountain ranges). The rest of the film is less impressive, both ponderous and predictable (and something of an ego trip for its producer-director-star). Having assembled various offbeat elements (biblical allusion, an undead hero, an evil version of the Magnificent Seven), Eastwood and his writers deploy them in an unimaginative, rather heavy-handed fashion. Befriending courageous prospector Hull Barret (fellow jazz pianist Michael Moriarty), Preacher finds himself desired by both Sarah Wheeler (Carrie Snodgress), a widow loved by Barret, and her fourteen year-old daughter Megan (a miscast Sydney Penny), who even makes sexual advances (needless to say, Preacher gently but firmly rejects the approaches of this 'teen temptress). Like the hero-worshiping son (Brandon De Wilde) in *Shane*, Megan enjoys the closest relationship with Eastwood's stranger, first summoning him with a prayer ('We need a miracle'), spouting handy biblical quotations ('Behold a pale horse. And his name that sat on him was death') and articulating the intended audience response ('We all love you, Preacher'.) A ghostly heaven-sent avenger having to do what no man can, Preacher destroys LaHood's mining operation with a fistful of dynamite, then rides into the nearby town for a showdown with LaHood's 'marshal', Stockburn (John Russell) and his six 'deputies', who all dress in the style of long coat favoured by the gunfighters in Leone's *Once Upon a Time in the West*. The ensuing shootout is well-enough staged (certainly an improvement on the first action scene where various thugs have to wait in line to be thumped by the newly arrived Preacher), but Eastwood overloads it with 'significant' detail. His six deputies dead, Stockburn is cornered by Preacher, finally recognizing the latter as a (deceased) face from the past ('You !'). Preacher shoots Stockburn seven times, the bullet wounds in his chest matching the scars seen on Preacher's back. Barret gets to shoot LaHood, earning his spurs as a worthy Eastwood/Stranger sidekick in the tradition of *Fistful*'s Silvanito and *Drifter*'s Mordecai. Paying one last homage to *Shane*, the film ends with Megan forlornly waving goodbye as Preacher rides off into the mountains.

Released in the United States in the summer of 1985, *Pale Rider* received generally favourable reviews, with no-one appearing to mind that Eastwood's character was about as convincing a preacher as John Doherty at the beginning of *Thunderbolt and Lightfoot*. Grossing over $20 million during the first ten days of its release, the film was hailed by some as marking the rebirth of the western, though the commercial failure of *Silverado* (1985) soon put paid to the idea (for six years or so).

What *Pale Rider* did signal was the reevaluation of Eastwood as a 'serious' film-maker in his native country (nearly ten years too late). Various film festivals held Eastwood retrospectives, the first such acclaim since the high-profile tribute from the New York Museum of Modern Art in 1980. When the star took his new western to the 1985 Cannes Film Festival, no-one batted an eyelid and Eastwood found himself at the receiving end of highbrow interrogation from various admiring critics (the French government had made Eastwood a Chevalier des Arts et Lettres earlier in the year). Aside from a brief blip in the late 1980s/early 1990s, Eastwood has retained his 'respectable' status to this day. On a more popular level, the mid 1980s also saw Eastwood emerge as the movies' favourite injoke/homage, usually in icon mode as either No Name or Harry Callahan. Eastwood references can be found in the likes of *La Balance* (1982), *Police Academy II* (1985), *Police Academy III* (1986), *Hollywood Shuffle* (1987), *Crocodile Dundee II* (1988), *The Naked Gun* (1988), *Red Heat* (1988), *Back to the Future II* (1989), *Back to the Future III* (1990), *London Kills Me* (1991), *Robin Hood: Men in Tights* (1993), *The Mask* (1994) and *Casper* (1995). Not adverse to raising a knowing smile or two himself, Eastwood has included a few self-referential moments in his own films. Aside from the *Tarantula* clips in *Coogan's Bluff* and *The Rookie*, and the *Good/Bad/Ugly* pastiches in *Kelly's Heroes* and *Every Which Way*, there are Eastwood injokes in *Play Misty for Me* (Dave Garver interviewed by a producer from Malpaso Television Productions), *Dirty Harry* (a cinema showing *Misty*), *Breezy* (Frank and Breezy go to see *High Plains Drifter*, which also turns up in the Universal/Jennings Lang disaster movie *Earthquake*), *Thunderbolt and Lightfoot* (*Kelly* co-star Don Rickles on television) and *Bronco Billy* (a nightwatchman whistles the

● *Pale Rider*: **Preacher goes to work.**

Every Which Way theme tune). Not that Eastwood has ever got too indulgent when it comes to self-quotation. While publicity stills for *High Plains Drifter* show the star standing in the Lago graveyard set next to markers bearing the names 'Sergio Leone', 'Don Siegel' and 'Brian Hutton', these morbid homages are nowhere to be seen in the finished film.

Eastwood's place among the film-makers' major league received a further boost in the form of an invitation from executive producer Steven Spielberg to direct an episode of his upmarket television fantasy series *Amazing Stories*. A co-production between Universal and Spielberg's own company, Amblin, *Amazing Stories* attempted to recreate the style of such small screen 'classics' as *The Twilight Zone* and *The Outer Limits*. Each 25 minute instalment related a tale of the uncanny or miraculous, usually with a twist at the end. The script on offer, *Vanessa in the Garden*, had been written by Spielberg himself, which no doubt helped persuade Eastwood to say yes, though he hadn't worked for television since the last dismal days of *Rawhide* twenty years earlier. Aside from the attraction of collaborating with the industry's most commercially successful talent, *Vanessa in the Garden* offered a good role for Sondra Locke, whose acting career had been a little quiet since *Sudden Impact*.

Though she claimed that being Eastwood's girlfriend could be as much of a hindrance as a help (always in the star's shadow, not being taken seriously as a professional actress etc), there is little doubt that Locke's career would have continued to go nowhere much very slowly without her Malpaso connection. Post *Josey Wales*, she had made only a couple of film appearances independently of Eastwood, *Death Game* (1977, aka *The Seducers*, filmed in 1974) and *Wishbone Cutter* (1978), neither of which made any impression. Her one substantial non-Malpaso leading role was in *Rosie* (1982), a made-for-television biopic of actress and cabaret singer Rosemary Clooney. Now it seemed that her Malpaso roles were drying up. Having enjoyed a career peak between 1976 and 1983, Locke had subsequently watched co-starring parts go to other actresses (Genevieve Bujold, Madeline Kahn, Carrie Snodgress). Perhaps Eastwood had become embarrassed by accusations of nepotism; perhaps he had finally noticed that his girlfriend lacked both charisma and versatility. Whether or not he intended *Vanessa in the Garden* as an appeasement to any hurt feelings, Eastwood had certainly found a part within Locke's range.

Set sometime during the late nineteenth century, *Vanessa in the Garden* is the tale of painter Byron Sullivan (Harvey Keitel), whose beloved wife and model Vanessa (Locke) is killed in a carriage accident. At first distraught (even destroying his pictures), Sullivan discovers that he can bring Vanessa back to life through his art: any portrayal of her on canvas will become reality. Thus the man who lives for art is able to (re)create life through art. The story ends with the triumphant reception of Sullivan's latest exhibition. The proud artist is accompanied by a mysterious woman, her face concealed by a veil. Set against an autumnal background (decay/fruition and so on), *Vanessa in the Garden* is mildly interesting without lingering in the mind. Keitel's performance is a little awkward (not helped by a blatantly false beard) and the script offers few surprises (what happens if one of the portraits is damaged?). Eastwood's direction, while adequate, lacks much sense of atmosphere or mystery, relying too much on the gliding effect of the Steadicam. In her final bow as an Eastwood player, Locke makes a passable ghost. An aspiring film director in her own right, Locke would extract one more professional favour from her boyfriend in the remaining years of their relationship. Eastwood agreed to her using the Malpaso facilities for her debut as a director-star, the fumbled satirical fantasy *Ratboy* (1986). Warner had owned the script for years, and Locke's finished film goes some way to explaining their reservations about putting it into production. That said, *Ratboy* merits a (small) niche in cinema history as the only Malpaso film made without any direct involvement from Clint Eastwood (he occasionally glanced at the daily rushes – the unedited footage shot during one day's filming).

Back in his adopted home town of Carmel, Eastwood found his local business ventures running a little less smoothly than his film work. Eager to develop the real estate he'd purchased in the town centre, he grew frustrated as his development plans were regularly rejected by the council. For all Eastwood's longstanding Republican inclinations, it appears to have been for this reason rather than any long term political ambitions that he declared himself a candidate for the position of mayor, up for election in April 1986. While the international press had a field day with the star's much publicized platform of ice creams, frisbees and high heels for all (a not entirely accurate summation of Eastwood's political agenda), his election campaign proved a relative pushover. Despite the inevitable accusations that Eastwood's development plans would bring crass commerce to Carmel, that he would neglect his mayoral duties in favour of his film career, that he wasn't a proper resident anyway, he won the election with a highly respectable majority. Appointed mayor for a two year term, Eastwood graciously accepted his official salary of $200 a month, and promised to reduce his Malpaso commitments while in office. A congratulatory phone call from Ronald Reagan hinted that the star's initial dip into small town politics might lead to much bigger things (not that Eastwood ever declared any serious interest in turning big time politician). In the event, his stint as mayor proved a definite one-off, despite overtures from then vice president George Bush, who apparently wanted to recruit Eastwood as his running mate for the 1988 presidential campaign (Bush had to make do with Dan Quayle.) Perhaps the star found the day-to-day business of civic administration a little duller than he'd imagined. He must also have realized that big-league political ambition required big-league funding, with no guarantee of a profitable return. Moreover, he would have to wave his film career goodbye, losing both the artistic satisfaction and a more dependable source of income. When Eastwood's term as Mayor of Carmel came to an end in April 1988, he declared himself satisfied with his period in office ('We got things built'), declining the opportunity to stand for re-election (in 1992, Eastwood voted for independent presidential candidate Ross Perot, which suggests a gradual disillusionment with his former party of choice.)

Having spent most of 1985 away from the movie business, Eastwood lost little time getting a new film into production once his term as mayor was secure (the Malpaso crew had been kept busy on *Ratboy*). Doubtless anxious to reaffirm his credentials as a loyal American, he picked the flagwaving war drama *Heartbreak Ridge*, written by James Carabatsos. The predictable story of a hardened drill sergeant transforming a misfit group of lazy, insubordinate recruits into dedicated fighting men, the script drew on recent history, depicting the marines as part of the US invasion force that stormed the island of Grenada in 1983. Filmed largely on location at Camp Pendleton, California during the summer of 1986, *Heartbreak Ridge* enjoyed the full co-operation of the United States Army. This official assistance did not come without conditions, one of them being that director-star Eastwood delete all the script's references to a terrorist bombing of US army barracks in Beruit in 1983 (bad publicity). Cast as hard-drinkin'/hard fightin' Gunnery Sergeant Thomas Highway, Eastwood got to try out a severe haircut and speak in a low growl. Approaching mandatory retirement age, Highway is a decorated veteran of both Korea and Vietnam, yet his refusal to play his career by the book has lost him the promotions he deserves. Treated with scorn by his uptight superiors, Highway is lumbered with the job of getting a multi-ethnic reconnaissance platoon into shape. Led by the ultra-hip Stitch Jones (Mario Van Peebles), these laidback marines are not initially impressed with their new commander and the relationship runs a well worn course of mutual hostility, grudging acceptance, respect and finally camaraderie (*Sands of Iwo Jima* did it better). By the time Highway's boys have kicked ass in Greneda, they are both good soldiers and better citizens. As with most of the star's more gung ho efforts, Eastwood's onscreen persona embodies America's confidence in itself: strong, morally upright, fair-minded and always ready for a beer with the boys after a hard day's work (much like fellow non-combatant John Wayne). Perhaps a bit too much swearing but nobody's perfect. The essential rightness of The American Way is reaffirmed with a vengeance.

The equally formulaic subplot of *Heartbreak Ridge* involves Highway's attempts to get back with his ex-wife Aggie (Marsha Mason). Anxious to become the kind of sensitive 'new' man Aggie wants, Highway takes to reading magazines such as *Femme*, *Woman* and *Bazaar*. This approach appears to work, as when the troops return home from Greneda to a heroes' welcome, Aggie is waiting at the airport. Best known (fairly or not) for being the ex-wife of playwright Neil Simon and for her starring roles in various film adaptations of his work (*The Goodbye Girl* 1977, *Chapter Two* 1979, *Only When I Laugh* 1981), Mason struggles to make something of the weak dialogue, with honours emerging about even.

When assorted army officials were given a preview of *Heartbreak Ridge*, instead of expressing grateful thanks for a gift of a recruiting poster, they objected to the swearing in the film and withdrew the official seal of approval. Eastwood's argument that the language used could be heard in any military barracks fell on uninterested ears. Audiences proved less prudish and *Heartbreak Ridge* scored an impressive box-office return (Eastwood's personal share of the profits amounted to more than $5 million.) Despite his non-involvement in Korea and avowed opposition to Vietnam, Eastwood appears to have taken the whole cliched enterprise seriously, perhaps feeling that anything less would be disrespectful to the American fighting man (back in 1982, he contributed $30,000 towards an unofficial (and unsuccessful) search for missing US prisoners of war thought to be held in Vietnam). James Carabatsos later redeemed himself a little with the script for *Hamburger Hill* (1987), one of the Vietnam hell-on-earth movies made to cash in on the surprise success of Oliver Stone's *Platoon* (1986). True to his promise on being elected mayor of Carmel, Eastwood waited for over a year before starting production on his next film, the jazz biopic *Bird*, an epic account of the short life and troubled times of alto saxophonist Charlie 'Yardbird' Parker (1920-1955).

Dating back to the late 1970s, the screenplay for *Bird* was the work of television writer Joel Oliansky (*The Senator* 1971, *Masada* 1980), who'd made an impressive film debut as the writer-director of *The Competition* (1981), a romantic drama starring Richard Dreyfuss as a temperamental pianist. Despite his obvious flair for musical themes, Oliansky had little immediate success with the Charlie Parker project, possibly because studios felt that the story of a womanizing, alcoholic drug addict who died at the age of 34 lacked popular appeal (the predominance of African-American characters may also have caused a little apprehension). Parker's brand of improvised 'bebop' jazz enjoyed a fiercely loyal cult following rather than mainstream success and there was no guarantee that his fans would turn up in their small droves for a film version of the man's life. Oliansky eventually made a deal with Columbia and veteran producer Ray Stark, whose company Rastar had a long-standing association with the studio. Having paid for an option on the script, Columbia and Stark proceeded to do nothing with it, until an offer came from Warner (on behalf of Malpaso) to acquire the property in exchange for one of their own screenplays.

A year or so before the *Bird* negotiations, Eastwood had apparently persuaded Warner to finance another jazz-themed film, Bertrand Tavernier's *Round Midnight* (1986). Shot largely in Tavernier's native France, it picked up favourable reviews and several awards but not much in the way of box-office returns. It says something about the strength of Eastwood's relationship with Warner that the studio agreed to him producing a similar project which stood very little chance of generating a profit (Robert Daley's new position as Warner Bros chairman can't have hurt.) Bearing in mind that the fifth Dirty Harry film, *The Dead Pool* was already underway before *Bird* finished post-production, it seems likely that Warner requested (or Eastwood offered) a little insurance before giving the green light. Columbia and Stark agreed to hand over Oliansky's screenplay in return for *Revenge*, a violent romantic thriller which became an unsuccessful vehicle for Kevin Costner two years later (his first starring flop).

As with *Honkytonk Man*, *Bird* obviously represented an important personal project for Eastwood, whose longstanding passion for jazz had been fired (in part at least) by witnessing Parker in concert forty years previously. Anxious to do his idol justice, he enlisted the help of Parker's widow, Chan, who provided previously unreleased recordings and gave her seal of approval to the production. The film also demanded a bigger than usual contribution from old friend Lennie Niehaus (a gifted saxophone player in his own right), who hit on the ingenious device of combining original Parker solos with newly recorded backing tracks. For the pivotal title role, Eastwood and casting director Phyllis Huffman selected character actor Forest Whitaker, who'd played supporting roles in films such as *The Color of Money* (1986), *Platoon* (1986), *Stakeout* (1987) and *Good Morning Vietnam* (1987). Niehaus taught Whitaker enough saxophone technique to make his miming to Parker's playing more than believable. Budgeted at $9.5 million, the film went into production in the autumn of 1987, with nine weeks of location shooting in and around New York.

Running over two and a half hours, *Bird* is a well-crafted, fairly straightforward biopic. Oliansky's script makes extensive use of flashbacks (even flashbacks within flashbacks) in its attempt to capture the chaotic, out of control feel of Parker's life, rendering the film a little convoluted and unfocussed itself at times. After a credits sequence where Parker progresses from a small boy playing a pipe on a Kansas street to a jazz legend in full flow at a New York nightclub, *Bird* covers most of the expected territory. Self destructive in both his personal and professional life, Parker alternately charms and maddens Chan (Diane Venora), his white, half-Jewish wife, as she attempts to keep her husband's career and health together. As a struggling young talent, Parker encounters jazz trumpeter and bandleader Dizzy Gillespie (Samuel E. Wright), who becomes both his friend and mentor, despite feeling that Parker's dissolute behaviour conforms to all the white prejudices regarding black musicians. In turn, Parker becomes a mentor and inspiration to white musician Red Rodney (Michael Zelniker), steering him away from the drug abuse that has blighted his own life. Early on in the film, a teenage Parker (Damon Whitaker) is shown the corpse of a junkie in a morgue. Already dabbling in drugs, Parker is warned that he will go the same way if he can't kick the habit (there's definitely a message here). This sense of fatalism is present throughout the film, made

● *Bird:* Eastwood directs Forest Whitaker and Samuel E. Wright. Jazz enthusiast Eastwood also served as executive producer on the feature length documentary *Thelonius Monk: Straight, No Chaser* (1988).

all the more tragic by the depiction of Parker as both caring family man and sensitive artist (he admires expatriate Russian composer Igor Stravinsky, happy just to stand outside the gates of the man's New York home). There are lighter moments, such as Parker and Chan riding through New York streets on a white horse (paid for by Parker pawning his saxophone) and Rodney being passed off as an albino when Parker's band tours the Deep South, yet these are only glimpses of the better life that might have been. When Parker finally expires (while watching a television comedy show), the implication is that jazz dies with him, superseded by rock 'n' roll as the dominant form of popular music.

Eastwood's careful direction of *Bird* makes good use of lengthy Steadicam shots and pseudo *film noir* touches (deep shadows, rain-drenched streets, hushed voiceover), hindered only by an element of self-consciousness in the more 'profound' moments, such as a recurring shot of a cymbal flying through the air in slow motion (conveying memories of Parker's humiliation as an ambitious young musician over-eager to impress; a symbolic cymbal, in fact). The film also seems a little uncertain as to how to convey Parker's greatness as an artist, other than numerous shots of him giving virtuoso solo performances in assorted nightclubs (which, in fairness, lets the music speak for itself). The period setting is well achieved, though Jack Green's crisp photography occasionally leans towards the slick rather than the atmospheric. Whitaker delivers an accomplished performance that earns audience understanding if not sympathy. Stuck with an unflattering (if historically accurate) hairstyle, Diane Venora is less fortunate, serving mainly as a reaction character (dud lines such as: 'I was born to drive men crazy' don't help). There are always drawbacks to making a biopic when some of the people involved in the events depicted are still alive (Chan Parker, Red Rodney and the now late Dizzy Gillespie in this instance). The less savoury aspects of Parker's life are discussed rather than shown, with little depiction of his numerous affairs and chronic drug abuse (his stomach ulcers appear to have been more traumatic). As the film draws to a close, a written epilogue assures us that Red Rodney is now living an exemplary drug-free life (good for him). If *Bird* ultimately works as a heartfelt homage to Parker rather than an unflinching warts-and-all portrait, it is still a praiseworthy, though flawed, achievement. Discussing the film in his *Man from Malpaso* tele-biography, Eastwood describes Charlie Parker as a man who refused to ration life over a normal period of time (rather than a sad loser whose personal problems stifled his talent) and this attitude is prevalent throughout *Bird*. Christopher Frayling interprets the film as the expression of one artist's empathy for another, though Eastwood the businessman would have little time for Parker's supremely unprofessional attitude to his work.

Accepting that *Bird* could only be marketed as specialized fare, Eastwood and Warner agreed on a small scale domestic release for the film, which eventually netted a minimal $2.2 million, nowhere near the production cost (overseas revenues, plus television and video sales, went some way to recouping the original investment). Thankfully, audience indifference was countered by general critical acclaim. Eastwood took his film to the 1988 Cannes Festival, where Forest Whitaker won the Best Actor Award. Back home, Lennie Niehaus received an Academy Award for Best Achievement in Sound, Malpaso's first Oscar. The film also gave Eastwood the opportunity to put right some of his past mistakes. While promoting *Bird* in Italy, he was contacted by Sergio Leone, who suggested they meet up. Twenty years after their last encounter, director and star put their old disagreements aside and parted friends. The following year, Leone died of a heart attack.

While the post-production on *Bird* continued through the early months of 1988 (in the safe hands of Joel Cox), Eastwood took to the streets of San Francisco one last time. Filmed on location during February and March, *The Dead Pool* made few demands on its star. Preoccupied with the finishing touches on *Bird*, Eastwood assigned *Harry* no.5 to occasional director Wayne Van Horn, with producer David Valdes overseeing the shooting (a Malpaso employee since the early 1980s, Valdes had worked his way up through the positions of assistant director, associate producer and executive producer). Like *The Enforcer*, *The Dead Pool* resembles a by-the-numbers television movie which just happens to have acquired a top box-office star. This time round, Harry is experiencing a little Mafia trouble (rapidly reduced to a dumb comedy subplot) and a series of killings that appear to be linked to trash horror film director Peter Swan (Liam Neeson with a very odd accent). Being a decadent media type of person, Swan assembled a list of local celebrities he thought likely to die in the near future (the 'dead pool' of the title). Needless to say, this tasteless speculation backfires on Swan, as the people on his list start to drop like flies, leaving him the chief suspect. Now something of a media star himself, Callahan is included in the dead pool, which lends a certain urgency to his investigation. That said, he still finds the time to romance earnest television reporter Samantha Walker (Patricia Clarkson), a role which might once have gone to Sondra Locke. At first pursuing Callahan for an exclusive on his life story, Walker learns that it is wrong for the media to exploit private tragedy in the name of higher ratings (wise words from the veteran policeman). The killer turns out to be a deranged horror fan, who at one point murders a uptight woman film critic (interpreted by some as Eastwood's revenge on longtime adversary Pauline Kael).

Aside from some competent shootouts, the only sequence of mild interest involves Callahan being pursued by a radio controlled car bomb. In the tedious finale, Harry temporarily mislays his Magnum .44 and has to despatch the psycho with a giant-sized harpoon gun, enabling a James Bond style throwaway sick joke as the man is pinned to a wall ('He's hangin' out back there.') Looking more than a little haggard (he claimed

● *Bird:* **Charlie Parker takes flight.**

that he could now play Callahan at the age originally envisaged by creators Harry and Rita Fink), Eastwood delivers a routine, uninterested performance. Faced with a poor script, the other actors mostly follow his lead. Only Evan Kim, cast as Callahan's Chinese-American sidekick Al Quan, attempts to bring a little enthusiasm to his role. Best remembered for his uncanny impersonation of Bruce Lee in the *Fistful of Yen* segment of *Kentucky Fried Movie* (1977), Kim also appeared in the underrated Vietnam war film *Go Tell the Spartans* (1978), one of director Ted Post's few notable post-*Magnum Force* efforts. As expected, *The Dead Pool* drew the crowds, grossing around $80 million. It is to be hoped that Inspector Callahan now stays in retirement for good. If his final bow attracts any future interest, it will probably be for the presence of actor-comedian Jim Carrey (cast as a doomed rock star named Johnny Squares), still five years away from stardom in *Ace Ventura, Pet Detective* (1993) and *The Mask*. Presumably impressed by Carrey (or unable to think of anyone else), Eastwood hired him for a split-second bit part in his next film, *Pink Cadillac*.

A slackly developed comedy-adventure, *Pink Cadillac* remains one of the most puzzling entries in the Eastwood filmography. Having just boosted his bank balance with *The Dead Pool*, the star can't have felt in pressing need of a big hit, yet commercial gain seems the only logical reason for this film's existence. John Escow's script is an unimaginative cross between the *Every Which / Any Which* films and *The Gauntlet*, as Eastwood's modern day bounty hunter helps a fugitive mother rescue her baby from a vicious gang of Neo Nazis. With Wayne Van Horn remaining in the director's chair (his last fling as a Malpaso auteur), *Pink Cadillac* was shot on location in California and Nevada, with a lengthy sequence set in the gambling mecca of Reno. For the co-starring role of Lou Ann McGuinn, Eastwood selected Bernadette Peters, a forty year old actress with some interesting credits (*The Jerk* 1979, *Pennies from Heaven* 1981, *Heartbeeps* 1981) and an affordable price tag. For the smaller part of Lou Ann's sister, he cast Frances Fisher, a daytime television soap opera star with a little film experience (*Tough Guys Don't Dance*

1987, *Heart* 1987, *Patty Hearst* 1988). Peters may have got the bigger role, but Fisher caught Eastwood's personal interest. Within a short space of time they would be an established Hollywood couple, once Eastwood had dealt with the small obstacle of Sondra Locke.

Indifferently made and at least half an hour too long, *Pink Cadillac* displays a sad lack of imagination or ambition. An employee of 'Buddy's Bail Bonds', Tommy Nowack (Eastwood) is a seasoned professional with a penchant for rather feeble disguises: disc jockey, chauffeur, rodeo clown, casino manager (in gold lame jacket and spats) and good ole boy racist. While still in good shape, Eastwood looks too old for his role, and the inevitable romance between Nowack and Lou Ann lacks any credibility (Peters' little-girl-cutesy persona doesn't improve things). The leading villain, psycho-nazi Alex (Michael Des Barres), is no more interesting than Bobby Maxwell in *The Enforcer* and cameos from Geoffrey Lewis, Bill McKinney and Mara Corday serve only as reminders of older, better films. The Cadillac of the title is the vehicle stolen by Lou Ann when she flees from her useless husband and his politically dubious friends (it turns out to be filled with money intended to finance their evil schemes). Outsized, gaudy and a little sluggish, the car is at least in keeping with the rest of the film.

There appear to be two not entirely compatible accounts of *Pink Cadillac*'s box-office fate. The best known version is that the film went down so badly with American audiences that Warner decided not to give it a cinema release in Britain, where *Pink Cadillac* belatedly emerged as an unheralded straight-to-video release in late 1991. Malpaso and Warner take a slightly different line, claiming that while their film had in fact done perfectly respectable business in the United States, they felt that a lightweight caper movie would spoil the build-up to the more weighty *White Hunter Black Heart*, due for release in 1990. While this might demonstrate a laudable sensitivity to Eastwood's artistic ambition, it somehow fails to ring true. Business is business and marketable product is not left on the shelf for fear of it somehow tainting another, far less commercial release. Unless, of course, Eastwood felt so embarrassed by *Pink Cadillac* that he wanted no more to do with it. Any controversy over the film's curtailed distribution quickly evaporated in the face of far more interesting developments offscreen. Having bought the *White Hunter Black Heart* script in 1988 (a year after the death of its inspiration, John Huston), Eastwood looked forward to starting production on the film in June 1989. First he would have to contend with Sondra Locke, as their faltering relationship came to a messy and very public end.

13

Souls in Torment

You were right Pete. The ending is all wrong.
John Wilson, *White Hunter Black Heart*

When something is no good to me I just cut it off and throw it away.
Liesl, *The Rookie*

If you want a guarantee, buy a toaster.
Nick Pulovski, ditto

The final instalment in the Eastwood-Locke saga got underway in late 1988 during a less than festive Christmas vacation. An apparently furious row brought their already waning relationship to a sad end (Locke later denied the rumours of a violent 'showdown'). Thirty years previously, Eastwood's not so merry Christmas had been miraculously salvaged by news of *Rawhide*'s impending television premiere. This time round, there would be no happy ending, and media exposure was the last thing either Eastwood or Locke needed. By the spring of 1989, the erstwhile lovers were looking at eachother from opposite sides of a courtroom, as Locke attempted to stake a claim on Eastwood's personal fortune (estimated at nearly $150 million). Needless to say, the case attracted worldwide media coverage, exposing the star's personal life to a level of public scrutiny he'd previously managed to confine to his onscreen adventures. If the Locke story wasn't enough for the scandal hungry, 1989 would also see the public airing of the Roxanne/Kimber Tunis saga, as the latter went public over her celebrity dad. Five years earlier, Kimber had incurred Eastwood's displeasure by naming her son Clinton Eastwood (the third ?); now he would cut her out of his life altogether, breaking off contact from his oldest child and only grandson.

The reasons behind the Eastwood-Locke breakup are doubtless many and various. It may have been a simple case of Locke discovering after 13 years what Maggie had taken twice that long to conclude: she couldn't be content with a relationship where her supposedly devoted partner felt free to get involved with other women. It has been suggested that Locke expected Eastwood's divorce from Maggie to result in a second marriage to her, though the brief 1980 separation indicates a certain unhappiness with his attitudes fairly early on in their affair (Locke claims that Eastwood also resented her growing independence as a film-maker in her own right.) Moreover, Locke was still married to Gordon Anderson, who remained an important figure in her life. The Eastwood-Locke-Anderson triangle comes across as a faintly bizarre arrangement, which nevertheless suited all three of them for a while. Eastwood purchased a Hollywood house, ostensibly for Locke's use, which sculptor Anderson used as his base of operations. Locke supposedly stayed overnight with Anderson at the house on numerous occasions, though she claimed that their marriage had never been consummated, the relationship being more akin to sister and brother than husband and wife. Apparently unconcerned with this arrangement (or just preoccupied elsewhere), Eastwood was happy to socialize with Anderson and buy a number of his sculptures.

By the time the Eastwood-Locke bust-up reached court, Gordon Anderson had become just another factor in their financial tussle. Having already lost her professional relationship with Eastwood, Locke resigned herself to the end of their private life together and requested a relatively modest palimony settlement of around $1.3 million. Back in 1979, a case involving former Eastwood co-star Lee Marvin had established a precedent for the level of financial payouts when film stars ditched their long-term live-in girlfriends and Locke's claim seemed in line with earlier handouts. Had Eastwood gone along with this deal, the case could have been dealt with quickly and quietly with no public exposure. Instead he turned Locke down flat and ended up fighting a lawsuit which threatened to remove half his wealth. During the ensuing court punch-up, sad and sordid accusations flew from both sides. Locke claimed that Eastwood had promised her that their relationship was for keeps, then coerced her into having two abortions, followed by a sterilization operation. Eastwood countered by swearing that these decisions had not only been entirely Locke's, but also a great disappointment to him: he wanted more children; Locke had made it very clear that she did not (as Minty Clinch has pointed out, it seems a little odd that two people of such obvious intelligence should be so inept at contraception). Worse, she had little regard for either Kyle or Alison Eastwood (allegedly badmouthing them), devoting most of her time and Eastwood's money to Gordon Anderson. Showing a modicum of sense, the sparring ex-lovers eventually agreed on an out of court settlement in 1991, with Locke receiving an estimated $5.5 million. In return, Eastwood bought Locke's permanent silence on most matters regarding their relationship (confining her media exposure to superficial, regurgitant magazine profiles). In addition to the cash, Locke negotiated a supposed boost to her fledgling directing career in the form of an undertaking from Warner: the studio would take up a provisional option on any project ideas over a three year period. Nothing seems to have come of this (aside from Locke suing Warner for alleged breach of agreement) and Locke's last feature film to date is the passable undercover-cop-turns-bad thriller *Impulse* (1990), put into production with Warner backing before the protracted Eastwood settlement even got underway. Oddly enough, two of the film's co-stars, Jeff Fahey and George Dzundza, also appear in *White Hunter Black Heart*, a thinly veiled account of John Huston's offscreen antics during the filming of *The African Queen* (1951).

More than happy to escape to Africa in the summer of 1989, Eastwood and his production team arrived in Zimbabwe for eight weeks of location shooting around Lake Karibu, to be followed by two weeks work based at Pinewood Studios, near London. The story of an irresponsible, egocentric (if gifted) film director taking time off from his movie-making to go elephant hunting, *White Hunter Black Heart* stood no more chance of pulling in a sizeable audience than *Honkytonk Man* or *Bird*, yet Eastwood spared no expense, lavishing $24 million on the project. Presumably the chance to play a pseudonymous version of the late John Huston (described by Eastwood as one of the 'ultimate' film directors) outweighed mere financial considerations. As with Charlie Parker, Huston's less than professional approach during the *African Queen* shoot would have prompted little sympathy from the ever budget conscious Eastwood, and the attraction must have been one of opposites. There has been some suggestion that Eastwood originally wanted to go one further and produce a 'straight' remake of *The African Queen*, presumably with himself in the Bogart role. This is not an entirely happy thought.

White Hunter Black Heart started life as a novel by Peter Viertel, an occasional Hollywood screenwriter hired by Huston to rework the *African Queen* script following the departure of original writer James Agee. A respected talent, Viertel's credits include Alfred Hitchcock's *Saboteur* (1942), *The Sun Also Rises* (1957) and *The Old Man and the Sea* (1958), plus an earlier Huston collaboration, *We Were Strangers* (1949). Whatever the extremes of drinker-gambler-womaniser Huston's behaviour on that production, Viertel retained enough respect for the man to work on *The African Queen* without taking a screen credit. Stuck on location in Uganda and the Belgian Congo while Huston did his elephant-hunting thing, Viertel acquired plentiful first hand experience of the director's often maddening behaviour and its effect on the film's stars, Humphrey Bogart and Katherine Hepburn, who later wrote her own account of the production. Written with Huston's semi-approval, the 'factional' *White Hunter Black Heart* was published in 1953, immediately attracting considerable industry interest (despite the use of pseudonyms, everyone knew the inspiration behind the story). Having produced another uncredited rewrite on Huston's follow-up film, *Beat the Devil* (1953), Viertel turned his novel into a script, which he sold straight away. For whatever reason (potential libel?), the initial enthusiasm did not result in any production deal and Viertel's screenplay was optioned and reoptioned a number of times, undergoing several rewrites but no studio green light.

Eastwood first came across Viertel's book during his time at Universal-International, thanks to the recommendation of a producer friend (Arthur Lubin?) By the early 1980s, the film rights were jointly owned by Columbia and Rastar Productions (again). Ray Stark had worked with Huston on several of his later films (*Night of the Iguana*, *Reflections in a Golden Eye*, *Fat City*, *Annie*) and planned to produce a screen version of *Hunter* with writer-director James Bridges. Bridges dropped out and the script fell into the hands of director Burt Kennedy, who changed the ending (following his work as a screenwriter with director Budd Boetticher, Kennedy had turned writer-director with westerns such as *Return of the Seven*, *Welcome to Hard Times* 1967, *The War Wagon* 1967 and *Support Your Local Sheriff* 1968). When Eastwood bought the property three years later, he found that a repeat of the *Bird* deal was not possible. Rastar would not relinquish all rights to *White Hunter Black Heart*, with the result that the film became a Malpaso/Rastar co-production (distributed by Warner). Recruiting Peter Viertel as an on location consultant (which must have produced a strong sense of *deja vu* for Viertel), Eastwood decided to use both Bridges' and Kennedy's rewrites, or at least enough of them to merit a three-way screenplay credit.

Retaining the 'fictional' veneer of the book, director-star Eastwood did not want to attempt a straightforward impersonation of Huston, yet felt it necessary to draw on the latter's vocal and physical mannerisms, studying footage of the late director and interviewing former colleagues and members of his family (including daughter Anjelica Huston). The resulting performance as 'John Wilson' is one of the few times in Eastwood's career when he is very obviously acting. His attempt to capture Huston's self-consciously paternal/patronizing/outrageous style of speaking is not really successful. Never less than enthusiastic in his performance, Eastwood lacks the range for such a character part, remaining defiantly miscast. In any case, if Eastwood really didn't want Wilson to be taken for Huston, his attempt at a Huston-style persona lacks any real point. This rather schizophrenic attitude runs through the whole film. While Viertel may have had good reason for changing names back in 1953, twenty seven years on the whole exercise seems much elaborate ado about nothing. We know that 'Phil

● *White Hunter Black Heart:* **John Wilson meets Big Tusker.**

Duncan' and 'Kay Gibson' are really Bogart and Hepburn. We know that Wilson's film, 'The African Trader' is really *The African Queen* (amalgamated with the earlier jungle epic *Trader Horn* 1930). There is no need to pretend otherwise. Unimaginatively renamed 'Pete Verill' in the script, Viertel is not close enough to actual events to tell the real story nor further enough away to create an entertaining fiction loosely based on the events. Making absolutely no concessions to popular taste, *White Hunter Black Heart* is both intelligent and amusing entertainment in parts, but if the time was ever right to make a film version of the book, it had long passed when Eastwood and Malpaso finally arrived on the scene.

Opening in 1950s London, *White Hunter Black Heart* begins with a spoken introduction to Wilson, accompanied by shots of the latter galloping along in full fox-hunting gear. This man, we are told, is a self-destructive maverick, sustaining his career through sheer luck as much as talent. Bankrupt to the sum of $300,000, Wilson needs to make 'African Trader' a hit, but seems more preoccupied with shooting a bull elephant. All this is witnessed by bemused writer Verrill (Jeff Fahey), who views Wilson with a mixture of awe and contempt. Once in Africa, the latter rows with his producer, Paul Landers (George Dzundza), argues about art (citing Hemingway, Flaubert, Tolstoy, Melville and Stendhal as prime examples of keeping it simple), fights with racist British expatriates (indulging in an unsuccessful spot of *Every Which Way* style fisticuffs) and generally avoids doing any work. For the elephant expedition, Wilson recruits native hunting guide Kivu (Boy Mathias Chuma). Asked by Verrill to explain this quest/obsession, Wilson comes out with purest bullshit: 'It's a sin to kill an elephant...the only sin you can buy a licence and go out and commit.' Finally faced with the Big Tusker of his dreams, Wilson hesitates, the elephant charges and Kivu is killed trying to save his employer (a clumsily staged and edited scene). As the local natives send out news of Kivu's death (the enigmatic message 'White Hunter Black Heart'), a distraught Wilson returns to the film location, sits down in his director's chair and finally calls out 'Action', the last line in the film (Burt Kennedy's idea).

Solidly directed by Eastwood, *White Hunter Black Heart* features fair period detail and the minimum of African travelogue. If the camerawork gets a little fidgety at times, the director redeems himself with a striking shot of Wilson brooding in the foreground of the frame, while his cast and crew socialize over dinner in the background, oblivious to their leader's inner turmoil. The best performance in the film is given by Marisa Berenson, cast as Kay Gibson. A former fashion model, Berenson enjoyed an impressive 'arthouse' film career in the early 1970s, working with the directors Luchino Visconti (*Death in Venice* 1971), Bob Fosse (*Cabaret* 1972) and Stanley Kubrick (*Barry Lyndon* 1975), before ending up in dross such as *Killer Fish* (1975). Here, she wisely avoids attempting to mimic Katherine Hepburn's rather eccentric acting style, creating a likeable character who amounts to more than a 'guess who?' nudge and a wink.

If *Bird* had done negligible business at the US box-office, *White Hunter Black Heart* keeled over and died, grossing a laughable $1 million. Reviews were mixed, ranging from euphoric praise to puzzled dismissal, critics regarding Eastwood's performance as either the finest of his career or a blatant piece of miscasting. Eastwood retained his faith in the film, putting it into competition at the 1990 Cannes Film Festival. It is a measure of Eastwood's dedication to the project that he was prepared to shut down production on his next film, *The Rookie*, in order to attend (a five day break at a cost of $1.5 million). While *Hunter* didn't walk away with any top awards, its direc-tor-producer-star got the chance to meet *Yojimbo* director Akira Kurosawa, who like John Sturges had played a significant, if indirect, part in launching Eastwood's career back in 1964. Communicating through an interpreter, they apparently got on well, laughing at the late Sergio Leone's brazen nerve in 'borrowing' Kurosawa's script without so much as a murmur about remake rights.

Described by its director-star as 'a good shoot 'em up', *The Rookie* certainly fea-tures a lot of shooting. Filmed on location in Los Angeles during the summer of 1990, this 'buddy' cop movie exhibits all the expected drawbacks of Eastwood's post 1980 urban action vehicles: a mediocre script (by newcomers Boaz Yakin and Scott Spiegel), sluggish story development, absurd violence, cartoonish stunts, cardboard characters and an overextended running time (121 minutes). That said, *The Rookie* is not quite the dreary disaster of reputation, featuring enough bright(ish) moments to place it a notch above *Sudden Impact*, *City Heat* and *The Dead Pool*. Eastwood is veter-an policeman Nick Pulovski, a divorced loner (again) working towards his retire-ment in the Grand Theft Auto division. Regarding his career achievements as strict-ly small-time, Pulovski still hopes for the one case that will make his name. He sees such an opportunity in the form of Strom (Raul Julia), the arrogant German leader of a car hijacking gang. When Strom murders Pulovski's partner, it becomes even more personal (again).

Obviously fans of *The Enforcer*, Pulovski's superiors team him up with inexperi-enced 'rookie' cop David Ackerman (Charlie Sheen, son of Martin). A law graduate from a wealthy family, Ackerman is riddled with self-doubt and estranged from his millionaire father ('Where were you when I was hurting ?'). He also feels guilt over the accidental death of his brother many years before, manifested in an interesting precredits dream sequence where an interview for Ackerman's promotion turns into a nightmare interrogation (one of the accusers is played by Mara Corday). Inevitably,

● *White Hunter Black Heart:* Kay Gibson (Marisa Berenson), Phil Duncan (Richard Vanstone) and Mrs Duncan (Jamie Koss). Any resemblance to Katherine Hepburn, Humphrey Bogart and Lauren Bacall is absolutely blatant.

this odd-couple combination begins in wary, antagonistic fashion, with Pulovski and Ackerman ending up as the best law enforcement team in the entire universe. Armed with a mild dose of flair and verbal interplay, they go after the bad guys, taking on Strom, his chief psycho-sidekick Loco (Marco Rodriguez) and his right-hand *femme fatale* Liesl (Sonia Braga), a rapacious sadist who gives Pulovski an interesting time while he is handcuffed to a chair. Paying homage to *Dirty Harry* (a $2 million ransom for the kidnapped Pulowski), *Coogan's Bluff* (motorbike chases and poolroom brawls), *Blazing Saddles* ('Candygram for Mr Mongo'), *Marathon Man* (an attempted garroting), *Bullitt* (a climactic airport shootout) and *A Fistful of Dollars* ('Aim for the heart'), *The Rookie* comes to fitful life, though the mix of knockabout self-parody and blood-spurting brutality doesn't really gel. Why Eastwood thought that the Puerto Rican Julia and the Brazilian Braga would make convincing German *schweinehund* is difficult to determine, with Braga in particular suffering the indignities of awful dialogue, poor costumes and a generally dumb character. There were rumours at the time that Eastwood looked on Braga as rather more than an actress-for-hire, though the off-camera presence of Frances Fisher during shooting would indicate that his romantic interests lay elsewhere. The bits of the film worth stealing are confidently swiped by Charlie Sheen, who after starring roles in *Platoon*, *Wall Street* (1987), *Eight Men Out* (1988) and the street-punks-on-the-range western *Young Guns* (1988) looked set to be one of the big names of the nineties. Poor professional judgment and a hectic private life took their toll. By no means a high point in anyone's career, *The Rookie* did launch one promising talent, albeit belatedly. After a five year silence, co-writer Boaz Yakin re-emerged as writer-director of the French-financed *Fresh* (1995), the impressive tale of a street-hardened twelve year old drug courier surviving (and triumphing) in a New York ghetto.

Opening in late 1990, *The Rookie* generated a reasonable profit but little else, grossing just over $10 million during the first month of its American release. If the box-office response suggested public indifference, the reviews were actively hostile, with British critic Philip French delivering a particularly damning verdict: 'Clint Eastwood has forgotten how to make popular entertainment.' While this epitaph was later proved a little hasty by the successes of *Unforgiven* and *In the Line of Fire*, at the time the sixty year old star did appear in some danger of following old friend Burt Reynolds into leading man oblivion. Eastwood hadn't enjoyed a fully fledged hit since *The Dead Pool*, which had relied heavily on lingering audience affection for Harry Callahan, plus the bonus attraction of a tantalizing trailer for the forthcoming Warner production *Batman* (1989). No longer top of the movie star league, he might well have chosen to cut his losses and retire with dignity (unlike the 68 year old Charles Bronson, still churning out tediously violent dross such as *Death Wish IV* 1987 and *Kinjite* 1989). Fortunately, there was still the small matter of the *William Munny Killings* script, which had now been lingering in the Malpaso offices for close on seven years. Eastwood waited for over twelve months after the *Rookie* shoot before putting his western into production, leaving Warner without a Malpaso release for 1991, the first year Eastwood had been absent from American cinema screens since 1967 (cameraman Jack Green kept busy working on the Goldie Hawn thriller *Deceived* (1991), distributed by Warner). The wait proved to be more than worthwhile.

Inexperienced prostitutes.

Do not laugh at a client's small penis.

He will become irate.

Worse, he will cut your face open with a Bowie knife.

Setting in motion a series of violent events.

Culminating in all-out carnage.

Have a care.

Such is the basic message of *Unforgiven*, a compelling tale of drunken macho pride, reckless vengeance and empty justice in a world where nothing is settled except by killing. Looking more gaunt and squinty-eyed than ever, Clint Eastwood is former hired gun and bounty hunter William Munny, whose 'notoriously vicious and intemperate disposition' was transformed by the love of a good woman, his late wife Claudia Feathers Munny. Left with two young children, Munny now struggles to survive as an honest pig farmer in 1880 Wyoming, still haunted by his 'wicked' past. When he learns of a bounty on two whore-slashing cowboys in Big Whisky, Munny (money ?) sees the chance for One Last Job. Matching Eastwood in age if not bone structure, Gene Hackman is William 'Little Bill' Daggett, sheriff of Big Whisky. Priding himself on being fairminded, progressive and above all civilized (building his own house), Daggett regards the attack on young whore Delilah (Anna Thomson) as a business matter pure and simple. A mutilated prostitute is merely her pimp's damaged property, to be paid for by her cowboy attackers ('hard workin' boys that was foolish') with seven quality ponies. Rather less tolerant of 'troublesome' outsiders, Daggett bans firearms from the precincts of Big Whisky, subjecting any gun-toting strangers to psycho violence. Frances Fisher is Strawberry Alice, spokeswoman for the whores at Big Whisky's bar/brothel, where Delilah works. Incensed when her employer, Skinny (Anthony James), agrees to Daggett's 'justice', Alice puts the $1000 bounty on the two cowboys. Morgan Freeman is Ned Logan, a former colleague of Munny who also got married and turned farmer (with a little more success). On hearing of the Big Whisky incident (much exaggerated by this stage), Ned decides that hunting the cowboys is as much a matter of fair retribution as financial gain: 'I guess they got it coming.' Richard Harris is English Bob, a self-styled aristocrat who makes his money killing errant Chinese labourers for the railroad companies ('It's uncivilized shooting persons of substance'.) Beating Munny and Logan to Big Whisky, Bob finds himself on the wrong end of Daggett's fists, eventually driven out of town bloodied and humiliated. Backed by his most impressive supporting cast since *The Outlaw Josey Wales*, Eastwood turned *Unforgiven* into his finest film for over a decade, nearly 10 years after seeing the script.

Starting off with the unsavoury, if accurate title *The Cut-Whore Killings*, David Webb Peoples wrote the first draft of *Unforgiven* in the mid-1970s, not expecting much response from a western-hostile film industry. Inspired by *The Wild Bunch* (anachronistic outlaws attempt a final heist in 1914 Texas) and Robert Altman's *McCabe and Mrs Miller* (1971, sex is merely small scale private enterprise, capitalism is corrupt and destructive), he continued to work on the script, eventually attracting the interest of Francis Coppola in the early 1980s. Coppola couldn't attract any studio backing and let his option lapse (the director's major career problems following the mega-budget mega-flop romance *One From the Heart* (1982) wouldn't have helped). By the time Eastwood picked up the rights, Peoples had found something of a career break as co-writer on Ridley Scott's cult science-fiction thriller *Blade Runner* (1982). While *Blade Runner* didn't make much money on its original release, the film did display ample evidence of screenwriting talent (which is more than can be said for Peoples' script contributions to the aquatic *Alien* rip-off, *Leviathan* 1989, or his directoral debut *Blood of Heroes* aka *Salute of the Jugger* 1990). Eastwood felt no need to call on Peoples for any rewrites on *Unforgiven* (or hire another writer), and the latter didn't even get to meet the director-producer-star of his script until shooting had been completed.

Budgeted at a typically modest $14.4 million (plus whatever Eastwood chose to pay himself), *Unforgiven* was filmed over seven weeks during September and October 1991, using picturesque areas of Sonora, Arizona and Alberta, Canada as the principal locations. Back with Eastwood for the first time since *High Plains Drifter*, production designer Henry Bumstead worked on the major exterior set, the town of Big Whisky, which the Malpaso crew built in only 32 days (a record for Bumstead according to the 'Making of...' video promo). Casting for the film presented only a few minor hitches, notably Gene Hackman's initial reluctance to take on the role of Daggett. An acquaintance of Eastwood for nearly twenty years (they were near neighbours in Carmel for a time), Hackman had grown tired of violent films, whether good (*The French Connection* 1971), mediocre (*March or Die* 1977) or awful (*The Domino Principle* 1977). Eastwood convinced him that *Unforgiven* would offer a strong condemnation of violence, with no sense of glamour or glorification to the numerous killings. Given the choice of either Strawberry Alice or Delilah, Frances Fisher opted for the former, presumably because Alice is the stronger (if less sympathetic) role. The performances in the film are all first rate, with Richard Harris in particular proving that the talent on display back in the 1960s (*This Sporting Life* 1963, *Major Dundee*) hadn't been dissipated by subsequent embarrassments (*Orca -Killer Whale* 1977, James Fargo's *Game for Vultures* 1979, *Tarzan the Ape Man* 1981) and a five year voluntary absence from the big screen (brought to an end by an acclaimed 'comeback' in *The Field* 1990). Understandably keen to get as much out of his character as possible, Harris felt that the scene where English Bob first arrives in Big Whisky (with illegal sidearm) didn't flow properly and persuaded Eastwood to work out a minor rewrite/rearrangement. Otherwise, the production proceeded smoothly, though the last few set-ups (over 20 hours of filming) had to be completed without a break in order to avoid a rapidly approaching blizzard.

Opening with a long shot of Munny's modest farmhouse perched on the distant horizon (silhouetted against a sunset), *Unforgiven* is a stylish and thoughtful piece of film-making, put together with great care and a curious sense of integrity. Eastwood's enduring preference for the understated, low key approach works to his film's advantage, though there is a case for arguing that even this anti-violence story eventually succumbs to the conventions of the genre, a man having to do what a man has to do. Jack Green's photography, with its predominantly red/brown hues, golden wheatfields and whiter-than-white snow recalls the visual styles of *McCabe and Mrs Miller* and *Heaven's Gate*, both photographed by top cameraman Vilmos Zsigmond. As with *White Hunter Black Heart*, Eastwood the director overindulges his fondness for the gliding Steadicam, resulting in a number of sequences which would have benefited from more restrained handling (along the lines of *The Outlaw Josey Wales*). Perhaps the most touching scene in the film is a conversation between Munny and the nervous, kindly Delilah (a role once intended for Sondra Locke ?), set against the tranquil, purifying backdrop of recent snowfall. Munny has recently been beaten senseless by Daggett (business as usual) and Delilah tends to his injuries (sewn up by Ned Logan). As the bounty killer complements the whore as a still beautiful lady (true enough), Eastwood offers a striking image, placing Delilah in close-up on the left side of the Panavision frame, while Munny sits to the

● *Unforgiven:* Strawberry Alice (Frances Fisher) argues with 'Little Bill' Daggett (Gene Hackman) over his peculiar notions of justice.

right of the picture in medium shot. Skinny has ordered the scarred Delilah to buy a veil, just in case any clients still want to 'hump' her (to Skinny, all whores are just 'stupid bitches'). Here we see the person rather than the abused professional, to be considered only in terms of potential lost earnings. Having no sexual interest in Delilah (Claudia was the only woman for him), Munny treats her with a kindness that no previous man has offered.

The meditation on violence that lies at the heart of *Unforgiven* is provocative and largely successful. News of the bounty offered by Alice is first brought to Munny by the Schofield Kid (Jaimz Woolvett), nephew of an old shooting partner. Reminiscent of the Sam Bottoms character in *Josey Wales*, the cocky, self-confident Kid (named after a make of pistol) intends to claim a share of the money himself. Despite his skill at shooting Ned Logan's water canteen full of holes (a homage to Tuco's desert antics in *The Good The Bad and The Ugly*), Kid is soon revealed as an inept novice with hopelessly poor eyesight. Having actually managed to kill one of the guilty cowboys (the man is sitting on an outhouse latrine at the time), Kid is so traumatized by the experience that he quits the bounty business on the spot, using his share of the reward money to buy a decent pair of glasses. After eleven years without firing a shot, Munny appears no more cut out for a return to the profession. Hopelessly inaccurate with a pistol (which in reality were less than precision weapons in the best of hands), Munny relies on a shotgun. His first attempt to ride a horse again is undignified to say the least, the animal no more co-operative than the pigs he now breeds. We assume that Munny's skill will return with practice, yet he insists that it was always this way. The man who draws first is invariably in too much of a hurry and will make mistakes. Keeping a level head is all-important. A weapon fired in haste is as likely to blow up in its owner's hand as kill his opponent (try telling that to Joe the Stranger). Munny based his career on this knowledge and a bottle of whisky for courage. Anything else is lies. Despite the beating from Daggett, Munny is prepared to forget the whole business and head for home once his injuries are healed. It takes the sheriff's murder of Ned Logan (whipped to death) to change his

179

mind. On an appropriately dark and stormy night, a shotgun barrel in the foreground of the frame announces Munny's arrival in Big Whisky's bar/brothel, where Daggett and his deputies are waiting. Having gunned down an unarmed Skinny ('the owner of this shithole'), Munny deals out the same fate to the rest of them, resorting to a pistol and Ned's rifle when the shotgun misfires. Successful, if hardly triumphant, Munny dismisses his victory with a line that sums up the character, the film and most of Eastwood's career: 'I've always been lucky when it comes to killing folks.' As the two Williams face eachother for the last time, the dying Daggett protests the unfairness of his fate: 'I don't deserve to die like this. I was building a house' (very badly). Munny hasn't the time for such sentiment ('Deserve's got nothing to do with it') and shoots the sheriff in the head.

Unforgiven has its flaws. The elegiac style of the film (with written prologue and epilogue) is perhaps a little selfconscious and the comedy elements are overplayed (Munny falling about in the mud as he chases his pigs, Daggett's awful attempts at carpentry). The script is repetitive in parts (especially Munny's tributes to his saintly dead wife) and the inclusion of dime novelist W.W. Beauchamp (Saul Rubinek) to act as a sounding board first for English Bob, then Daggett is a redundant device (Beauchamp also gets to piss himself when cornered by Daggett's pistol-toting deputies.) Indeed, impressive as Harris' portrayal is, his character is awkwardly incorporated into the script, making up a largely self-contained episode which could have been reduced to a single glimpse of his undignified departure as Munny, Logan and Kid ride into town. Still, these are not fatal drawbacks by any means, and this must be the only Malpaso production where a supporting actor (Freeman) gets to ask Eastwood if he masturbates (apparently not). If, as seems likely, *Unforgiven* proves to be Eastwood's last major effort as a director-star, the film is a fitting climax to his career, ending with the dedication to Sergio Leone and Don Siegel. That said, exactly who or what is 'unforgiven' ?

Released in August 1992, towards the end of the lucrative Summer season, *Unforgiven* proved an immediate hit with audiences and critics alike, enjoying a record opening weekend. Back in the cinemas and back in the saddle, Eastwood saw his film

● *Unforgiven:* **William Munny takes aim.**

gross over $100 million in the United States alone, making *Unforgiven* the first of his westerns to challenge the box-office supremacy of Harry Callahan. Whatever the reasons for the film's unexpected runaway success (the western nostalgia revitalized by *Dances with Wolves*, public affection for Eastwood, sunspot activity), it didn't stop with the cash. When the Academy Award nominations were announced for 1993, *Unforgiven* scored in nine categories: Best Picture, Actor, Director, Supporting Actor, Original Screenplay, Production Design, Photography, Editing and Sound. All too aware of the class opposition, notably the Merchant-Ivory production *Howard's End* (1992), Eastwood turned up at the ceremony on March 29 1993 for the first time in twenty years, accompanied by his mother Ruth, his sister Jean and Frances Fisher. *Unforgiven* took the awards for Best Picture, Best Director, Best Supporting Actor (Gene Hackman, who had more than one reason to be grateful to Eastwood) and Best Editing (Joel Cox, rewarded for many years of loyal service to Malpaso). Eastwood received the Best Director statuette from Barbra Streisand, who had doubtless forgiven/forgotten the small business of Eastwood swiping the *Gauntlet* script a few years back. All things considered, a pretty good night out.

14

Senior Citizen a Go Go

Always tell a man by his eyes.
Frank Horrigan, *In the Line of Fire*

Win, lose or draw, this is my ship.
Red Garnett, *A Perfect World*

It's been one hell of a ride.
Robert 'Butch' Haynes, ditto

Having done his bit to revitalize the Great American Western, Eastwood switched his attention to the thriller genre, leaving others to cash in the success of *Unforgiven* (*Heartbreak Ridge* co-star Mario Van Peebles directed the African American oriented horse opera *Posse*.) Written with Eastwood in mind, Jeff Maguire's script for *In the Line of Fire* offered the role of veteran FBI agent/bodyguard Frank Horrigan, a man haunted by his failure to take the bullets that shredded President John Fitzgerald Kennedy on the fateful afternoon of November 22 1963. Thirty years on, Horrigan is working his way through a batch of routine 'crank' threats against the current President when he discovers one he believes to be deadly serious. Maguire sent his screenplay to Warner, who for whatever reason neglected to bring it to Eastwood's attention. Shrugging off this unexpected lack of interest, Maguire found a more sympathetic response at Columbia, who shared his thoughts regarding casting and offered the film to Eastwood. Something of a specialist in burned out, world weary semi-failures since the mid 1980s and *Heartbreak Ridge*, Eastwood recognized an ideal role and accepted, finally getting to work for Columbia instead of just lifting its projects. For the first time since *Bronco Billy*, there would be no Malpaso involvement and only two of the star's regular team on board: David Valdes and Wayne Van Horn. With Eastwood acting largely as a 'humble' star-for-hire, principal control of the film fell to executive producer and director Wolfgang Petersen, a German film-maker who'd achieved international acclaim with his television drama *Das Boot/The Boat* (1981), the depressing tale of a U-Boat crew during World War II (worlds away from the Boy's Own style of *Where Eagles Dare*). Originally intended for Don Siegel, *Das Boot* enjoyed a mildly successful theatrical release overseas (in an abridged version), leading to offers from Hollywood. Petersen's subsequent films, *The Neverending Story* (1983), *Enemy Mine* (1985) and *Shattered* (1991), hadn't quite put him among the front rank of Los Angeles-based directors, and *In the Line of Fire* would be his first project with a major star.

For the co-starring role of Mitch Leary, ex-CIA assassin turned freelance nutter, Columbia selected stage actor John Malkovich, who'd previously graced the big screen with appearances in *The Killing Fields* (1983), *Empire of the Sun* (1987), *Dangerous Liaisons* (1988) and *The Sheltering Sky* (1990). Obviously feeling that Eastwood needed a little romantic interest (62 or not), Maguire had written in the role of fellow agent Lily Raines, to be played by Rene Russo. Warmish (as opposed to hot) after co-starring roles in *Major League* (1989), *One Good Cop* (1991) and *Lethal Weapon 3* (1992), Russo faced the rather thankless task of breathing life into a dull part. If Eastwood felt a little short of old friends during filming on location in Washington and Los Angeles, he could at least console himself with the knowledge that the film's music lay in the safe hands of Ennio Morricone, sharing a credit roll with the star for the first time since *Two Mules for Sister Sara*. After a commercially hesitant start in American movies during the 1970s (*Exorcist II: The Heretic* 1977, *Days of Heaven* 1978, *Bloodline* 1979, *The Island* 1980, *The Thing* 1981), Morricone had finally hit his Hollywood stride a decade on, scoring films such as *The Untouchables* (1987), *Frantic* (1988), *Casualties of War* (1989) and the Mel Gibson *Hamlet* (1990). Eastwood also got to perform a token stunt, hanging from the edge of a roof during a chase sequence (a homage to James Stewart in Hitchcock's *Vertigo*?), which presumably compensated for having to shoot less 'authentic' interior scenes at the Sony Pictures Studios (Sony being Columbia's parent company.)

An efficient, if overlong and unsurprising piece of work, *In the Line of Fire* is a two hour battle of wits between Horrigan and Leary, with the President's life (and Horrigan's self-respect) as the prize. A lonely divorcee and dried-out alcoholic, Horrigan has existed in a self-created limbo since the Kennedy assassination. JFK's favourite bodyguard, he helped the 'martyred' President out of an awkward situation when one of the latter's girlfriends was discovered in the White House, yet couldn't react fast enough after the first shot in Dallas. Blaming himself for failing in his duty, Horrigan also fears that he might not have had the guts (so to speak) to lay down his life (a youthful Eastwood is incorporated into archive film of John and Jacqueline Kennedy via computer generated mixing and matching). Leary plays on this self-doubt, alternating between sympathy ('The world can be a cruel place to an honest man, Frank') and malicious taunts (afflicted by both a death wish and a lousy taste in poetry, Kennedy wasn't worth saving anyway). Armed with a custom-built plastic handgun (no worries about metal detectors), Leary has devised an elaborate scheme for blowing away the

● *In the Line of Fire:* **Mitch Leary (John Malkovich) takes Horrigan on a rooftop tour of the nation's capital.**

President during an election dinner (down in the opinion polls, the President can't afford to lose his public profile, whatever Horrigan's suspicions). Casually slaughtering anyone who inconveniences him (six in all), Leary is 'obliged' to kill Horrigan's rookie partner, Al D'Andrea (Dylan McDermott), during the rooftop pursuit. As Horrigan had only recently persuaded a reluctant D'Andrea to remain with the service, this doesn't do much to improve his mood. Needless to say, Horrigan saves the President with split-second timing, taking the bullet fired by Leary (no fool, Horrigan is wearing body armour). Leary ends up hanging from an exterior glass elevator, from which he deliberately drops to his messy death rather than surrender to Horrigan.

While the basic plot of *In the Line of Fire* is sound enough, it is weighed down by tediously predictable subplots and a misplaced sense of being more than a mere thriller. Occasionally lapsing into his John Wilson voice (which didn't really work first time round), Eastwood's character is fleshed out (unlike the star) with a love of jazz and the piano, paying spurious homage to *Casablanca* (1942) with a passable rendition of 'As Time Goes By'. A card-carrying chauvinist of the old school (mistaking Agent Lily Raines for a secretary on their first meeting), Horrigan finds himself out of step with the new-look FBI, antagonizing his much younger boss, who looks on the veteran agent as 'a borderline burnout with questionable social skills' (Horrigan's words). Having convinced Lily that he is really as progressive in his outlook as the next man, Horrigan gets to respect the professional and love the woman, though in truth Eastwood is just a little too old for his romance with Russo to be credible (the script clumsily alternates between the Russo and McDermott characters, no doubt breathing a sigh of relief when the latter gets a bullet in the head). Eastwood could play this kind of material with all four limbs tied behind his back, and the star only gets a real chance to shine in the short scene where Horrigan talks to Lily about the Kennedy murder and its effect on him. Specializing in smooth-tongued menace and cold carnage (toned down by the British censor), Malkovich makes an admirable villain, though Leary's reasons for the attempted assassination are barely explained (an expression of disgust at the state of the nation, his own exploitation by the CIA or just a game ?) A more serious drawback is Leary's risible use of 'disguises' (a wig, a false nose) that would fool no-one not registered blind (yet only the still-sharp Horrigan sees through them). Petersen's direction is adequate, using tight close-ups of Malkovich's mouth and eyes during Leary's telephone conversations with Horrigan and a swirling camera as an ailing Horrigan becomes disoriented during a presidential rally, and Morricone's score keeps things moving (though it borrows a little too freely from his *Untouchables* theme).

Premiered in July 1993, *In the Line of Fire* equalled *Unforgiven*'s commercial success, raking in $102 million at the US box-office. Eastwood nevertheless felt that it could have been even more profitable, criticizing Columbia for putting the film into direct competition with Warner's major summer release, *The Fugitive* (1993), a big-budget reprisal of the 1960s television series starring Eastwood's old (now dead) friend David Janssen. By the time his Columbia excursion hit the cinemas, Eastwood was back with Warner (and Malpaso), working on a new project entitled *A Perfect World*. Oddly enough, this film features the same 'humorous' moment where Eastwood's seasoned lawman mistakes his new female colleague for a secretary as *In the Line of Fire*. It isn't much funnier second time round.

At the time, the deal for *A Perfect World* must have seemed a star combination made in heaven: Kevin Costner in the leading role, backed by Clint Eastwood as both director and co-star. Having first come to notice in the amiable, if unsuccessful western

● *In The Line of Fire:* **Frank Horrigan.**

Silverado, Costner quickly assumed serious star status with leading roles in *The Untouchables*, *Bull Durham* (1988), *Field of Dreams* (1989), the genre revitalizing *Dances With Wolves*, which he also directed and co-produced, and *Robin Hood – Prince of Thieves* (1991). There was the small matter of *Revenge*, a deserved flop with both audiences and critics, yet no-one appeared seriously concerned that the Eastwood-Costner combo might go the same way as the Eastwood-Reynolds team-up a decade earlier.

Set during the 1960s (with a John Kennedy reference or two), *A Perfect World* is the tale of convicted criminal Robert 'Butch' Haynes (Costner), who busts out of jail (a sequence reminiscent of *Escape from Alcatraz*) and goes on the run, taking eight year old Phillip Perry (T.J. Lowther) hostage after breaking into Mrs Perry's house. The instant rapport between Butch and Phillip suggests that the latter will treat his kidnapping as an adventure rather than an ordeal, and for the bulk of the film this proves to be the case. Both raised with a minimum of paternal influence or love, they find in eachother a father-son relationship neither has experienced before. The law takes a less than tolerant view of this unconventional male-bonding and Haynes is pursued throughout the film by aged Texas Ranger Red Garnett (Eastwood). A passionate advocate of decorative cow horns and Geritol, Garnett is reluctantly teamed up with youthful criminologist Sally Gerber (Laura Dern), a run-of-the-mill 'odd couple' relationship that develops into mutual respect and understanding (again). Garnett is in part to blame for the present situation, as he once persuaded a judge to put the teenage Haynes in prison for three years on the minor charge of joyriding, reasoning that it would keep the boy out of reach from his career-criminal father. Not such a hot idea.

Despite having been raised in a whorehouse and shooting a man dead when only Phillip's age (in defence of his mother), Haynes appears a generally decent person, instilling the value of loving family relationships in his 'hostage' as they drive along (as with most 'road movies', this is also a journey of self-discovery). Having escaped with fellow convict Terry Pugh (Keith Szarabajka), Haynes grows increasingly disgusted at the man's evil, abusive behaviour. When Pugh molests Phillip, Haynes puts a bullet in his brain. Free to develop their relationship undisturbed, man and boy appear to be doing just fine, with frank talk about 'peckers' and regular shopping trips (kidnapped in his nightwear, Phillip is in serious need of trousers for the first hour of the film). A bizarre, uncomfortably prolonged scene involving a black nightwatchman and his family sees the friendship begin to fall apart. Having witnessed the man knock his child around, Haynes goes berserk, beating the man up and threatening to kill him. Panicking, Phillip shoots Haynes in the gut. In the drawn out, not to say bathetic climax, convict and hostage are cornered by Garnett's team, with the injured Haynes finally shot dead by a smug FBI marksman, leaving Phillip to weep.

Filmed on location in Austin, Texas during the summer of 1993, *A Perfect World* is a peculiar misfire, absurdly overlong at 138 minutes, and mostly going nowhere slowly for no discernible reason. John Lee Hancock's script opens with Haynes' peaceful-looking dead body, filmed by Eastwood as a series of close-ups intercut with slow motion shots of the convict's stolen money blown through the air by whirring helicopter blades. This flashback structure adds little in the way of depth or understanding to the proceedings, reflecting an uncertainty on Eastwood's part as to how he should approach the material, throwing in sentiment, social comment, slapstick, high tragedy, psycho-nastiness and even a *Bull Durham* injoke. The Eastwood and Dern characters are largely redundant, the former not even getting to speak with Haynes until close on two hours into the film. Gerber serves mainly as Garnett's confidant, providing some crass 'analysis' of Haynes for not-so-good measure (that said, Laura Dern is at least more restrained than her over-the-top father in *Hang 'Em High*). In the central role, Costner appears a little ill-at-ease, relying on a handy pair of sunglasses for much of his performance. The script doesn't help him a great deal, alternately depicting Haynes as a good man dealt a particularly lousy hand by fate and a borderline psychotic posing a danger to anyone who deviates from his vision of the ideal family. Photographed by Jack Green, the film does at least look quite attractive, with plentiful rural scenery, and Lennie Niehaus' score makes effective use of a melancholy harmonica theme (the bagpipes are not such a good idea).

Having endured rainstorms and floods during the shooting of *A Perfect World*, Eastwood and Costner found their hopes for the film further dampened by its disappointing reception in the United States. Released to so-so reviews in December 1993, it grossed a mere $31 million. Overseas revenue eventually added up to a more impressive $100 million, yet for Costner *A Perfect World* marked the end of his reign as the star with the (largely) golden touch. Intending to bounce back with the epic western *Wyatt Earp* (1994), co-starring Gene Hackman, he took a further box-office dive (audiences didn't want yet another version of the OK Corral story so soon after *Tombstone*). Third and fourth times unlucky, Costner then bombed with *The War* (1994), a dull Viet-Vet drama, and *Waterworld* (1995), a $200 million damp squib of a sci-fi epic, placing his star status on precarious ground. If Eastwood felt put out by the verdict on *A Perfect World*, he already had more important matters than mere movies on his mind, with the birth of his third daughter, Francesca Ruth Fisher Eastwood, in August 1993 (nearly thirty years after the arrival of Kimber Tunis). Whatever one's opinion of fatherhood at the age of 63, Eastwood certainly isn't afraid of a challenge. Kimber Eastwood (as she now calls herself) was subsequently interviewed for the British television series *Hollywood Kids* (1994), offering the expected thoughts on her father ('I grew up reading about him and watching him...I don't know any other way') and a wistful reference to Francesca: 'It's weird having a new baby half-sister I've never met...I'm anxious to meet her...but our schedules don't allow it.' Sad, perhaps, but no sadder than any other fractured family.

A combination of advancing years and parenthood have slowed down the Malpaso production line since *A Perfect World*, though Eastwood has maintained a high industry profile by other means. In 1994 he made a fourth trip to the Cannes Film Festival, this time to serve as President of the Festival Jury. Flying his native flag with as much fervour as ever, Eastwood successfully lobbied for Quentin Tarantino's exuberant, if empty crime melodrama *Pulp Fiction* (1994) to receive the main 'Best Picture' prize, the esteemed *Palme d'Or*. Tarantino repaid the compliment, citing *Where Eagles Dare* as his favourite 'Guys on a Mission' movie.

While hardly in need of additional funds (unless the cost of baby clothes had suddenly gone through the roof), Eastwood wanted to make his next film a safer commercial bet. As *In the Line of Fire* and *A Perfect World* demonstrated, he'd shed some of his old reluctance to collaborate with other major film-makers and companies, and agreed to a ten-years-on reunion with executive producer Steven Spielberg for a big-screen adaptation of the bestselling novel *The Bridges of Madison County*. Written by Robert James Waller, an economics teacher from Iowa, this 1960s tale of a passionate, if doomed rural small town romance between dashing *National Geographic* photographer Robert Kincaid and middled-aged Italian-American housewife Francesca Johnson had proved a runaway success on its original publication. Described by *Movieline* critic Yvette Mason as 'weepy, damp-panty piffle', the book still sold nearly 11 million copies worldwide, turning Waller into a millionaire several times over (he gave up the day job). Spielberg acquired the screen rights for Amblin Entertainment, and offered Eastwood a co-production deal, a starring role and the director's chair (vacated by Spielberg, Bruce Beresford and Sydney Pollack), with distribution through Warner (as part of the 1995 Summer line-up).

Appreciating that Waller's original didn't provide the strongest dialogue or narrative thrust (Eastwood called the book 'a skeleton of a great idea'), Eastwood and Spielberg hired respected scriptwriter Richard LaGravenese to make a few improvements, no doubt impressed by his Academy Award nominated screenplay for Terry Gilliam's romantic fantasy *The Fisher King* (1991). Frances Fisher let it be known that she wanted to co-star alongside her lover and erstwhile employer, only to face disappointment. Miscasting aside, Eastwood did not intend to repeat the mistakes of the Sondra Locke era (his personal relationship with Fisher ended soon after). Besides, a rather more famous leading lady had expressed interest. Impressed by LaGravenese's adaptation/rewrite, Meryl Streep signed on the dotted line. Perhaps the most acclaimed female star of the 1980s, with films such as *The French Lieutenant's Woman* (1981), *Sophie's Choice* (1982), *Silkwood* (1983), *Out of Africa* (1986) and *A Cry in the Dark* (1988), Streep then stumbled a little, unwisely accepting roles in two dumb comedies (*She Devil* 1989, *Death Becomes Her* 1992) and a laughable 'arthouse' effort, *The House of the Spirits* (1993). Having clawed back a little commercial ground with the outdoor action movie *The River Wild* (1994), Streep hoped to consolidate her return to box-office favour with a surefire leave-'em-weeping slushfest. She might not look particularly Italian but she could certainly do accents (English, Polish, Danish and Australian).

What neither Streep nor Eastwood could conjure up onscreen was any real sense of passion, even allowing for the latter's mature age, which rather undermined the central premise of the story: intense romantic/sexual attraction need not be confined to those under forty (that said, they only get four day's worth, to be followed by years of wistful memories/regrets). The idea of two lonely people finding love and fulfillment when they least expect it, only to realize that it has come too late in their lives for them to start again together is not without appeal, yet *Bridges* fails to ring true. It is typical of the film's problems that an undeniably striking shot of Kincaid standing in the pouring rain, struggling to control his emotions as he and Francesca say goodbye, seems merely a way of getting round the fact that Eastwood is just too much of a man to cry onscreen (though he came close in *The Outlaw Josey Wales*). Thirty years previously, the star had responded to another simulated downpour by lighting up a cigarillo and going in search of some mean hombres to shoot. Fairly or not, Eastwood's camera-toting New Man With a Name doesn't have the same authenticity, whatever his improvements to Waller's story.

The film did pick up a few respectable reviews, with the *New York Times* hailing it as 'vastly better than the book', though some might regard this as damning with faint praise. Unlike Eastwood's previous 'package' outing, *City Heat*, the target audience did show up in reasonable numbers, generating over $70 million in the US alone. Tasteful, restrained (apart from Streep's mannerisms) and filled with pleasant scenery, *Bridges* is painless, if overlong. The many-years-later scenes where Francesca's now adult children discover their dead mother's infidelity via several volumes of in-depth journals don't help.

At least the intended follow-up, a screen version of Michael Murphy's allegorical novel *Golf in the Kingdom*, sees Eastwood staying firmly behind the camera, his third director-only effort after *Breezy* and *Bird* (1995 saw Eastwood's second producer-only credit, the small-town drama, *Stars Fell on Henrietta*, starring Aidan Quinn, Robert Duvall and Frances Fisher). And he does know a little bit about golf. Whether or not this ambitious project sees the light of day, there appears to be a general feeling within the film industry that Eastwood's career is drawing to a close. Not bothering to wait for the release of *Bridges* (perhaps just as well), the Academy of Motion Picture Arts and Sciences honoured him with the life-achievement-pat-on-the-back Irving G. Thalberg Memorial Award at the 1995 Oscars ceremony. Always ready with a handy quip, Eastwood injected a little humour into the proceedings by wondering aloud if he might not be the biological father of hyper-macho (yet amusing) action-star Arnold Schwarzenegger. (According to a bullshit rumour of older vintage, this would make Schwarzenegger the 'natural' grandson of the late Stan Laurel.)

However Eastwood chooses to spend the twilight years of his career, he can rest safe in the knowledge that his existing body of work should ensure him a place in whatever cel-luloid heaven awaits those film-makers with a genuine love of their craft. The biggest disappointment of his career is that this goal was achieved twenty years ago, as *The Outlaw Josey Wales* rode off into the sunset. The subsequent decades may have produced interesting or offbeat work among the routine (*Escape from Alcatraz*; *Tightrope*; *Bird*; *White Hunter Black Heart*) yet only *Unforgiven* can be regarded as a (more or less) uncompro-mised success. While Harry Callahan might be keen on every man knowing his limita-tions, this has plainly not been the case for Eastwood, his admittedly bold changes of paces seldom offering more than curiosity value (*Honkytonk Man* springs to mind). From this perspective, his post-1976 attempts to alternate between lucrative action fodder and 'quality' projects have by and large failed. For all the praise heaped on the likes of Wes Block and John Wilson, Eastwood's much lauded desire to experiment with his star image is far better manifested in earlier films such as *The Beguiled* and *Thunderbolt and Lightfoot* (both prime examples of the star entrusting himself to another gifted director). Even the acclaimed *Bird* is ultimately lacking the hard edge and sureness of touch that would have made it more than another well-crafted, sentimental biopic. Clint Eastwood was born to play two roles: Joe the Stranger and Inspector Harry Callahan of the San Francisco Police Department. No other actor could have been so unarguably right for the characters, and in partnership with Sergio Leone and Don Siegel Eastwood created two of the cinema's most enduring icons (though it's regrettable that Harry ended up as just another hackneyed product on the Malpaso production line). The other career highs, his performances as John McBurney in *The Beguiled*, John 'Thunderbolt' Doherty, Josey Wales and William Munny; the direction of *High Plains Drifter*, *The Outlaw Josey Wales* and *Unforgiven*, are among the finest moments in modern American cinema. If Eastwood is to be admired, it should be for the period when his star power was at its height, offering a unique combination of old-fashioned heroism (one can imagine a 1940s version of Eastwood churning out endless westerns, cop movies and war films under the studio system regime) and decidedly post-1960s attitudes (an ambitious, independently-minded actor/film-maker with a cynical, darkly humorous screen image). For all its own merits, *Unforgiven* is perhaps most valuable as a reminder of the old Eastwood, before the odd combination of laziness (endless dull shoot-em-ups) and ill-placed ambition got the better of him. For most, this should be enough.

Filmography

REVENGE OF THE CREATURE

1955 82 mins
United States
Universal-International
Producer: William Alland, Director: Jack Arnold, Screenplay: Martin Berkeley, Photography: Charles S. Welbourne (black and white), Art direction: Alexander Golitzen, Alfred Sweeney, Editing: Paul Weatherwax, Sound: Leslie I. Carey, Jack Bolger, Music: Herman Stein, Music supervisor: Joseph Gershenson, Special effects (Creature design): Bud Westmore, Jack Kevan.
Cast: John Agar (Clete Ferguson), Lori Nelson (Helen Dobson), John Bromfield (Joe Hayes), Grandon Rhodes (Foster) [Clint Eastwood uncredited as laboratory technician Jennings].

TARANTULA

1955 80 mins
United States
Universal-International
Producer: William Alland, Director: Jack Arnold, Screenplay: Robert Fresco, Martin Berkeley, Photography: George Robinson (black and white), Art direction: Alexander Golitzen, Alfred Sweeney, Editing: William M. Morgan, Sound: Leslie I. Carey, Frank Wilkinson, Music: Henry Mancini, Music supervisor: Joseph Gershenson, Special photographic effects: Clifford Stine.
Cast: John Agar (Dr. Matt Hastings), Mara Corday (Stephanie Clayton), Leo G. Carroll (Professor Deemer), Nestor Paiva (Sheriff) [Clint Eastwood uncredited as bomber pilot].

LADY GODIVA (UK title: LADY GODIVA OF COVENTRY)

1955 89 mins
United States
Universal-International
Producer: Robert Arthur, Director: Arthur Lubin, Screenplay: Oscar Brodney, Harry Ruskin, Photography: Carl Guthrie (Technicolor), Art direction: Alexander Golitzen, Robert Boyle, Editing: Paul Weatherwax, Sound: Leslie I. Carey, Joe Lapis, Music: Hans Salter, Music supervisor:
Joseph Gershenson.
Cast: Maureen O'Hara (Lady Godiva), George Nader (Lord Leofric), Eduard Franz (King Edward), Leslie Bradley (Count Eustace), Victor McLaglen (Grimald), Torin Thatcher (Lord Godwin), Clint Eastwood (First Saxon).

FRANCIS IN THE NAVY

1955 80 mins
United States
Universal-International
Producer: Stanley Rubin, Director: Arthur Lubin, Screenplay: Devery Freeman, Photography: Carl Guthrie (black and white), Art direction: Alexander Golitzen, Bill Newberry, Editing: Milton Carruth, Ray Snyder, Sound: Leslie I. Carey, Frank H. Wilkinson, Music supervisor: Joseph Gershenson.
Cast: Donald O'Connor (Lieutenant Peter Stirling/Bosun's Mate Slicker Donevan), Chill Wills (voice of Francis), Martha Hyer (Betsy Donevan), Jim Backus (Commander Hutch), David Janssen (Lieutenant Anders), Martin Milner (Rick), Paul Burke (Tate), Clint Eastwood (Jonesy).

NEVER SAY GOODBYE

1955 96 mins
United States
Universal-International
Producer: Albert J. Cohen, Director: Jerry Hopper, Screenplay: Charles Hoffman, Photography:
Maury Gertsman (Technicolor), Art direction: Alexander Golitzen, Robert Boyle, Editing: Paul
Weatherwax, Sound: Leslie I. Carey, Frank Wilkinson, Music: Frank Skinner, Music supervisor:
Joseph Gershenson.
Cast: Rock Hudson (Dr. Michael Parker), Cornell Borchers (Lisa), George Sanders (Victor), David
Janssen (Dave), Shelley Fabares (Suzy Parker), Clint Eastwood (Will).

THE FIRST TRAVELING SALESLADY

1956 92 mins
United States
Radio-Keith-Orpheum / Arthur Lubin Productions Incorporated.
Producer: Arthur Lubin, Director: Lubin, Screenplay: Stephen Longstreet, Devery Freeman,
Photography: William Snyder (Technicolor), Art direction: Albert S. D'Agostino, Editing:
Otto Ludwig, Sound: Stanford Houghton, Terry Kellum, Music: Irving Gertz, Costumes:
Edward Stevenson.
Cast: Ginger Rogers (Rose Gillray), Barry Nelson (Charles Masters), Carol Channing (Molly Wade),
David Brian (James Carter), James Arness (Joel Kingdom), Clint Eastwood (Jack Rice).

STAR IN THE DUST

1956 80 mins
United States
Universal-International
Producer: Albert Zugsmith, Director: Charles Haas, Screenplay: Oscar Brodney, Photography: John
L. Russell (Technicolor), Music: Frank Skinner.
Cast: John Agar (Bill Jordan), Mamie Van Doren (Ellen Ballard), Richard Boone (Sam Hall), Leif
Erikson (George Ballard), Harry Morgan (Lew Hogan), James Gleason (Orval Jones) [Clint
Eastwood uncredited as ranch hand].

AWAY ALL BOATS

1956 114 mins
United States
Universal-International
Producer: Howard Christie, Director: Joseph Pevney, Screenplay: Ted Sherdeman (based on the
novel by Kenneth M. Dodson), Photography: William Daniels, Clifford Stine
(Technicolor / Vistavision), Music: Frank Skinner.
Cast: Jeff Chandler, Julie Adams, George Nader, Lex Barker, Keith Andes, Richard Boone, Frank
Faylen, David Janssen [Clint Eastwood uncredited as marine]

ESCAPADE IN JAPAN

1957 93 mins
United States
Radio-Keith-Orpheum / Arthur Lubin Productions Incorporated
Producer: Arthur Lubin, Director: Lubin, Screenplay: Winston Miller, Photography: William Snyder
(Technicolor / Technirama), Art direction: George W. Davis, Walter Holscher, Editing: Otto Ludwig,
Sound: Francis J. Scheid, Terry Kellum, Music: Max Steiner.
Cast: Teresa Wright (Mary Saunders), Cameron Mitchell (Dick Saunders), Jon Provost (Tony
Saunders), Roger Nakagawa (Hiko), Philip Ober (Lieutenant Colonel Hargrave) [Clint Eastwood
uncredited as rescue pilot One Dumbo Victor].

LAFAYETTE ESCADRILLE (UK title:HELL BENT FOR GLORY)

1957 93 mins
United States
Warner
Producer: William Wellman, Director: Wellman, Screenplay: A.S. Fleischmann (based on a story by
Wellman), Photography: William Clothier (black and white), Art direction: John Beckman, Editing:
Owen Marks, Sound: John Kean, Music: Leonard Rosenman.
Cast: Tab Hunter (Thad Walker), Etchika Choreau (Renee), Marcel Dalio (Drillmaster), David
Janssen (Duke Sinclaire), Will Hutchins (Dave Putnam), Clint Eastwood (George Moseley), William
Wellman Jr. (William Wellman).

AMBUSH AT CIMARRON PASS

1957 73 mins
United States
Regal/Twentieth Century Fox
Producer: Herbert E. Mendelson, Director: Jodie Copelan, Screenplay: Richard Taylor, John Butler,
Photography: John M. Nickolaus Jr. (black and white/RegalScope), Art direction: John Mansbridge,
Editing: Carl L. Pierson, Sound: Harold Hanks, Harry Leonard, Music: Paul Sawtell, Bert Shefter.
Cast: Scott Brady (Sergeant Matt Blake), Margia Dean (Teresa), Clint Eastwood (Keith Williams),
Irving Bacon (Stanfield).

A FISTFUL OF DOLLARS/PER UN PUGNO DI DOLLARI

1964 (US/UK release: 1967) 100 mins
Italy/West Germany/Spain
Jolly Film/Constantin/Ocean. English language versions distributed by United Artists
Producers: Arrigo Colombo, Giorgio Papi, Director: Sergio Leone, Screenplay: Leone, Duccio
Tessari (based on the film *Yojimbo*, scripted by Akira Kurosawa and Ryuzo Kikushima), English dia-
logue: Mark Lowell, Photography: Massimo Dallamano (Technicolor/Techniscope), Art direction:
Giancarlo Simi, Editing: Roberto Cinquini, Sound: Elio Pacella, Edy Simson, Music: Ennio
Morricone, Costumes: Simi, Title sequence: Luigi Lardani.
Cast: Clint Eastwood (Joe the Stranger/The Man with No Name), Gian Maria Volonte (Ramon
Rojo), Marianne Koch (Marisol), Pepe Calvo (Silvanito), Sieghardt Rupp (Don Miguel Rojo),
Antonio Prieto (Esteban Rojo), Wolfgang Lukschy (John Baxter), Margherita Lozano (Consuela
Baxter), Bruno Carotenuto (Antonio Baxter), Josef Egger (Piripero), Benito Stefanelli (Rubio),
Mario Brega (Chico), Daniel Martin (Julian).

FOR A FEW DOLLARS MORE/PER QUALCHE DOLLARI IN PIU

1965 (US/UK release: 1967) 130 mins
Italy/Spain/West Germany
Produzioni Europee Associate (P.E.A.)/Gonzales/Constantin. English language versions distributed
by United Artists.
Producer: Alberto Grimaldi, Director: Sergio Leone, Screenplay: Leone, Fulvio Morsella (based on
an original story by Leone and Luciano Vincenzoni), Dialogue: Vincenzoni, Photography: Massimo
Dallamano (Technicolor/ Techniscope), Art direction: Giancarlo Simi, Editing: Eugenio Alabiso,
Georgio Serralonga, Sound: Oscar De Arcangelis, Music: Ennio Morricone, Musical director: Bruno
Nicolai, Costumes: Simi, Assistant director: Tonino Valerii.
Cast: Clint Eastwood (Manco/The Man with No Name), Lee Van Cleef (Colonel Douglas
Mortimer), Gian Maria Volonte (Indio), Luigi Pistilli (Graghi), Mario Brega (Nino), Klaus Kinski
(Wild, the hunchback), Josef Egger (Prophet), Maria Krup (Hotel Manageress), Rosemary Dexter
(Mortimer's sister).

THE WITCHES/LE STREGHE

1966 110 mins
Italy/France
Producer: Dino de Laurentiis, Directors: Luchino Visconti, Pier Paolo Pasolini, Mauro Bolognini, Franco Rossi, Vittorio De Sica.
A compendium film consisting of five self-contained episodes, all starring Silvana Mangano. Eastwood appears in the fifth, A NIGHT LIKE ANY OTHER/UNA SERA COME LE ALTRE, directed by De Sica. The credits for this 19 minute episode are as follows: Screenplay: Cesare Zavattini, Fabio Carpi, Enzo Muzzi, Photography: Giuseppe Rotunno, Giuseppe Maccari (Technicolor), Music: Ennio Morricone, Piero Piccione.
Cast: Silvana Mangano (Giovanna), Clint Eastwood (Mario).

THE GOOD THE BAD AND THE UGLY/IL BUONO IL BRUTTO IL CATTIVO

1966 (US/UK release: 1968) 175 mins (Italian version)/161 mins (standard English language version)/148 minutes (UK cinema version)
Italy
Produzioni Europee Associate. English language versions distributed by United Artists
Producer: Alberto Grimaldi, Director: Sergio Leone, Screenplay: Leone, Luciano Vincenzoni, Agenore Incrocci and Furio Scarpelli [Age-Scarpelli was one of the Italian cinema's top comedy writing teams of the 50s, 60s and 70s.], English dialogue: Mickey Knox, Photography: Tonino Delli Colli (Technicolor/Techniscope), Art direction: Giancarlo Simi, Editing: Nino Baragli, Eugenio Alabiso, Music: Ennio Morricone, Musical director: Bruno Nicolai, Costumes: Simi, Special effects: Eros Bacciucchi, Title sequence: Luigi Lardani.
Cast: Clint Eastwood (Blondie/The Good), Lee Van Cleef (Setenza [Italian version]/Angel Eyes [English version]/The Bad), Eli Wallach (Tuco Benedicto Pacifico Juan Maria Ramirez/The Ugly), Aldo Giuffre (Union Captain), Luigi Pistilli (Father Pablo Ramirez), Mario Brega (Sergeant Wallace), Al Mulloch (Bounty hunter).

HANG 'EM HIGH

1968 114 mins
United States
Malpaso/Leonard Freeman Productions/United Artists
Producers: Leonard Freeman, Clint Eastwood (uncredited), Associate producer: Irving Leonard, Director: Ted Post, Screenplay: Freeman, Mel Goldberg, Photography: Leonard South, Richard Kline (De Luxe Color), Art direction: John B. Goodman, Editing: Gene Fowler Jr., Music: Dominic Frontiere.
Cast: Clint Eastwood (Jed Cooper), Inger Stevens (Rachel), Ed Begley (Captain Wilson), Pat Hingle (Judge Adam Fenton), Arlene Golonka (Jennifer), James MacArthur (Priest), Bruce Dern (Miller), Alan Hale Jr. (Stone), James Westerfield (Prisoner), Ben Johnson (Marshal Dave Bliss), Dennis Hopper (Prophet), L.Q. Jones (Loomis), Charles McGraw (Jenkins), Bert Freed (Hangman), Mark Lenard (Prosecuting lawyer).

COOGAN'S BLUFF

1968 94 mins
United States
Malpaso/Universal
Executive producer: Richard Lyons, Producer: Don Siegel, Associate producer: Irving Leonard, Director: Siegel, Screenplay: Herman Miller, Howard Rodman, Dean Riesner (based on an original story by Miller), Photography: Bud Thackery (Technicolor), Art direction: Alexander Golitzen, Robert C. MacKichan, Editing: Sam Waxman, Music: Lalo Schifrin, Music supervisor: Stanley Wilson, Dialogue coach: Scott Hale, Camera operator: Bruce Surtees, Stunts: Wayne 'Buddy' Van Horn.

Cast: Clint Eastwood (Deputy Sheriff Walt Coogan), Lee J. Cobb (Detective McElroy), Susan Clark (Julie), Don Stroud (James Ringerman), Tisha Sterling (Linny Raven), David Doyle (Pushie), Betty Field (Mrs Ringerman), Tom Tully (Sheriff McCrea), Albert Popwell (Wonderful Digby), Skip Battyn (Omega), Marya Henriques (Go-Go dancer), Melodie Johnson (Millie), John Coe (Bellboy), James McCallion (Room clerk), Jess Osuna (Prison hospital guard), Louis Zorich (Taxi driver), Rudy Diaz (Running Bear).

WHERE EAGLES DARE

1968 155 mins
Great Britain
Winkast Productions/Metro Goldwyn Mayer
Producer: Elliott Kastner, Director: Brian G. Hutton, Screenplay: Alistair MacLean, Hutton (uncredited), Photography: Arthur Ibbetson (Metrocolor/Panavision), Art direction: Peter Mullins, Editing: John Jympson, Sound: Jonathan Bates, Music: Ron Goodwin, Special photographic effects: Tom Howard, Second unit director/Stunt arranger: Yakima Canutt.
Cast: Richard Burton (Major John Smith), Clint Eastwood (Lieutenant Morris Schaffer), Mary Ure (Mary Ellison), Anton Diffring (Colonel Kramer), Derren Nesbitt (Major Von Hapen), Ferdy Mayne (Reichsmarschal Rosemeyer), Michael Hordern (Vice-Admiral Rolland), Patrick Wymark (Colonel Turner), Ingrid Pitt (Heidi), Robert Beatty (General Carnaby/Cartwright-Jones), Peter Barkworth (Berkeley), Donald Houston (Olaf Christiansen), Neil MacCarthy (Jock MacPherson), William Squire (Lee Thomas), Brook Williams (Sergeant Harrod), Vincent Ball (Pilot Carpenter).

PAINT YOUR WAGON

1969 164 mins
United States
Alan J. Lerner Productions/Paramount, in association with the Malpaso Company
Producer: Alan J. Lerner, Director: Joshua Logan, Screenplay: Lerner (based on the 1951 Broadway musical; book and lyrics by Lerner, score by Frederick Loewe), Adaptation: Paddy Chayefsky, Photography: William A. Fraker (Technicolor/Panavision), Production design: John Truscott, Art direction: Carl Braunger, Editing: Robert C. Jones, Sound: William Randall, Music: Loewe (original score only), Andre Previn (additional songs), Musical direction: Nelson Riddle, Costumes: Truscott, Titles: David Stone Martin.
Cast: Lee Marvin (Ben Rumson), Clint Eastwood (Sylvester Newel aka 'Pardner'), Jean Seberg (Elizabeth), Harve Presnell (Rotten Luck Willie), Ray Walston (Mad Jack Duncan), Tom Ligon (Horton Fenty), Alan Dexter (Parson), William O'Connell (Horace Tabor), Alan Baxter (Mr Fenty), Paula Trueman (Mrs Fenty), John Mitchum (Jacob Woodling), Sue Casey (Sarah Woodling), Eddie Little Sky (Indian), Karl Bruck (Schermerhorn), Roy Jenson (Hennessey).

TWO MULES FOR SISTER SARA

1969 116 mins
United States
Malpaso/Universal, in association with Sanen Productions (Mexico)
Producers: Martin Rackin, Carroll Case, Director: Don Siegel, Screenplay: Albert Maltz (based on an original story by Budd Boetticher), Photography: Gabriel Figueroa (Technicolor/Panavision), Art direction: Jose Rodriguez Granada, Editing: Robert F. Shugrue, Juan Jose Marino, Sound: Waldon Watson, Jesus Gonzalez Gancy, Ronald Pierce, Music: Ennio Morricone, Music supervision: Stanley Wilson, Costumes: Helen Colvig, Carlos Chavez, Camera operator: Bruce Surtees, Stunt arranger: Wayne 'Buddy' Van Horn.
Cast: Shirley MacLaine (Sister Sara), Clint Eastwood (Hogan), Manolo Fabregas (Colonel Beltran), Alberto Morin (General Leclair), Armando Silvestre (First American), John Kelly (Second American), Enrique Lucero (Third American), Pedro Armendariz (Young French Officer).

KELLY'S HEROES

1970 143 mins

United States/Yugoslavia

The Warriors Company/Avala Films/Metro Goldwyn Mayer

Producers: Gabriel Katzka, Sidney Beckerman, Associate producer: Irving Leonard, Director: Brian G. Hutton, Screenplay: Troy Kennedy Martin, Photography: Gabriel Figueroa (Metrocolor/Panavision), Art direction: Jonathan Barry, Editing: John Jympson, Sound: Cyril Swern, Harry Tetrick, Music: Lalo Schifrin, Lyrics (*Burning Bridges*): Mike Curb, Second unit director: Andrew Marton, Stunt arranger: Alf Joint.

Cast: Clint Eastwood (Kelly), Telly Savalas (Big Joe), Don Rickles (Crapgame), Donald Sutherland (Oddball), Carroll O'Connor (General Colt), Gavin MacLeod (Moriarty), Hal Buckley (Maitland), Stuart Margolin (Little Joe), Jeff Morris (Cowboy), George Savalas (Mulligan), David Hurst (Colonel Dankhopf), [Harry] Dean Stanton (Willard), George Fargo (Penn).

THE BEGUILED

1970 105 mins

United States

Malpaso/Universal

Executive producer: Julian Blaustein, Producer: Don Siegel, Associate producer: Claude Traverse, Director: Siegel, Screenplay: 'John B. Sherry', 'Grimes Grice' (pseudonyms for Albert Maltz and Irene Kamp) and Traverse (uncredited) (based on the novel by Thomas Cullinan), Photography: Bruce Surtees (Technicolor), Production design: Ted Haworth, Art direction: Alexander Golitzen, Editing: Carl Pingitore, Sound: Waldon Watson, John Mack, Music: Lalo Schifrin, Costumes: Helen Colvig, Dialogue coach: Scott Hale.

Cast: Clint Eastwood (John McBurney), Geraldine Page (Martha Farnsworth), Elizabeth Hartman (Edwina Dabney), Pamelyn Ferdin (Amy), Mae Mercer (Hallie), Jo Ann Harris (Carol), Darleen Carr (Doris), Melody Thomas (Abigail), Peggy Drier (Lizzie), Pattye Mattick (Janie), Matt Clark, Wayne Van Horn (Confederate soldiers).

PLAY MISTY FOR ME

1971 102 mins

United States

Malpaso/Universal

Producer: Robert Daley, Director: Clint Eastwood, Screenplay: Jo Heims, Dean Riesner (based on an original story by Heims), Photography: Bruce Surtees (Technicolor), Art direction: Alexander Golitzen, Editing: Carl Pingitore, Sound: Walden Watson, Robert Martin, Robert Hoyt, Music: Dee Barton, Songs: Erroll Garner (*Misty*), Roberta Flack (*The First Time Ever I Saw Your Face*), Clint Eastwood's wardrobe by Brad Whitney of Carmel.

Cast: Clint Eastwood (Dave Garver), Jessica Walter (Evelyn Draper), Donna Mills (Tobie Williams), James McEachin (Al Monte), Clarice Taylor (Birdie), Donald Siegel (Murphy), John Larch (Detective McCallum), Irene Hervey (Madge Brenner), Duke Everts (J.J.), Jack Ging (Frank Dewan), Britt Lind (Anjelica), Ginna Paterson (Madelyn), George Fargo (Man).

DIRTY HARRY

1971 102 mins

United States

Malpaso/Warner

Executive producer: Robert Daley, Producer: Don Siegel, Associate producer: Carl Pingitore, Directors: Siegel, Clint Eastwood (one scene, uncredited), Screenplay: Harry Julian Fink, Rita M. Fink, Dean Riesner, John Milius (uncredited) (based on *Dead Right*, an original story by Fink and Fink), Photography: Bruce Surtees (Technicolor/Panavision), Art direction: Dale Hennessy, Editing: Pingitore, Sound: William Randall, Music: Lalo Schifrin, Stunt arranger: Wayne 'Buddy' Van Horn,

Dialogue coach: Scott Hale, Assistant to the producer: George Fargo.
Cast: Clint Eastwood (Inspector Harry Callahan), Andy Robinson (Scorpio), Reni Santoni (Chico Gonzales), Harry Guardino (Lieutenant Bressler), John Vernon (Mayor), John Larch (Chief of Police), John Mitchum (Frank De Georgio), Mae Mercer (Mrs Russell), Lyn Edgington (Norma), Ruth Kobart (School bus driver), Woodrow Parfrey (Mr Jaffe), Josef Sommer (Rothko), Albert Popwell (Bank robber), Wayne Van Horn (Rooftop jumper), Charles Washburn (Steve).

JOE KIDD

1972 87 mins
United States
Malpaso/Universal
Executive producer: Robert Daley, Producer: Sidney Beckerman, Director: John Sturges, Screenplay: Elmore Leonard, Photography: Bruce Surtees (Technicolor/Panavision), Art direction: Alexander Golitzen, Henry Bumstead, Editing: Ferris Webster, Sound: Walden Watson, James Alexander, Music: Lalo Schifrin, Stunt arranger: Wayne Van Horn, Assistant director: James Fargo.
Cast: Clint Eastwood (Joe Kidd), Robert Duvall (Frank Harlan), John Saxon (Luis Chama), Stella Garcia (Helen Sanchez), Don Stroud (Lamarr), James Wainwright (Mingo), Paul Koslo (Roy), Gregory Walcott (Sheriff Mitchell), John Carter (Judge), Lynne Marta (Elma), Dick Van Patten (Hotel manager), Joaquin Martinez (Manolo), Ron Soble (Ramon), Pepe Callahan (Naco), Gil Barreto (Emilio), Maria Val (Vita), Ed Deemer (Bartender), Pepe Hern (Priest).

HIGH PLAINS DRIFTER

1972 105 mins
United States
Malpaso/Universal
Executive producer: Jennings Lang, Producer: Robert Daley, Director: Clint Eastwood, Screenplay: Ernest Tidyman, Photography: Bruce Surtees (Technicolor/Panavision), Art direction: Henry Bumstead, Editing: Ferris Webster, Sound: James Alexander, Music: Dee Barton, Stunt arranger: Wayne Van Horn, Assistant director: James Fargo.
Cast: Clint Eastwood (The Stranger), Verna Bloom (Sarah Belding), Mariana Hill (Callie Travers), Billy Curtis (Mordecai), Geoffrey Lewis (Stacy Bridges), John Quade (Jake Ross), Dan Vadis (Dan Carlin), John Mitchum (Prison warden), Paul Brinegar (Lutie Naylor), John Hillerman (Bootmaker), Mitchell Ryan (Dave Drake), Jack Ging (Morgan Allen), Stefan Gierasch (Major Jason Hobart), Ted Hartley (Lewis Belding), Scott Walker (Bill Borders), Walter Barnes (Sheriff Sam Shaw), Richard Bull (Asa Goodwin), Robert Donner (Preacher), William O'Connell (Barber), Wayne Van Horn (Marshal Jim Duncan).

BREEZY

1973 107 mins
United States
Malpaso/Universal
Executive producer: Jennings Lang, Producer: Robert Daley, Associate producer: Jo Heims, Director: Clint Eastwood, Screenplay: Jo Heims, Photography: Frank Stanley (Technicolor), Art direction: Alexander Golitzen, Editing: Ferris Webster, Sound: James Alexander, Music: Michel Legrand, Assistant directors: James Fargo, Tom Joyner.
Cast: William Holden (Frank Harmon), Kay Lenz (Breezy), Roger C. Carmel (Bob Henderson), Marj Dusay (Betty Tobin), Joan Hotchkis (Paula Harmon), Jamie Smith Jackson (Marcy).

MAGNUM FORCE

1973 122 mins
United States
Malpaso/Warner

Producer: Robert Daley, Director: Ted Post, Screenplay: John Milius, Michael Cimino (based on an original story by Milius), Photography: Frank Stanley (Technicolor/Panavision), Art direction: Jack Collis, Editing: Ferris Webster, Sound: James Alexander, Music: Lalo Schifrin, Second unit director: Wayne Van Horn.

Cast: Clint Eastwood (Inspector Harry Callahan), Hal Holbrook (Lieutenant Neil Briggs), Felton Perry (Early Smith), David Soul (Ben Davis), Robert Urich (John Grimes), Tim Matheson (Phil Sweet), Kip Niven (Red Astrachan), Mitchell Ryan (Charlie McCoy), Christine White (Carol McCoy), John Mitchum (Frank De Georgio), Adele Yoshioka (Sunny), Albert Popwell (Sidney the Pimp), Margaret Avery (Prostitute), Richard Devon (Carmine Ricca), Tony Giorgio (Frank Palancio).

THUNDERBOLT AND LIGHTFOOT

1974 114 mins
United States
Malpaso/United Artists
Producer: Robert Daley, Director: Michael Cimino, Screenplay: Cimino, Photography: Frank Stanley (De Luxe Color/Panavision), Art direction: Tambi Larsen, Editing: Ferris Webster, Sound: Bert Hallberg, Norman Webster, Music: Dee Barton, Title song (*Where Do I Go From Here ?*): Paul Williams, Stunt arranger: Wayne Van Horn.
Cast: Clint Eastwood (John 'Thunderbolt' Doherty), Jeff Bridges (Lightfoot), George Kennedy (Red Leary), Geoffrey Lewis (Goody), Gary Busey (Curly), Roy Jenson (Dunlop), Bill McKinney (Crazy driver), Gregory Walcott (Used car salesman), Catherine Bach (Melody), Dub Taylor (Gas station attendant), Jack Dodson (Bank vault manager), Vic Tayback (Mario), Luanne Roberts (Housewife).

THE EIGER SANCTION

1975 128 mins (US), 118 mins (UK)
United States
Malpaso/Universal
Executive producers: Richard Zanuck, David Brown, Producer: Robert Daley, Director: Clint Eastwood, Screenplay: Warren B. Murphy, Hal Dresner, Rod Whitaker (based on the novel by Trevanian), Photography: Frank Stanley (Technicolor/Panavision), Mountain photography: John Cleare, Jeff Schoolfield, Peter Pilafian, Pete White, Art direction: George Webb (US), Aurelio Crugnola (Switzerland), Editing: Ferris Webster, Sound: James Alexander, Music: John Williams, Climbing advisor: Mike Hoover, Assistant directors: James Fargo (US), Craig Hughes, Victor Tourjansky.
Cast: Clint Eastwood (Jonathan Hemlock), George Kennedy (Ben Bowman), Vonetta McGee (Jemima Brown), Thayer David (Dragon), Elaine Shaw (Miss Cerberus), Gregory Walcott (Pope), Brenda Venus (George), Jack Cassidy (Miles McHough), Reiner Schoene (Freytag), Michael Grimm (Meyer), Jean-Pierre Bernard (Montaigne), Heidi Bruhl (Anna Montaigne), Candace Rialson (Art student).

THE OUTLAW JOSEY WALES

1976 135 mins (US), 134 mins (UK)[*]
United States
Malpaso/Warner
Producer: Robert Daley, Associate producers: James Fargo, John G. Wilson, Director: Clint Eastwood, Screenplay: Philip Kaufman, Sonia Chernus (based on the book *Gone to Texas* by Forrest/Asa Carter), Photography: Bruce Surtees (De Luxe Color/Panavision), Production design: Tambi Larsen, Editing: Ferris Webster, Sound: Keith Stafford, Music: Jerry Fielding, Stunt arranger: Walter Scott, Assistant directors: Fargo, Win Phelps, Alan Brimfield, Assistant editor: Joel Cox, Production assistant: Fritz Manes.
Cast: Clint Eastwood (Josey Wales), Chief Dan George (Lone Watie), Sondra Locke (Laura Lee),

John Vernon (Fletcher), Bill McKinney (Terrill), Paula Trueman (Grandma Sarah), Geraldine Keams (Little Moonlight), Sam Bottoms (Jamie), Woodrow Parfrey (Carpetbagger), Will Sampson (Ten Bears), John Quade (Comanchero leader), John Russell (Bloody Bill Anderson), Joyce Jameson (Rose), Sheb Wooley (Travis Cobb), Royal Dano (Ten Spot), William O'Connell (Slim Carstairs), John Mitchum (Al), Charles Tyner (Luke Zimmer), Matt Clark (Kelly), Cissy Wellman (Josey's wife), Kyle Eastwood (Josey's son).

*Warner trimmed the scene where Laura is assaulted by comancheros in order to obtain an 'AA' certificate (over fourteens only) from the British Board of Film Censors, who regarded the original version as suitable for adults only ('X' rated). The unedited American print is currently available on television and video.

THE ENFORCER

1976 96 mins
United States
Malpaso/Warner
Producer: Robert Daley, Director: James Fargo, Screenplay: Stirling Silliphant, Dean Riesner, Photography: Charles W. Short (De Luxe Color/Panavision), Art direction: Allen E. Smith, Editing: Ferris Webster, Joel Cox, Sound: Bert Hallberg, Music: Jerry Fielding, Stunt arranger: Wayne Van Horn, Production assistant: Fritz Manes.
Cast: Clint Eastwood (Inspector Harry Callahan), Tyne Daly (Inspector Kate Moore), Harry Guardino (Lieutenant Bressler), Bradford Dillman (Captain McKay), John Mitchum (Frank DeGeorgio), DeVeren Bookwalter (Bobby Maxwell), Samantha Doane (Wanda), Albert Popwell (Big Ed Mustapha), Adele Proom (Irene DeGeorgio), John Crawford (Mayor), M.G. Kelly (Father John).

THE GAUNTLET

1977 109 mins
United States
Malpaso/Warner
Producer: Robert Daley, Associate producer: Fritz Manes, Director: Clint Eastwood, Screenplay: Michael Butler, Dennis Shryack, Photography: Rexford Metz (De Luxe Color/Panavision), Art direction: Allen E. Smith, Editing: Ferris Webster, Joel Cox, Sound: Bert Hallberg, Music: Jerry Fielding, Stunt arranger: Wayne Van Horn, Special effects: Chuck Gaspar.
Cast: Clint Eastwood (Ben Shockley), Sondra Locke (Augusta 'Gus' Mally), Pat Hingle (Josephson), William Prince (Blakelock), Michael Cavanaugh (Feyderspiel), Bill McKinney (Constable), Mara Corday (Prison warden), Samantha Doane (Lesbian biker), Roy Jenson (Bearded biker), Dan Vadis (Biker with legal knowledge), Fritz Manes (Helicopter marksman).

EVERY WHICH WAY BUT LOOSE

1978 114 mins
United States
Malpaso/Warner
Producer: Robert Daley, Associate producers: Fritz Manes, Jeremy Joe Kronsberg, Director: James Fargo, Screenplay: Kronsberg, Photography: Rexford Metz (De Luxe Color), Art direction: Elayne Ceder, Editing: Ferris Webster, Joel Cox, Sound: Bert Hallberg, Music supervisor: Snuff Garrett, Music director: Steven Dorff, Stunt arranger: Wayne Van Horn, Special effects: Chuck Gaspar, Camera operator: Jack Green, Orang Utan trainer: Bobby Beronsini.
Cast: Clint Eastwood (Philo Beddoe), Manis (Clyde), Sondra Locke (Lynn Halsey-Taylor), Geoffrey Lewis (Orville), Ruth Gordon (Ma), Beverly D'Angelo (Echo), Gregory Walcott (Putman), James McEachin (Herb), John Quade (Cholla), Roy Jenson (Woody), Dan Vadis (Frank), William O'Connell (Elmo), Bill McKinney (Dallas), Hank Worden (Trailer Park Manager), Walter Barnes ('Tank' Murdoch), Jeremy Joe Kronsberg (Bruno), Fritz Manes (Bartender).

ESCAPE FROM ALCATRAZ

1979 112 mins
United States
Malpaso/Paramount
Executive producer: Robert Daley, Producer: Don Siegel, Associate producer: Fritz Manes,
Director: Siegel, Screenplay: Richard Tuggle (based on the book by J. Campbell Bruce),
Photography: Bruce Surtees (De Luxe Color), Production design: Allen E. Smith, Editing: Ferris
Webster, Joel Cox, Sound: Bert Hallberg, Music: Jerry Fielding, Special effects: Chuck Gaspar.
Cast: Clint Eastwood (Frank Lee Morris), Patrick MacGoohan (Prison Warden), Roberts Blossom
(Chester 'Doc' Dalton), Jack Thibeau (Clarence Anglin), Fred Ward (John Anglin), Paul Benjamin
(English), Larry Hankin (Charley Butts), Frank Ronzio (Litmus), Bruce M. Fischer (Wolf), Don
Siegel (Doctor), Danny Glover, Carl Lumbly (Inmates).

BRONCO BILLY

1980 116 mins
United States
Second Street Films/Warner
Executive producer: Robert Daley, Producers: Dennis Hackin, Neal Dobrofsky, Associate producer:
Fritz Manes, Director: Clint Eastwood, Screenplay: Hackin, Photography: David Worth (De Luxe
Color), Art direction: Eugene Lourie, Editing: Ferris Webster, Joel Cox, Sound: Bert Hallberg,
Music supervisor: Snuff Garrett, Music director: Steven Dorff, Camera operator: Jack Green.
Cast: Clint Eastwood (Bronco Billy McCoy), Sondra Locke (Antoinette Lily), Scatman Crothers
(Doc Lynch), Sam Bottoms (Leonard James), Geoffrey Lewis (John Arlington), Bill McKinney (Lefty
LeBow), Dan Vadis (Chief Big Eagle), Sierra Pecheur (Lorraine Running Water), Walter Barnes
(Sheriff Dix), Woodrow Parfrey (Dr Canterbury), Beverlee McKinsey (Irene Lily), Hank Worden
(Garage mechanic), Kyle Eastwood, Alison Eastwood (Orphans).

ANY WHICH WAY YOU CAN

1980 116 mins
United States
Malpaso/Warner
Executive producer: Robert Daley, Producer: Fritz Manes, Director: Wayne 'Buddy' Van Horn,
Screenplay: Stanford Sherman, Photography: David Worth (De Luxe Color), Production design:
William J. Creber, Editing: Ferris Webster, Ron Spang, Sound: Bert Hallberg, Music supervisor:
Snuff Garrett, Music director: Steven Dorff, Special effects: Chuck Gaspar, Jeff Jarvis, Camera oper-
ators: Jack Green, Douglas Ryan.
Cast: Clint Eastwood (Philo Beddoe), Sondra Locke (Lynn Halsey-Taylor), Geoffrey Lewis (Orville
Boggs), Ruth Gordon (Ma), William Smith (Jack Wilson), Harry Guardino (James Beekman),
Michael Cavanaugh (Patrick Scarfe), Barry Corbin (Fat Zack), John Quade (Cholla), Bill McKinney
(Dallas), Dan Vadis (Frank), William O'Connell (Elmo), Roy Jenson (Woody) ['Clyde' uncredited]

FIREFOX

1982 136/124 mins (shorter version used for video release)
United States
Malpaso/Warner
Executive producer: Fritz Manes, Producer: Clint Eastwood, Director: Eastwood, Screenplay: Alex
Lasker, Wendell Wellman (based on the book by Craig Thomas), Photography: Bruce Surtees (De
Luxe Color/Panavision), Art direction: John Graysmark, Elayne Ceder, Editing: Ferris Webster, Ron
Spang, Sound: Don Johnson, Music: Maurice Jarre, Special visual effects: John Dykstra, Special
effects: Chuck Gaspar, Karl Baumgartner, Camera operator: Jack Green.
Cast: Clint Eastwood (Mitchell Gant), Freddie Jones (Kenneth Aubrey), David Huffman (Buckholz),
Nigel Hawthorne (Piotr Baranovitch), Dimitra Arliss (Natalia Baranovitch), Warren Clarke (Pavel

Upenskoy), Ronald Lacey (Semelovsky), Kenneth Colley (Colonel Kontarsky), Klaus Lowitsch (General Vladimirov), George Pravda (General Borov), Clive Merrison (Major Lanyev), Oliver Cotton (Dimitri Priabin), George Orrison (Leon Sprague).

HONKYTONK MAN

1982 122 mins
United States
Malpaso/Warner
Executive producer: Fritz Manes, Producer: Clint Eastwood, Director: Eastwood, Screenplay: Clancy Carlile (based on his novel), Photography: Bruce Surtees (Technicolor), Production design: Edward Carfagno, Editing: Ferris Webster, Joel Cox, Michael Kelly, Sound: Don Johnson, Music supervisor: Snuff Garrett, Music director: Steven Dorff, Camera operator: Jack Green.
Cast: Clint Eastwood (Red Stovall), Kyle Eastwood (Whit), John McIntire (Grandpa), Alexa Kenin (Marlene), Verna Bloom (Emmy), Matt Clark (Virgil), Barry Corbin (Derwood Arnspriger), John Russell (Jack Wade), Marty Robbins (Smoky), Roy Jenson (Dub), Sherry Allurd (Dub's wife), George Orrison, Glenn Wright (Jailbirds).

SUDDEN IMPACT

1983 117 mins
United States
Malpaso/Warner
Executive producer: Fritz Manes, Producer: Clint Eastwood, Associate producer: Steve Perry, Director: Eastwood, Screenplay: Joseph C. Stinson (based on a story by Earl E. Smith and Charles B. Pierce), Photography: Bruce Surtees (Technicolor/Panavision), Production design: Edward Carfagno, Editing: Joel Cox, Sound: Don Johnson, Music: Lalo Schifrin, Special effects: Chuck Gaspar, Stunt arranger: Wayne Van Horn, Camera operator: Jack Green.
Cast: Clint Eastwood (Inspector Harry Callahan), Sondra Locke (Jennifer Spencer), Pat Hingle (Chief Jannings), Albert Popwell (Horace King), Bradford Dillman (Captain Briggs), Paul Drake (Micky), Audrie J. Neenan (Ray Parkins), Jack Thibeau (Kruger), Nancy Parsons (Mrs Kruger), Mara Corday (Coffee Shop Waitress), James McEachin (Detective Barnes).

TIGHTROPE

1984 114 mins
United States
Malpaso/Warner
Producer: Clint Eastwood, Director: Richard Tuggle, Screenplay: Tuggle, Photography: Bruce Surtees (Technicolor), Production design: Edward Carfagno, Editing: Joel Cox, Sound: William Kaplan, Music: Lennie Niehaus, Stunt arranger: Wayne Van Horn, Camera operator: Jack Green.
Cast: Clint Eastwood (Detective Wes Block), Genevieve Bujold (Beryl Thibodeaux), Alison Eastwood (Amanda Block), Jennifer Beck (Penny Block), Dan Hedaya (Inspector Molonari), Marco St John (Leander Rolf), Rebecca Clemons (Woman with whip).

CITY HEAT

1984 97 mins
United States
Malpaso/Deliverance/Warner
Producer: Fritz Manes, Director: Richard Benjamin, Screenplay: Blake Edwards (credited as 'Sam O. Brown'), Joseph C. Stinson, Photography: Nick McLean (Technicolor/Panavision), Art direction: Edward Carfagno, Editing: Jacqueline Cambas, Sound: C. Darin Knight, Music: Lennie Niehaus, Stunt arranger: Wayne Van Horn.
Cast: Clint Eastwood (Lieutenant Speer), Burt Reynolds (Mike Murphy), Jane Alexander (Addy), Madeline Kahn (Caroline Howley), Rip Torn (Primo Pitt), Irene Cara (Ginny Lee), Richard

Roundtree (Dehl Swift), Tony Lo Bianco (Leon Coll), Robert Davi (Nino), Bruce M. Fischer (Bruiser), Jack Nance (Aram Strossell).

PALE RIDER

1985 115 mins
United States
Malpaso/Warner
Executive producer: Fritz Manes, Producer: Clint Eastwood, Associate producer: David Valdes, Director: Eastwood, Screenplay: Michael Butler, Dennis Shryack, Photography: Bruce Surtees (Technicolor/Panavision), Art direction: Edward Carfagno, Editing: Joel Cox, Sound: C. Darin Knight, Music: Lennie Niehaus, Stunt arranger: Wayne Van Horn, Special effects: Chuck Gaspar, Camera operator: Jack Green.
Cast: Clint Eastwood (Preacher), Michael Moriarty (Hull Barret), Carrie Snodgress (Sarah Wheeler), Sydney Penny (Megan Wheeler), John Russell (Marshal Stockburn), Richard Dysart (Coy LaHood), Christopher Penn (Josh LaHood), Richard Kiel (Club), Doug McGrath (Spider Conway), John Dennis Johnston (Deputy Tucker), Billy Drago (Deputy Mather), Wayne Van Horn (Stage driver).

STEVEN SPIELBERG'S AMAZING STORIES: VANESSA IN THE GARDEN

1985 25 mins
United States
Amblin/Universal Television
Executive producer: Steven Spielberg, Producer: David E. Vogel, Director: Clint Eastwood, Screenplay: Spielberg, Music: Lennie Niehaus.
Cast: Harvey Keitel (Byron Sullivan), Sondra Locke (Vanessa Sullivan), Beau Bridges (Teddy Colman).

HEARTBREAK RIDGE

1986 130 mins
United States
Malpaso/Jay Weston Productions/Warner
Executive producer: Fritz Manes, Producer: Clint Eastwood, Director: Eastwood, Screenplay: James Carabatsos, Photography: Jack Green (Technicolor), Art direction: Edward Carfagno, Editing: Joel Cox, Sound: William Nelson, Music: Lennie Niehaus, Special effects: Chuck Gaspar, Stunt arranger: Wayne Van Horn.
Cast: Clint Eastwood (Gunnery Sergeant Thomas Highway), Marsha Mason (Aggie), Everett McGill (Major Powers), Moses Gunn (Sergeant Webster), Eileen Heckart (Little Mary), Bo Svenson (Roy Jennings), Mario Van Peebles (Stitch Jones), Tom Villard (Profile).

BIRD

1988 160 mins
United States
Malpaso/Warner
Executive producer: David Valdes, Producer: Clint Eastwood, Director: Eastwood, Screenplay: Joel Oliansky, Photography: Jack Green (Technicolor), Art direction: Edward Carfagno, Editing: Joel Cox, Sound: Willie D. Burton, Bobby Fernandez, Music supervisor: Lennie Niehaus.
Cast: Forest Whitaker (Charlie 'Yardbird' Parker), Diane Venora (Chan Parker nee Richardson), Michael Zelniker (Red Rodney), Samuel E. Wright (Dizzy Gillespie), Keith David (Buster Franklin), Michael McGuire (Brewster), James Handy (Esteves), Diane Salinger (Nica), Damon Whitaker (Young Charlie Parker).

THE DEAD POOL

1988 91 mins
United States
Malpaso/Warner
Producer: David Valdes, Director: Wayne 'Buddy' Van Horn, Screenplay: Steve Sharon, Photography: Jack Green (Technicolor), Art direction: Edward Carfagno, Editing: Joel Cox, Ron Spang, Sound: Richard S. Church, Bobby Fernandez, Music: Lalo Schifrin, Special effects: Chuck Gaspar, Stunt arranger: Richard Farnsworth.
Cast: Clint Eastwood (Inspector Harry Callahan), Patricia Clarkson (Samantha Walker), Evan C. Kim (Al Quan), Liam Neeson (Peter Swan), David Hunt (Harlan Rook), Michael Currie (Captain Donnelly), Michael Goodwin (Lieutenant Ackerman), Anthony Charnota (Lou Janero), James Carrey (Johnny Squares), Ronnie Claire Edwards (Molly Fisher).

PINK CADILLAC

1989 122 mins
United States
Malpaso/Warner
Executive producer: Michael Gruskoff, Producer: David Valdes, Director: Wayne 'Buddy' Van Horn, Screenplay: John Eskow, Photography: Jack Green (Technicolor), Production design: Edward Carfagno, Editing: Joel Cox, Music: Steven Dorff, Stunt arranger: Richard Farnsworth.
Cast: Clint Eastwood (Tommy Nowack), Bernadette Peters (Lou Ann McGuinn), Timothy Carhart (Roy McGuinn), Michael Des Barres (Alex), John Dennis Johnston (Waycross), Jimmy E. Skaggs (Billy Dunston), William Hickey (Mr Burton), Geoffrey Lewis (Ricky Z), Paul Benjamin (Judge), Frances Fisher (Dinah), Cliff Remis (Jeff), Mara Corday (Stick Lady), Bill McKinney (Bartender), James Carrey (Elvis impersonator).

WHITE HUNTER BLACK HEART

1990 112 mins
United States
Malpaso/Rastar/Warner
Executive producer: David Valdes, Producer: Clint Eastwood, Co-producer: Stanley Rubin, Director: Eastwood, Screenplay: Peter Viertel, James Bridges, Burt Kennedy (based on the book by Viertel), Photography: Jack Green (Technicolor), Production design: John Graysmark, Art direction: Tony Reading, Editing: Joel Cox, Sound: Peter Handford, Music: Lennie Niehaus, Costumes: John Mollo, Second unit director (wildlife sequences): Simon Trevor, Stunt arranger: George Orrison, Camera operators: Green, Peter Robinson.
Cast: Clint Eastwood (John Wilson [John Huston]), Jeff Fahey (Pete Verrill [Peter Viertel]), Marisa Berenson (Kay Gibson [Katherine Hepburn]), Richard Vanstone (Phil Duncan [Humphrey Bogart]), Jamie Koss (Mrs Duncan [Lauren Bacall]), George Dzundza (Paul Landers [Sam Spiegel]), Timothy Spall (Hodkins), Boy Mathais Chuma (Kivu), Charlotte Cornwell (Miss Wilding), Alun Armstrong (Ralph Lockheart), Mel Martin (Margaret MacGregor), Clive Mantle (Harry), Edward Tudorpole (Reissar).

THE ROOKIE

1990 121 mins
United States
Malpaso/Warner, in association with Kazanjian/Siebert Productions.
Producers: Howard Kanzanjian, Steven Siebert, David Valdes, Director: Clint Eastwood, Screenplay: Boaz Yakin, Scott Spiegel, Photography: Jack Green (Technicolor/Panavision), Production design: Judy Cammer, Art direction: Ed Verreaux, Editing: Joel Cox, Sound: Don Johnson, Music: Lennie Niehaus, Second unit director: Wayne Van Horn, Stunt arranger: Terry Leonard, Car stunts: Bill Young's Precision Driving Team, Second second assistant director: Jeffrey Wetzel.

Cast: Clint Eastwood (Nick Pulovski), Charlie Sheen (David Ackerman), Raul Julia (Strom), Sonia Braga (Liesl), Tom Skerritt (Eugene Ackerman), Lara Flynn Boyle (Sarah), Pepe Serna (Lieutenant Ray Garcia), Marco Rodriguez (Loco), Mara Corday (Interrogator).

UNFORGIVEN

1992 131 mins
United States
Malpaso/Warner
Executive producer: David Valdes, Producer: Clint Eastwood, Director: Eastwood, Screenplay: David Webb Peoples, Photography: Jack Green (Technicolor/Panavision), Production design: Henry Bumstead, Editing: Joel Cox, Sound: Rob Young, Music: Lennie Niehaus, Technical consultant: Wayne Van Horn.
Cast: Clint Eastwood (William Munny), Gene Hackman (William 'Little Bill' Daggett), Morgan Freeman (Ned Logan), Richard Harris (English Bob), Jaimz Woolvett (Schofield Kid), Frances Fisher (Strawberry Alice), Anna Thomson (Delilah), Saul Rubinek (W.W. Beauchamp), Anthony James (Skinny Dubois), Cherrilene Cardinal (Sally Two Trees).

IN THE LINE OF FIRE

1993 128 mins
United States
Castle Rock Entertainment/Columbia
Executive producers: Wolfgang Petersen, Gail Katz, David Valdes, Producer: Jeff Apple, Co-producer: Bob Rosenthal, Director: Petersen, Screenplay: Jeff Maguire, Photography: John Bailey, Mark Vargo (Technicolor/Panavision), Production design: Lilly Kilvert, Art director: John Warnke, Editing: Ann Coates, Steven Kemper, Sound: Willie Burton, Music: Ennio Morricone, Stunt arranger: Wayne Van Horn.
Cast: Clint Eastwood (Frank Horrigan), John Malkovich (Mitch Leary), Rene Russo (Lily Raines), Dylan McDermott (Al D'Andrea), Gary Cole (Bill Watts), Fred Dalton Thompson (Harry Sargent), John Mahoney (Sam Campagna), Clyde Kusatsu (Jack Okura), John Heard (Professor Riger).

A PERFECT WORLD

1993 138 mins
United States
Malpaso/Warner
Producers: Mark Johnson, David Valdes, Director: Clint Eastwood, Screenplay: John Lee Hancock, Photography: Jack Green (Technicolor/Panavision), Production design: Henry Bumstead, Editing: Joel Cox, Ron Spang, Sound: Jeff Wexler, Bobby Fernandez, Music: Lennie Niehaus, Stunt arranger: Wayne Van Horn.
Cast: Kevin Costner (Robert 'Butch' Haynes), Clint Eastwood (Red Garnett), Laura Dern (Sally Gerber), T.J. Lowther (Phillip Perry), Keith Szarabajka (Terry James Pugh), Leo Burmester (Tom Adler), Jennifer Griffin (Gladys Perry), Leslie Flowers (Naomi Perry), Belinda Flowers (Ruth Perry).

THE BRIDGES OF MADISON COUNTY

1995 135mins
United States
Amblin Entertainment/Malpaso/Warner
Executive producer: Steven Spielberg, Producers: Clint Eastwood, Kathleen Kennedy, Director: Eastwood, Screenplay: Richard LaGravenese (based on the book by Robert James Waller), Photography: Jack Green (Technicolor), Art direction: William Arnold, Editing: Joel Cox, Music: Lennie Niehaus.
Cast: Clint Eastwood (Robert Kincaid), Meryl Streep (Francesca Johnson), Annie Corley, Victor Slezak, Jim Haynie.

Bibliography

Atkins, Thomas R. (ed.), *Graphic Violence On the Screen*, Monarch Press, New York, 1976.

Bach, Steven, *Final Cut*. Faber & Faber, London, 1986.

Boorman, John and Donohue, Walter (eds.), *Projections 4 1/2*, Faber & Faber, London, 1995

Bragg, Melvyn, *A Man Called Clint*, Esquire Volume 5, No 7, September 1995.

Brosnan, John, *Movie Magic* (Revised edition), Sphere Books Ltd, London, 1977.

Clinch, Minty, *Clint Eastwood*, Hodder & Stoughton, London, 1994.

Frayling, Christopher, *Clint Eastwood*, Virgin, London, 1992.

Gallafent, Edward, *Clint Eastwood Actor and Director*, Studio Vista, London, 1994.

Halliwell, Leslie, *Halliwell's Filmgoer's Companion* (ninth edition), Paladin, London, 1989.

Katz, Ephraim, *The International Film Encyclopedia*, Macmillan, London, 1980.

Malcolm, Derek, *Giving good Clint* [interview], The Guardian, September 1 1995.

Maltin, Leonard (ed.), *Leonard Maltin's Movie and Video Guide 1995*, Signet, New York, 1994.

Masheter, Philip, *Broadsword Calling Danny Boy, The Making of WHERE EAGLES DARE*, Movie Collector Volume 2, Issue 1, Christmas 1994/Volume 2, Issue 2, March 1995.

McBride, Joseph (ed.), *Hawks on Hawks*, University of California Press, Los Angeles, 1982.

Medved, Harry and Medved, Michael, *The Hollywood Hall of Shame*. Angus & Robertson, London, 1984.

Mitchum, John, *Them Ornery Mitchum Boys*. Creatures at Large Press, Pacifica, 1989.

Mordden, Ethan, *Medium Cool, The Movies of the 1960s*, Alfred A. Knopf, New York, 1990.

Norman, Barry, *Talking Pictures: The Story of Hollywood*. Arrow Books, London, 1991.

Rensin, David, John Milius Interview, Playboy Vol 38 no 6 June 1991.

Siegel, Donald, *A Siegel Film*. Faber & Faber, London, 1993.

Thompson, Douglas, *Clint Eastwood: Sexual Cowboy*, Warner Books, London, 1993.

Walker, John (ed.), *Halliwell's Film Guide* (ninth edition), HarperCollins, London, 1993.

Index